The
STARSHIP
and the
CANOE

ALSO BY KENNETH BROWER

With Their Islands Around Them

KENNETH BROWER

The
STARSHIP

and the
CANOE

Holt, Rinehart and Winston • New York

Library of Congress Cataloging in Publication Data
Brower, Kenneth (date)
The starship and the canoe.
1.   Dyson, Freeman J. 2. Dyson, George Bernard   I.   Title.
TL789.85.D9B76   629.4'092'4 [B]   77-15200
ISBN 0-03-039196-2

Many of Freeman Dyson's quotations in Chapter 6 were
taken from two articles by Freeman Dyson—"The Sellout"
and "Letter from Armenia"—both first published by
The New Yorker and quoted here by permission of
New Yorker Magazine, Inc.

First Edition
Designer: Amy Hill
Printed in the United States of America
10 9 8 7 6 5 4 3 2 1

For my mother and father

Boom Boom Boom

As long as Freeman Dyson can remember, his thoughts have been on the stars. Those thoughts have not been commonplace. Dyson is one of the foremost theoretical physicists this planet has produced. At the very top of the ivory tower, among the membership of that preternaturally brilliant, uncombed fraternity who doodle equations on napkins, who forget to wear their galoshes, and who tend in midsentence to depart conversation, and the world, for new calculations on how the universe is put together, Dyson is regarded as a man with a special gift. More than one of his colleagues have described his place as "stellar." He is a principal architect of the theory of quantum electrodynamics. He has made contributions to the theories of statistical mechanics and matter in the solid state. He has worked in pure mathematics and in particle physics. He helped design a very successful nuclear reactor.

But Dyson's preoccupation has been space. He has not been content, like Einstein, to probe space with his phenomenal intuition, nor, though he writes well, to travel there, like Asimov, by his pen and imagination. He wants to go in person. He has helped design a craft to take him.

In 1958 Dyson took a leave of absence from the Institute of Advanced Studies at Princeton and moved to La Jolla, California, where he joined a group of forty scientists and engineers working on a project called Orion. His colleagues in La Jolla were all brilliant and were all dead serious. They intended to explore space themselves, bodily. They had no hope for conventional rocketry as a means for reaching much of anything beyond the moon. The enormous energy required for a voyage to the planets and beyond could only be nuclear. They worked out a system they called nuclear-pulse propulsion. From a hole in the bottom of the Orion spaceship, nuclear bombs would be dropped at intervals and detonated. The shock of each shaped charge, and debris from it, would strike a pusher plate at the ship's bottom, sending the ship forward. Orion would bomb itself through space at enormous speeds. It would be equipped with shock absorbers to protect crew and machinery from the nuclear jolts, and with shielding against the heat and radiation.

It was crazy, of course, except apparently it wasn't. Orion was supported by the Nobel laureates Harold Urey, Niels Bohr, and Hans Bethe. General Curtis LeMay liked the idea, and Werner von Braun followed its progress respectfully. Even NASA contributed some money.

Dyson and the others worked out detailed plans for a ship that would quickly carry eight men and a hundred tons of equipment to Mars and back. This solar-system model became the heart of the project, and most of Dyson's energy went into it. He was personally curious about Mars, and about Saturn as well, for these were places he hoped to visit in the flesh. But Dyson is a man much concerned with human destiny, and his attention soon ranged beyond his own solar system and his own lifespan. Immortality for the human race requires colonization of the stars, he believes, or at very least, of the comets. He sketched out plans for a gargantuan ark, a starship the size of a city and powered by hydrogen bombs. Riding a monstrous concatenation of explosions, thundering silently through the void, leaving behind it a trail brighter than a thousand suns, this vessel would centuries hence take his descendants, frozen if necessary, to Alpha Centauri or another star.

George Dyson, Freeman's only son, has another idea. George wants to build a canoe, a great ocean-going kayak.

Almost a Mad Stare

Freeman Dyson is a slender man of middle height. His hair is dark, still, and he moves youthfully. His head is long, but not oversized in any futuristic way. His nose is large. He dresses without eccentricity or absentmindedness, but he dresses a bit drably. He is not a man much concerned with appearances. He does have one mannerism of the sort that the world associates with its physicists—that tendency to retire from companionship, from the human plane and from sentences in progress, while he pursues some thought. He was born in England and spent his youth there, and he speaks still with a trace of his native accent.

Dyson's eyes are his striking feature. They are dominated by the irises. The pupils seem too small, as if he were gazing always into a very bright light. His eyes are large, gray, and steady, and he holds them wide open. "Almost a mad stare—I have to say it," one of his Orion colleagues has said.

Freeman's son George is slender too. He stands about four inches taller than his father, and is a shade darker. In the summertime on the waterways of British Columbia, where George has lived from the time he was seventeen, the long days and the refracted sunlight tan him so darkly that he is taken for an Indian. He dresses entirely in wool, which stays warm when wet, and he is impatient with Northerners who don't dress that way. His taste, or his necessity, runs to long woolen underwear, baggy oft-patched wool trousers, ragged wool sweaters, and wool watch caps. He often goes barefoot. His hair is moderately long and it hangs scraggly in the rain. He is in his early twenties, and his beard is still sparse. It's a Northwest Indian beard—Nootka or Kwakiutl. "They have either no beards at all," wrote Captain Cook, "which was most commonly the case, or a small thin one upon the point of the chin; which does not arise from any defect on that part, but from plucking it out more or less." George achieves the effect naturally. He looks less like the son of a British physicist than the bastard of a French-Indian trapper.

But under the beard, the long hair, and the tan, George bears strong resemblance to his father. He has the same long face. His cranium, on the outside at least, is identical. He has the big nose. Both Freeman Dyson and George Dyson have broken their noses, but George's break is more spectacular. His nose takes several turns before finishing. He is homely-handsome. His features are strong, but they lack the nice symmetry and proportion that break young girls' hearts.

His eyes are his extraordinary feature. They are so dominated by the irises that the pupils seem pinpricks. His eyes are large, green, and steady, and he holds them wide open.

—— 3 ——

Comets

"First I have to clear away a few popular misconceptions about space as a habitat," said Freeman Dyson, lecturing in London in 1972. "It is generally considered that planets are important. Except for Earth, they are not. Mars is waterless, and the others are for various reasons basically inhospitable to man. It is generally considered that beyond the sun's family of planets there is absolute emptiness extending for light-years until you come to another star. In fact, it is likely that the space around the solar system is populated by huge numbers of comets, small worlds a few miles in diameter, rich in water and the other chemicals essential to life. We see one of these comets only when it happens to suffer a random perturbation of its orbit which sends it plunging close to the sun. It seems that roughly one comet per year is captured into the region near the sun, where it eventually evaporates and disintegrates. If we assume that the supply of distant comets is sufficient to sustain this process over the thousands of millions of years that the solar system has existed, then the total population of comets loosely attached to the sun must be numbered in the thousands of millions. The combined surface area of these comets is then a thousand or ten thousand times that of Earth. I conclude from these facts that comets, not planets, are the major potential habitat of life in space. If it were true that other stars have as many comets as the sun, it then would follow that comets pervade our entire galaxy. We have no evidence either supporting or contradicting this hypothesis. If true, it implies that our galaxy is a much friendlier place for interstellar travelers than it is popularly supposed to be. The average distance between habitable oases in the desert of space is not measured in light-years, but is of the order of a light-day or less.

"I propose to you then an optimistic view of the galaxy as an abode of life. Countless millions of comets are out there, amply supplied with water, carbon, and nitrogen, the basic constituents of living cells. We see when they fall close to the sun that they contain all the common elements necessary to our existence. They lack only two essential requirements for human settlement, namely warmth and air. And now, biological engineering will come to our rescue. We shall learn to grow trees on comets.

"To make a tree grow in airless space by the light of a distant sun is basically a problem of redesigning the skin of its leaves. In every organism the skin is the crucial part which must be most delicately tailored to the demands of the environment. The skin of a leaf in space must satisfy four requirements. It must be opaque to far-ultraviolet radiation to protect the vital tissues from radiation damage. It must be impervious to water. It must transmit visible light to the organs of photosynthesis. It must have extremely low emissivity for far-infrared radiation, so that it can limit loss of heat and keep itself from freezing. A tree whose leaves possess such a skin should be able to take root and flourish upon any comet as near to the sun as the orbits of Jupiter and Saturn. Farther out than

Saturn the sunlight is too feeble to keep a simple leaf warm, but trees can grow at far greater distances if they provide themselves with compound leaves. A compound leaf would consist of a photosynthetic part, which is able to keep itself warm, together with a convex mirror part, which itself remains cold but focuses concentrated sunlight upon the photosynthetic part. It should be possible to program the genetic instructions of a tree to produce such leaves and orient them correctly toward the sun. Many existing plants possess structures more complicated than this.

"Once leaves can be made to function in space, the remaining parts of a tree—trunk, branches, and roots—do not present any great problems. The branches must not freeze, and therefore the bark must be a superior heat insulator. The roots will penetrate and gradually melt the frozen interior of the comet, and the tree will build its substance from the materials which the roots find there. The oxygen which the leaves manufacture must not be exhaled into space; instead it will be transported down to the roots and released into the regions where men will live and take their ease among the tree trunks. One question still remains. How high can a tree on a comet grow? The answer is surprising. On any celestial body whose diameter is of the order of ten miles or less, the force of gravity is so weak that a tree can grow out for hundreds of miles, collecting the energy of sunlight from an area thousands of times as large as the area of the comet itself. Seen from far away, the comet will look like a small potato sprouting an immense growth of stems and foliage. When man comes to live on the comets, he will find himself returning to the arboreal existence of his ancestors."

—— 4 ——

Flying Squirrels

George Dyson lives ninety-five feet above the ground in a Douglas fir in British Columbia. His tree stands on land leased by friends from the provincial government. It is the last tree before the water, and the front window of his tree house looks down into Indian Arm of the Strait of Georgia. The tree is the biggest around, and its foliage is dense. Through his seaward windows George can look out unseen at the traffic on the strait. Through his landward windows he can study anyone approaching from that direction. At night the city of Vancouver glows on the horizon.

George built his house in 1972, the year his father lectured on comets and the hospitality of interstellar space.

George's stairs are the tree's branches. They make a spiral staircase, leading him round and round the trunk as he ascends. The first branches begin some distance above the ground, so at the foot of the tree George has nailed a ladder. Climbing from the top rung to the first branch is difficult, and George intended it that way. He likes his privacy. The hands of any visitor are covered with pitch by the time he reaches George's door, but George knows where to put his own hands, and they stay clean. For visitors, even those young and nimble, the first few climbs up to the tree house are scary, but George runs up as if his Douglas fir lay horizontal on the ground. He has climbed it drunk and he has climbed it in winter storms. He could climb it in his sleep. All the motions— swinging around this branch, reaching for that one, pulling up— have been burned by repetition into his autonomic nervous system. He hauls up his firewood by rope. When he wants to descend he rappels.

The house is lashed to the tree, not nailed, for the treetop sways in the wind and the attachment must be flexible to endure. George has confidence in the lashings. In 1975 the worst storm in many years hit British Columbia, and George, who at the time had been living elsewhere, moved back into his tree to see how a big storm felt. The storm did its best; the tree whipped wildly about; George fell asleep.

The house is shingled, inside and out, with red-cedar shakes. The outside shakes have weathered as dark as the tree trunk, fine camouflage. The inside shakes, protected from the weather, look fresh split, retaining the warm red-blond of the heart of the log they came from. The house has a single tiny room. The ship-tight, red-blond interior is free-form, for George built to include fourteen branches as structural members. His ingenuity does not call attention to itself, and the number of incorporated branches is a surprise when you total it up. The door's hinges are screwed into the main trunk. Above the hinges, the biggest of the inner limbs forks from the trunk, thick as a man's thigh, passes over George's bed and exits through the wall. In the morning, George's eyes open wide and green on living bark, and he can pull himself out of bed on the limb's solidness.

The bed is Procrustean. George is six feet tall, and the house is two or three inches narrower than that, so he must sleep slightly bent. The bed's hard planks are softened somewhat by a mattress of two blankets, thin and nondescript, which are covered by a Persian rug, thick and beautiful. At the head is a handmade leather cushion that George uses as a pillow. Like most of the things he has owned for a while, the cushion has begun to have the look of a talisman. It is round, shallow, and worn. It might be a Kwakiutl or Haida artifact that he stole from a museum. On the wall above the bed a barometer is nailed, and next to it hangs a pair of binoculars in a leather case that George made himself. An octagonal window with leaded panes is inset in the wall beside the bed, and an identical octagonal window is inset at the foot. George can lie in bed and watch, through his binoculars and his leaded panes, any boats moving on the inlet. He has three rectangular windows, too. No point of the compass is hidden to him.

Across from the bed is a small, cast-iron, wood-burning stove. Stamped on the front is NEW ALBION STOVE WKS, and beneath that is the raised emblem of a fish, and beneath that is VICTORIA.

Against the seaward wall is a tiny desk. On the desk are candles, a kerosene lamp, a small jar of flowers, another jar full of pens, a vial of washable blue ink, and a wooden letter seal. The seal was carved by a friend of George's. It is titled LING COD and shows a cod swimming among the stalks of a kelp forest. On the wall above the desk hangs a silver letter-opener with Arabian designs on the scabbard and handle. Stored beneath the desk are a big jar of nuts, a few pots and utensils, and a coffee mug. The mug is thick, white, and plain. It came from an Alaska ferry. It is the kind of mug, says George, that a man on watch can take out on deck. It is the kind of mug that, on the bridge of a seiner, a man can set down heavily and satisfactorily, then return his attention to the helm.

On the landward wall hangs a frying pan and a whiskbroom and a toothbrush.

When I visited, two books lay under the bed. One was the *U.S. Coast Pilot for the Pacific Coast,* tenth edition, 1968. The other was the *Bering Sea and Strait Pilot,* first edition, 1920. George is especially fond of the old 1920 volume. He chooses old books over new ones when he can. The old guides, assembled in the days of sailing ships, have better information on the winds—"Wait for SE wind and stay close-hauled on the port tack"—and they tell George where, in 1913, the Indians rendezvoused in their canoes.

Inside the old pilot book was a sketch of a canoe rudder George was planning. In the margin of the sketch was a note I have puzzled over, and have never been able to decipher. It said,

 DAWN TREADER

DAWN TREADER

 THIRD PLANET

 MARIEM

I would take this for a list of possible names for a canoe, except for the odd placement on the page. The note looks more like a crude map. Are these sailing instructions to some obscure region? *Dawn Treader* is the ship in C. S. Lewis's *Narnia* books, but is "Mariem" a misspelling of the Latin *marem?* I don't know. When I asked George the meaning of the note, he claimed to have forgotten.

Outside the door, on the landward side of the house, hang two buckets for rainwater. They are brimful through most of the year, for maritime British Columbia is a rainy country. On a seaward branch is a birdhouse.

Henry Thoreau was proud of building a grounded house at Walden for $28.12½. George built higher, and for $20.00 less. He split all his shakes from a single drift log he found at sea and towed to shore. His two octagonal windows, his three rectangular windows, and most of his other materials are gifts or salvage. He spent $2.00 on a stovepipe and $6.00 on the string for his lashings.

Sometimes George *looks* alarmingly like Thoreau, even in the style of his beard and the cut of his hair. From the old daguerreotypes it is impossible to tell the color of Thoreau's eyes, but his gaze in black and white is as wide and arresting as the Dyson gaze. George, like Thoreau, suffers and enjoys a heightened sense of solitude. George has the same rawboned ego, inflated to fill the solitude. His personality, like Thoreau's, is sharp with edges that companionship has not had opportunity to wear away. If George is Henry reincarnate, then their soul has made some progress since 1845, but entirely in matters of economy.

Like Thoreau, George is a bean-eater. When George's body is entirely finished with the beans he has eaten, or the brown rice or fish or sprouts, he rappels down the tree and disappears briefly in the forest. In nature he answers nature's call. Sometimes, when it's raining hard, or when he just doesn't feel like making the trip to earth, he selects a red-cedar shingle, uses it, then sails it like a Frisbee out over the canopy of trees.

In the autumn George has trouble with flying squirrels. In that season they besiege him like paratroopers. When he is home, there's no problem, for on hearing them bang into his windows or land on his doorsill, he shouts, and they jump off to glide elsewhere. But when he is gone, they enter and burglarize his place. In British Columbia, 1974 was a bad year for flying squirrels.

"They were driving me crazy," George told me afterward. "They were flying down from the hill into my tree and messing up my house."

"Eating your food?"

"Yes. That I could tolerate. They shit all over my floors, and I could take that. But then they began taking the insulation from my walls to make their *own* nests. They began taking the insulation from my *sleeping bags*. That was too much. I was seriously thinking of getting a shotgun."

This, from George Dyson, is a powerful admission. George is a pacifist who first came to Canada at the height of the Vietnam War. The squirrels were testing his creed. They were bending his essential nature. He never got the shotgun, but he began practicing with a slingshot and became, in a purely theoretical way, deadly with it. He honed his skill down very fine, continually postponing the day of the massacre. Then came an idea for a new sort of trap.

Conventional rattraps don't work with flying squirrels, according to George, because the squirrels know how to set them off harmlessly. Had he proceeded conventionally, he says, bomb squads of squirrels would have eased into his house, defused his devices, then whistled an all-clear. George believes that living in trees boosts intelligence, and that squirrels are smart, like primates. Arboreal life had sharpened George's wits too, of course. He designed a cage with a door like a guillotine blade, a mousetrap for a trigger, and power supplied by rubber bands. He trapped three squirrels, transported them thirty miles, and released them. They were the ringleaders, apparently, for he had no more trouble that year.

Raccoons sometimes bother George in his tree. Most of his trouble is with the juveniles. "They're bad then. It's their teen-age period or something. They challenge each other to go up my tree. 'I dare you to go up to George's house.' One night they wouldn't let me in until four in the morning. There were five of them, all from the same litter. I threw rocks at them and everything."

"Did you hit them?" I asked.

"Yes. But they're tough. They wouldn't move. I don't know where they are now. I guess they broke up."

Winter is George's favorite time in the tree house. In that season, fogs roll in from the cold strait and obliterate everything but the Douglas fir. George is perfectly alone then, his tree rising from the immaculateness. He sits high and detached, like a Moslem in his minaret, or an astronaut orbiting a planet of clouds.

On being fired up, the small stove warms his small space

instantly. He passes stormy winter days reading, thinking, and swaying slightly in the wind. At night, high in the dark, wet motion of the Canadian fir forest, his hidden fire burns.

—— 5 ——

Wunderkind

"My repute is that of a good technician, happy with words, but not markedly original," George Dyson once wrote. Not the George Dyson of the wool cap and the tree house, but his grandfather, *Sir* George Dyson, director of the Royal College of Music. "I am familiar with modern idioms, but they are outside the vocabulary of what I want to say. I am really what the eighteenth century called a *kapellmeister*, an untranslated word which means a musician equipped both to compose and produce such music as is needed in his position or environment."

Sir George Dyson was a gifted, busy, forceful man. In 1923, when he was forty, his only son, Freeman, was born.

If, as is often suggested, music and mathematics arise from a single aptitude, or from two very similar aptitudes, then Freeman inherited that. By the age of six, his great interests were mathematics and astronomy. He was more than a little mathematical kapellmeister, however. He was a *wunderkind*.

"It is said," Sir George wrote, "that the mental processes of a mathematical prodigy differ in no essential respect from those of ordinary folks who can handle more modest problems. The prodigy's gift is the power of incessant concentration on more and more complicated mental calculations, until his brain can instantly recall the end products of the thousands of factors with which his mind has been busy." Sir George was writing here about genius in music, and he was going to math for analogy. It is not hard to guess which mathematical prodigy had aroused his wonder.

"In Mozart you hear this fantastic intricacy," says Brian Dunne, one of Freeman Dyson's colleagues on Project Orion. "You know he has to hold a whole series of things in balance, in order to make it come out right. Freeman has this. He has a wonderful ability to carry his train of thought through fantastic numbers of logical steps."

If Freeman's synapses sparked more electric than his father's, his personality was somewhat less forceful. This is, at any rate, Freeman's own view of things. Others who know the Dyson history seem to share it. Sir George was the country boy who made good by determination. Freeman, because of the social advantage provided by his father's success, and because of his own dazzling, force-of-nature gift, never had to develop that determination. Freeman will admit that as a boy he was competitive. He enjoyed doing anything he could do well. He excelled at Latin and history, as well as at math, but he avoided sports, except for distance running—the steeplechase—for which his slender frame was suited. He was mostly an indoorsman. He lived in books.

English schools advanced students according to ability, not age, and Freeman was usually three years or so ahead of his contemporaries. His older classmates did not mind this precociousness, but his age-mates did, and Freeman suffered black eyes from small fists.

"Why?" I asked, when I learned this. "Why did they resent you?"

For a time the physicist was lost for an answer. "Well," he said at last. "Well, I suppose I was quite unbearable." He insisted that he likes the English system, in spite of the black eyes. They were a small price for the freedom to grow at his own speed.

"I was lucky," he has written, "to go through high school and college in England during World War II when there was an acute shortage of paper. In England, oral examinations are not part of the system. No paper, no examinations. So the regular examination routine was disrupted and we were free to get ourselves an education. In my last year of high school I sat in class for a total of seven hours a week. We made good use of our freedom. I learned higher mathematics (and French) from three fat and dusty volumes of Jordan's *Cours d'Analyse* which I found in the school library. I often wondered who had had the vision to put these marvelous books into our library. Nobody on the teaching staff ever looked at them. The famous mathematician Hardy had been a boy at the same school forty years earlier, so perhaps he had had something to do with it. He wrote in his book, *A Mathematician's Apology*, that his eyes were opened to the beauty of mathematics by reading Jordan's *Cours d'Analyse*. How many American high-school libraries have a copy? And how many American high schools would give the children enough time to read it if they had it?

"When I came to Cambridge University in the middle of the war I was again lucky, because the war had swept away all the graduate students. The mathematicians Hardy, Littlewood, Besicovitch gave courses of advanced lectures in a small room with three or four undergraduates sitting around a table. The geophysicist Harold Jeffreys gave his course to an audience of one. Mondays, Wednesdays, and Fridays at nine, I was always there punctually so that he would not begin talking to an empty room. It was a great time to be a student."

—— 6 ——

Fire Storm

Then the war caught up with Freeman. At the end of his second year at Cambridge, he was interviewed by C. P. Snow, whose wartime job was finding appropriate military uses for technical people. Freeman became, at the age of nineteen, a mathematician with the Royal Air Force Bomber Command.

This was irony, though an irony fairly common at the time. Freeman had been a "fierce pacifist" for most of his youth. He had grown up in the grim years after the First World War. "The older generation," he has written of that time, "were determined that we should be constantly reminded of their tragedy. And, indeed, our whole lives were overshadowed by it. Every year, on November 11, there was the official day of mourning. But much heavier on our souls weighed the daily reminders that the best and brightest of a whole generation had fallen.

"We of the class of 1941 were no fools. We saw clearly in 1937 that another bloodbath was approaching. We knew how to figure the odds. We saw no reason to expect that the next round would be less bloody than the one before. We expected that the fighting would start in 1939 or 1940, and we observed that our chances of coming through it alive were about the same as if we had belonged to the class of 1915 or 1916. We calculated the odds to be about ten to one that we would be dead in five years."

To Freeman and his small circle of fellow pacifists, the world was insane. Hitler was just a symptom. The German people were not enemies, but fellow victims; it was the times that were sick. The old men in power in Britain had no answers to any of the nation's problems. Chamberlain was a hypocrite. Hitler was no hypocrite, but he was insane. Churchill was a warmonger "planning the campaigns in which we were to die." The only world leader that Freeman's friends admired was Gandhi. They subscribed to *Peace News*. They boycotted OTC, the British equivalent of ROTC. "We raged against the hypocrisy and stupidity of our elders in the same way the young rebels are raging today, and for very similar reasons."

But the holocaust that Freeman's circle expected did not materialize. The war came, but proved not so bloody as they had calculated. Churchill won their grudging admiration. The non-violent, Hitler-accommodating Pétain-Laval government ended their Gandhism. "Pacifism was destroyed as a moral force as soon as Laval touched it," Freeman has written. He was no longer a fierce pacifist when he reported for duty with the RAF.

"I arrived at the headquarters of the Royal Air Force Bomber Command in July 1943, just in time for the big raids against Hamburg. On July 27, we killed forty thousand people and lost only seventeen bombers. For the first time in history, we had created a fire storm."

Fire storms were devastatingly effective accidents. No one understood, or understands today, what makes them. They seem to depend on a climatic instability with which the bombs interact. The storms travel very fast, generate enormous heat, and burn up the oxygen in large areas of a city. They kill people even inside bomb shelters.

"In every big raid, we tried to raise a fire storm, but we succeeded just twice—once in Hamburg and once, two years later, in Dresden." American forces had a similar success in bombing Japan, twice triggering fire storms, Freeman notes. A fire storm in Tokyo killed as many people as the Hiroshima bomb—a hundred thousand. It was more devastating than the atomic bomb that fell on Nagasaki.

Freeman did not work directly on the mathematics of the fire storm. He became the Bomber Command expert on collisions. British bombers flew at night, and occasionally in the darkness they ran into one another. The bomber crews resented dying by accident; they felt slightly better about dying by enemy fire. The problem was that loosely bunched formations, though they suffered fewer collisions, lost more planes to enemy fighters. Freeman's chore was to find the grim median.

"The ratio of lethal to nonlethal collisions over England proved to be about three to one. In this ratio, I had already allowed for the fact that some nonlethal collisions over England would have been lethal if they had occurred over Germany. So in the end I told the Command that our best guess at the number of lethal collisions over Germany was to multiply the number of nonlethal collisions by three. That was all the mathematics I had to do. In practical terms my information meant that we were losing only about one bomber to collisions in a thousand sorties. I told the Command that this was not nearly enough. I told them to increase the density of the bomber force five-fold, so that the collision losses would come up one-half percent. I told them that they would save much more than one-half percent in losses to fighters. The Command followed my advice and the crews reluctantly obeyed."

Freeman came to know more about the bombing campaign than most operational officers. He knew more even than most cabinet ministers. His knowledge appalled him.

"The defenses made it impossible for us to bomb accurately. We stopped trying to hit precise military objectives. Burning down cities was all we could do, so we did that. Even in killing the civilian population, we were inefficient. The Germans had killed one person for every ton of bombs that they dropped on England. To kill a German, we dropped three tons. I felt my responsibility deeply, being in possession of all this information that was so carefully concealed from the British public. Many times, I decided I owed it to the public to run out into the streets and tell them what stupidities were being committed in their name. But I never had the moral courage to do it. I sat in my office until the end, carefully calculating how to murder another hundred thousand people most economically.

"After the war ended, I read reports of the trials of men who had been high up in the Eichmann organization. They had sat in their offices writing memoranda and calculating how to murder people efficiently, just like me. The main difference was that they were sent to jail or hanged as war criminals and I went free. . . .

"In August, 1945, I was all set to fly to Okinawa. We had defeated the Germans, but Mr. Churchill had still not had enough. He persuaded President Truman to let him join in the bombing of Japan with a fleet of three hundred bombers, which he called Tiger Force. We were to be based in Okinawa, and since the Japanese had almost no air defenses, we were to bomb, like the Americans, in daylight. I found this new slaughter of defenseless Japanese even more sickening than the slaughter of well-defended Germans. Still I did not quit. By that time, I had been at war so long that I could hardly remember peace. No living poet had words to describe that emptiness of the soul which allowed me to go on killing without hatred and without remorse. But Shakespeare understood it, and he gave Macbeth the words:

I am in blood
Stepped in so far, that, should I wade no more,
Returning were as tedious as go o'er.

I was sitting at home eating a quiet breakfast with my mother when the morning paper arrived with the news of Hiroshima. I understood at once what it meant. 'Thank God for that,' I said. I knew that Tiger Force would not fly, and I would never have to kill anybody again."

Asked recently if his experience of the war figured in his drive for the stars, Freeman nodded. "Our strongest feelings are subconscious. I grew up in a time of despair—the late thirties. It was far worse than it is now. It was worse than we realized. I think we were incredibly lucky. I suppose that's where it really comes from." Twenty-five years after the war, he wrote, "In my personal view of the human situation, the exploration of space appears as the most hopeful feature of a dark landscape."

At the war's end, Freeman considered his prospects. Physics, he decided, would be the most vital science of the next twenty-five years. Physics needed him, too; it was in "more of a mess than mathematics or astronomy." He went to Cambridge, saw G. I. Taylor, and asked that great physicist for advice. Taylor immediately suggested that Freeman go to Cornell and work with Hans Bethe.

"It wasn't all that obvious at the time," says Freeman. "But it was the right decision. It was the perfect place. I had to get away from England, from my father. I needed a fresh start." In 1947 he came to the United States on a Commonwealth Fund Fellowship. He arrived in Ithaca in the rain.

"When I knocked on Bethe's door, and he opened it, and I looked down, the first thing I saw was a pair of very muddy boots. I found that very reassuring. It would not have happened at Cambridge. The students called him Hans. He ate with them in the cafeteria. Those were things no one would have thought to do at Cambridge."

Freeman learned his physics from Bethe and from Richard Feynman, who was also at Cornell. "From Bethe and Feynman," he writes, "I learned that mathematical elegance is not enough, a hard lesson for a pupil of Hardy to learn. To do good work in physics, one must also have an instinct for reality, an intuitive sense of the intrinsic importance of things. Bethe and Feynman had this instinct to a superlative degree. Some of it, though not enough, rubbed off on me. On the other side stood the great mathematician Herman Weyl, who once said to me, 'When I am forced to make the choice between truth and beauty, I always choose beauty.' "

It is said of Hans Bethe that he is less a great physicist than a great teacher of physicists. I once asked Dyson if this was true.

"Both are true. Bethe had a mind very much like my own. He is less a deep thinker than a problem-solver. He figured out the equations for what goes on in the sun. The sun is an interesting piece of machinery to Bethe." Of Freeman, Dr. Bethe says, "He was probably the most gifted graduate student I ever had. He was so good, he discouraged other graduate students from becoming theoretical physicists. Here was a man who could do everything with his left hand, and spend the rest of the day reading *The New York Times.* He's a superb mathematician. The rest of us physicists usually know only enough math to get by. When he was very young, still a graduate student, he solved a problem nobody else was able to solve."

The solution came to Freeman on a Greyhound bus.

The problem was one central to quantum electrodynamics, and the young physicist first spent a year at Cornell studying it, learning what approaches had failed. At the end of that year he closed his books, disconnected his cerebrum, got on a Greyhound, and headed west. His fondness for bus travel dates from that trip. Greyhounds had no toilets then, so every two or three hours the bus had to stop. Freeman stretched his legs and walked around. He really saw the country. He made no calculations, letting his mind go fallow. In Berkeley he got off and visited friends, then got on another Greyhound and headed east again.

America passed once more outside his window. The bus rattled down the highway, and the pieces of the electrodynamic puzzle jiggled in Freeman's head. It was a hard puzzle. Quantum electrodynamics is the theory that unifies Einstein's special relativity and quantum mechanics. It reconciles, in a few neat principles, a former chaos of laws on solid-state and plasma physics, on the creation and annihilation of particles, on maser and laser technology, and on optical and microwave spectroscopy. The bus droned past mesas and cacti and one-gas-pump towns, while formulae chased one another across Freeman's consciousness.

"We were driving home when it all fell into place," he says. "I saw how to do it. I got out in Chicago and spent a week writing the thing up."

Did any of the bus passengers notice? Shouldn't some kind of metaphysical crackling be audible as a body of physical law becomes seamless? Did a sleepy soldier or an irritable mother or a bored child see anything different in the stare of the slender young man by the window? Probably not. Of course, those people were not just anonymous bus-riders either, and may have been busy with calculations, or composing symphonies, of their own.

Freeman's discovery was one of those intuitive leaps so strenuous that physicists and mathematicians seldom make them after their midthirties. He has never made so daring a leap again.

"It must have been quite a sensation," I once suggested.

"Well," said Freeman. "Of course it's the greatest thing in the world."

From Cornell, Freeman moved to Princeton and the Institute for Advanced Studies. Strolling in Princeton one day, the shy young physicist struck up a conversation with a four-year-old named Katrina, who was riding her tricycle. He was then, as he is now, most comfortable in the company of children. Freeman and

Katrina went on meeting like that, outside her house, until one day she invited him in for tea. Inside he met her mother, Verena Haefeli-Huber, the Swiss mathematician who would become his wife.

"He was the budding young genius among the people at the institute," Verena remembers. "He was not shy so much as awkward. He enjoyed the social thing—to be among people—but there was a slight distance in him, a rigidity. He was quite attractive."

Three weeks later Freeman proposed. Verena thought this was a little hurried, but "Freeman was very determined. He isn't swayed by moods or insecurities. He was very rational." They were married. Katrina got the stepfather that she had wanted. She found Freeman very satisfactory. He spent a lot of time with her, taking her skating and on long walks. His looks were so youthful that people mistook him for her older brother, and that tickled her. His manner was strange sometimes—he would stop in the middle of sentences to make his calculations—but that was different and she liked it.

In 1951, the year Freeman became, at twenty-eight, a full professor at Cornell, Verena gave birth to Esther Dyson. In 1953, after Freeman was elected a fellow of the Royal Society, his second child, George Bernard Dyson, was born.

—— 7 ——

A Blue Smile

No nova appeared over the Cornell physics department to mark George's arrival. His intellect did not from infancy light up the night. One would not have guessed from his school grades that his parents had met as colleagues of Einstein. George was bright enough, but indifferent to formal learning. He showed no glimmer of genius in mathematics or music. In George, the Dyson thread, strung of quarter notes and equations, becomes difficult to trace.

"When I was little I played with boats more than anything," he says. "I remember in Maine I spent a whole summer building and sailing models. I made really fast catamarans. I painted them blue. I'd let them go, and that's the last you'd ever see of them."

George's earliest memory is of a bad dream.

"It's the first memory I have. Or one of the first. It's back in those memories where you can't tell which is first. I remember being woken up by Freeman in the middle of the night. I used to go to him when I had nightmares, but this time he came to me. He said he needed to talk to me. He had just had a dream where an airliner crashed. The plane was in flames. People were standing around outside, and some of them were running into the flames to rescue passengers. Freeman couldn't move. He was rooted to the spot. He told me it wouldn't mean anything to me now, but later it would. He told me that a father, though he seems powerful, is just a man, with weaknesses. He wanted me to remember, so that if I was ever in that situation, I would be able to move."

Katrina remembers her little brother as a boy so shy he never removed his shirt, even on the hottest days of summer. His shirts were always white. He insisted on that color. She remembers parsley: "Wherever we moved—Ithaca, Princeton, Berkeley—George would plant parsley. That was his territorial mark."

Freeman remembers his son's crying fits. "He would cry and cry, and sometimes I thought he would have to crack. I couldn't get him to stop." There was instability in both family lines, and the crying fits worried Freeman deeply. The fits were not the sort of problem for which he could work out a formula.

Verena remembers her boy's imagination. "He always had a lot of it. He was always building things with blocks. The boatbuilding started very early. He whittled models out of scraps of wood.

"I don't know how it began. He went to sea very early—that may have helped. In 1956, when George was three, I took the children to Switzerland and Austria on the Holland-America Line. It was when things were beginning to go bad with Freeman and me.

Freeman was making his first trip west to General Atomic, and he put us on the boat. The evening after waving good-bye to him, I was feeling a bit blue. I took the kids on deck to watch the sunset. It was a beautiful sunset over the Atlantic. Clear. Afterward, down below, George said, 'Mom, do you know what I saw? I saw a mermaid. I saw a blue smile without a face.'

"It happened on consecutive nights. He saw her again. He found out her name—Misty. Later on, she got mixed up in Carnegie Lake in Princeton. That winter, when the lake froze, he began to lose interest in her—she was locked up under the ice. After a while he no longer talked about her.

"George has this romantic streak, this poetic view of things. Everything he does turns out to be an adventure.

"His first expedition was in a rubber dinghy in Maine. It was after the divorce. George spent the summers with me, then, and I was teaching at Bowdoin. George saw this island in a little lake and he decided to visit it. He was always very methodical. He spent three days getting his food and provisions together. I dropped them off at the lakeshore—George and a friend, who was named Tom, I think—and they paddled in the dinghy over to the little island. They were going to spend three days.

"A terrific storm came up. After the second night I got a call from George, who was in a phone booth. They had paddled ashore. It wasn't the storm, it turned out; it was that George couldn't stand the guy. Tom was a compulsive marshmallow eater. George couldn't stand to watch him eat marshmallows. George had clammed up. He had that pale, drawn look he gets when he doesn't like someone.

"He wasn't a procrastinator about his expeditions, but he was so pedantic. Everything had to be wrapped right. It took him a long time, and he was always late. Once it was dusk before he got into the woods, and in the morning he found he was on a traffic island.

"He even had adventures when he took the subway. When I was in New York, teaching on Long Island, George would come to see me on the subway. He was eleven. He was good at finding his way, but one day he was an hour late. He came in worn and exhausted. He had opened the gate for somebody at Penn Station, and people started pouring through. He was so polite. He stood there holding the door. He couldn't shut it on anybody."

After the divorce, Freeman remarried, and most of the year George lived in Princeton with his father and stepmother.

Around the Institute for Advanced Studies was a margin of woodland, the institute's fief, and George rambled there with his friends. The small gang of institute children collected snakes from the woods and turtles from the river. ("This one guy, he really had guts. He'd catch cottonmouths. Bring them to class.") Black kids from beyond the pale hunted the same river for turtles, but the two tribes never mixed. The black kids snared turtles not for their collections, George thinks, but for the soup pot. George took violin lessons. His tutor, addicted to baseball, listened to George's violin with a radio earplug in place. It was not the screech of George's missed notes that caused the maestro to rise in his seat; it was the lift of distant home runs. On George's birthdays, his grandfather sent him messages in music from England. Freeman would pick out the notes on the piano. Sir George never sent *recordings* of his birthday messages. "My grandfather believed phonographs were the invention of the Devil," George says. "He fixed it with copyrights so no one could play his music on machinery. It was monotonous music—hymns and stuff." George fooled around with fireworks, disassembling a lot of small ones to make big bombs.

Ulli Steltzer, a photographer who then lived in Princeton and now lives in Vancouver, remembers George as a boy. Her fondness for him was in direct proportion to her dislike for the institute. ("A terrible place. A pretty-pretty place. It doesn't know it is in New Jersey. It's the mountain, and all the prophets are coming.") She first met George at a wine-and-cheese party at the Dysons'. "There were all sorts of notables there," she says. "George and I stayed away from everybody else. He was twelve, and tall for his age. Quiet, shy, and skinny. George was skinny no matter what he wore. He was like a bird—big nose and big eyes coming out of clothes that were invariably hanging from him. He was a little evasive. He disappeared as soon as I photographed him. He was very odd and charming."

The winter in Princeton when he was twelve, George and his best friend, Robert Fish, decided to camp out one night. "It was January," Freeman recalls. "It happened to be the coldest night of the year. Around zero. I didn't think it was a good idea, but I thought he should be allowed to learn from his own mistakes. I drove them there, to their spot deep in the woods. It looked to me like a pretty hopeless situation."

Remembering, Freeman laughs his odd, shy, silent laugh. His shoulders shake, but no sound comes out.

"I didn't sleep much all that night. Very early, when it got light, I drove back. They were fine, of course. They had a fire and were having a fine time in their tent. George had organized it very carefully."

—— 8 ——

Jail

The next year, when he was thirteen, George built a thirteen-foot plywood kayak. He had to build it in his room, for his father and stepmother would not let him use the garage. This remains a sore point with him. To make his kayak long enough, he had to extend it into the closet, and it was hell getting it out. The kayak was an idea before its time—not in human history, perhaps, but in the scheme of George's life. It was a premature budding of his genius. George paddled his kayak once on the river, then sold it.

It was not the kayak that George regards as epochal in his life. In his thirteenth year he went on a time voyage, and that weighs more heavily with him.

It began like this: George left a friend's house one evening in June and mounted his bike to go home. As his friend watched,

George fell and hit his head on the pavement. He rose, remounted, and pedaled home. On entering the door, he walked straight up to his room without speaking. His father noted this and found it peculiar. Later, at dinner, it seemed to Freeman that George was acting strangely.

George does not remember any of this. He remembers opening his eyes on an intensely bright light. He was lying on his back, and men in white coats were staring down at him. He was in a hospital. "All right," someone said, "what kind of dope did you take?"

Then they told him it was June.

"That scared me to death. I thought it was March. I remembered that back in March I was thinking of trying some of this marijuana everyone was talking about." Now it was June, and these men in white coats thought he had taken some bad dope. George assumed they were right. In the missing months, he thought, he must have gone from marijuana to something stronger, the very thing all the high-school propaganda warned against.

When George came home from the hospital, it was for him still March, yet he found all his term papers written. They were in his handwriting, so he must have done them, but he remembered not a word. They were a gift, written as if by magic. It was a painless way to have done two months of work. "It was great," George claims now. "It was like time travel."

At fourteen George was smoking marijuana for real. He had earned the name so now he played the game. He dressed all in black, cultivating a hoodlum's image. He became, without knowing it, the center of a big investigation. The local narcotics officers suspected him of being the California Connection, the main source of marijuana for his high school. Whether or not this was true, George does not say.

He had spent his recent summers in California visiting his mother, who was teaching there. He had hiked the Sierra Nevada and the Haight-Ashbury, meeting people in both places. Some of his acquaintances were a little shady. He was back in New Jersey, and the target of the investigation, when a package without return address came to him from California. It was opened in the post office and found to contain marijuana. George was at school when the police knocked at his family's door. They told his stepmother that he might be in trouble, and asked to look at his room. She let them in. Among George's things they found some marijuana seeds.

"They came and got me in class. That really raised my status around there. At that school the most exclusive clique was the people who had been to jail. They called each other by their old cell numbers. These three detectives came into the classroom and handcuffed me—my hands between my legs so I couldn't run. They were *strong*. They knew what they were doing. They really plan those things in advance." The detectives fingerprinted George and shaved his head. They showed him mugshots of a number of reprobates and warned him about following the same path.

George had lived a sheltered life at Princeton, and suddenly that was gone.

"You're really insulated at the institute," he says. "They don't want their people to worry about anything. They want you to spend your time thinking. When a staff member travels some-where, the institute works out all the details—passports and schedules and everything. They have limousines to take the wives shopping. There's a good cafeteria. You get a plate of prawns and crab and everything for two dollars." Jail was not like that. The jailhouse was inhabited by a real cross-section of New Jersey. At first his new cellmates scared him, then he got acquainted, and they no longer seemed so tough. The black kids taught him to play basketball, a game that George, temperamentally cool to team sports, had never learned. Jail was not a bad experience, he claims now. It taught him about a lot of things.

That his father would leave him in prison, for whatever reason, had shaken him, he admits. It seems to have marked the end of something between them.

The authorities told George he would be in jail for two years, and he made a decision. He knew he couldn't do that much time. A week later, when they released him, he was already planning his escape. He knew where he was going, once he broke out. He was going to the mountains.

The next summer found George in the mountains indeed. He was working as a pot washer for a Sierra Club base camp in Colorado. The white peaks of the Rockies had become the most hopeful feature in a dark landscape.

It was an ideal summer, except for the intrusion of a party of hunters. The hunters came on horseback, led by a packer and guide named Carol Martin. George and the Sierra Club people resented Martin's dilution of their wilderness experience; Martin resented the hikers for trampling the meadow where he always camped. Years later, he and George would meet again.

Susan Baxter, one of the girls who worked with George in the camp commissary, recalls him then: "I remember the sense of being alone—his aloneness. He was precocious. He seemed very grown for his age. Not so grown in his dealings with people, maybe, but he knew exactly where he was going. He knew what he wanted to experience."

The commissary girls, who were two and three years older than George, pulled him into their female mountain gaiety. To tease him, they braided his hair, and he shyly put up with it. Several of them remember hiking with George, his long hair braided, carrying an ice ax, wearing nothing but net long johns. Net long johns would become a trademark.

"His tarp!" Susan Baxter remembers. "He pitched an incredibly beautiful tarp in the aspens. It was clear plastic. One night we had this incredible storm and we all went to George's tarp to watch it. You could sit under it and watch the lightning and everything through the plastic. He had done just a beautiful job on it."

George had begun work on another trademark. He was building nests.

9

The Origin of Species

George left home for good at the age of sixteen. In the next five years he and his father saw each other only once. Occasionally they exchanged stiff letters. Their estrangement deepened. Somehow things had gone wrong. There is a variety of opinion as to why.

One Princeton colleague: "Freeman had a rough time. He had Sir George and his boy George at both ends—two male figures who have something he doesn't. Or thinks he doesn't. Freeman imagines he's a more timid soul."

Another Princeton colleague: "I have a hunch it was entirely George. The same thing happened with a lot of families in the late sixties and early seventies—during the Vietnam War. It's similar to difficulties I've had with two of my own children. I can't shed any light on it, because I never understood what happened between me and my own son and daughter. Pretty much a total disconnect."

A former Princeton resident: "Freeman is a very sentimental person, like many mathematicians. He lives by his fantasies, but he executes them. He dresses like Einstein now—a little sloppy. He doesn't grasp George. Freeman's an Establishment baby. He's an Establishment person who has sold out and is trying to retrieve his soul through George."

Verena Huber-Dyson: "Freeman couldn't really enjoy the animal warmth of his one and only son, because of the necessity to mold him. He felt a tremendous obligation, which was paralyzing."

George Dyson: "I felt completely molded into my undertakings by him. By his preconceptions of what his son should be. It was like I was his proxy. The atmosphere at home was cold, but any outward trip was reinforced. Like camping. I didn't particularly enjoy those first adventures. I felt I had to do them. It's not what you want as a kid at all."

Katrina (when I asked her how it was that her stepfather, who had been so good with her, could have had so much trouble with his son): "*He's good with little girls.* George was not a make-believe child. He was a real boy, with a strong spirit."

Freeman himself says little about the separation, aside from taking the blame. "These five years have been me. It's been my fault. He's been on the other side of the country. There was the expense and . . . and I thought it was important for George to get away, to be on his own."

But it is possible to find more about George between the lines of what Freeman writes. Freeman's confessional piece on his days with the RAF, published in 1971, during the Vietnam War and shortly after George had left the U.S. for Canada, seems addressed in part to his pacifist son. If the confession rings a little false, or rings at least peculiar—and certain of Freeman's acquaintances think it does—then the fault may lie in its undercover polemicism. George appears too, of all places, in the *Bulletin of Atomic Scientists.* In 1969, the year George left home, Freeman enumerated for that journal several facts of modern life:

". . . A third fact of life is drugs. By this I mean not the harmless legal drugs like aspirin and penicillin, bu the illegal ones, LSD, marijuana, and so forth. Many people no doubt have more experience with these than I do, but at least I have not brought up a couple of teen-agers without realizing that drugs are an important part of the landscape.

". . . I find the underlying pattern to be the propensity of human beings to function best in rather small groups. . . . Our pot-smoking teen-agers are unanimous in saying that the great thing about pot is not the drug itself but the comradeship which it creates. And to make the comradeship real, there must not only be a group of friends inside the circle but enemies outside, police and parents and authorities to be defied. This is human life the way it is: my son wearing his hair odiously long just because I dislike to be seen together with it in public, and we of the older generation fulfilling our duty as parents by keeping our hair short and marijuana illegal."

Freeman's solution was dramatic. The answer was in the new frontier of space. Out there, he wrote, "Man's tribal instincts will move back from the destructive channels of nationalism, racism, and youthful alienation, and find satisfaction in the dangerous life of a frontier society."

This, for someone searching for George between the lines, is startling. The generation gap suddenly becomes an interplanetary void. Freeman seems to have contemplated shooting his odiously long-haired son entirely off this globe.

In 1972, at Birkbeck College in London, Freeman gave a lecture he called "The World, the Flesh, and the Devil." He had borrowed the title from a book by the physicist J. D. Bernal, whom the occasion in London was honoring. Freeman acknowledged Bernal's influence on his own ideas, conceded that their shared view of the future was as unpopular now as in 1928, when Bernal first advanced it, and then roughly paraphrased it: Man would defeat the World, its limited resources and living space, by leaving the planet for free-floating colonies in space. Man would defeat the Flesh, its various diseases and infirmities, with the aid of bionic organs, biological engineering, and self-reproducing machinery. Man would defeat the Devil—the irrational in his nature—by reorganizing society along scientific lines and by learning intellectual control over his emotions. "Bernal understood," said Freeman, "that his proposals for the remaking of man and society flew in the teeth of deeply entrenched human instincts. He did not on that account weaken or compromise his statement. He believed that a rational soul would ultimately come to accept his vision of the future as reasonable, and that for him was enough. He foresaw that mankind might split into two species, one following the technological path which he described, the other holding on as best it could to the ancient folkways of natural living. And he recognized that the dispersion of mankind into the vastness of space is precisely what is required for such a split of the species to occur without intolerable strife and social disruption."

But did Bernal foresee that the split might appear between one generation and the next? Did it occur to Freeman, as he paraphrased in London, that this speciation might already have come to pass—that he and his son were different animals?

Two Years Before the Mast

When George was sixteen he attended, in a loose sense of the word, the University of California at San Diego. That campus did not agree with him. After a few weeks he moved north to Berkeley and loosely attended classes there. They did not hold his attention either, and he took to wandering away. One day his stroll brought him to the Berkeley marina. At one of the moorings was a small sailboat, and on it a For Sale sign. George stopped in his tracks. He could buy this boat, he calculated, and have something left over. His fortune was three thousand dollars, part of which his father had given him for expenses at school. He knew nothing about sailboats, and had never considered owning one. But if he bought, he reasoned, he would have both a place to live and a boat. He bought. He moved his things in and lived onboard. He cooked on a Primus stove, slept in one of his four narrow berths, and read on the tiny galley table. He came and went stealthily, for it was against marina rules to live on your boat.

Biologists have a word for this. They have found a new meaning for the old term *cryptozoic*, using it now to describe the life led by raccoons, possums, and the other wild animals that have adapted to civilization by learning to live secretly alongside it. George's style was cryptozoic. In the California nights, in the rows of darkened boats, his secret light was burning.

My family knew George then. My sister was one of the commissary girls who, two summers before, had braided his hair and watched the lightning storm through his clear plastic tarp. On arriving in Berkeley, George looked us up. He visited our house when he needed company, or when his ship's stores ran low. He was already suspicious of processed foods. Once my mother found him in her kitchen reading the ingredients on a bag of dogfood. "This is the only thing in the house that's fit to eat," he muttered. It was a line she has always remembered.

George learned to sail by simply casting off and setting out. San Francisco Bay became an extended home. When he studied, which was seldom, he liked to sail to Angel Island and stand off its coast while he read. He had suspected that he would not like higher education, and he was right. He did not last a semester at the university. He quit and made preparations to sail to Hawaii. He read books on navigation and learned that his boat, though small, was designed for open-ocean sailing.

When my mother heard of his plans, she urged him not to go. She believed that George was unhappy, that he didn't much care whether he reached Hawaii or not. She called his sister Katrina, who was living in Vancouver, and enlisted her aid. Together the two women leaned on George. Pleased at all the commotion, he let himself be dissuaded. He offered to sell his boat to my brothers and me, but we were broke, so he sold to a stranger at a considerable loss. He left Berkeley and headed up to British Columbia.

He has told me since that he's glad he didn't make the trip to Hawaii. "Knowing what I do now about the ocean, I think I would have ended at the bottom of it," he said. He laughed his odd, shy, silent laugh. The shoulders shake, but no sound comes out.

George has written an account of his new beginnings in Canada. It is part of an unpublished article on whales. His style then was nautical, and about a hundred and fifty years old. He must have been subsisting on a straight diet of sea classics, Melville and Richard Henry Dana:

At the age of seventeen, while seeking my place in the world through hard and persevering work, I was partner to the launching of the *D'Sonoqua*, a small vessel of forty-eight feet and twenty tons which I had helped build in the preceding months. She was launched at Vancouver, British Columbia, into waters that yearly see the migration and presence of numerous killer whales. This diminished but still thriving population visits the various straits and inlets to feed upon the gathering schools of salmon, and being the subject of much local legend and esteem, finds itself free from most harassment. This is a coastline rich and hospitable to all who learn its ways, and although worthy of the mariner's due respect, offers good shelter and safe traveling to the careful user of many kinds of watercraft.

Our little ship was in no way complete and we knew of her true habits solely that conjectured during her construction. *D'Sonoqua* was launched with the last of our meagre funds, so disregarding the preliminaries usual with such a new-born craft we accepted that very day the offer of a paying venture up the coast.

We were to load in Vancouver with five musicians, four assistants, and all their associated equipment, to travel in this manner a round trip of over six hundred miles, with the aim of performing in concert to an audience of killer whales. This was part of Dr. Paul Spong's research on this matter near Alert Bay, and I will not elaborate on this amazing journey other than to point out the occasion of my first finding myself approached by whales.

I *will* elaborate.

D'Sonoqua was a ferro-cement boat that George and her owner, Jim Bates ("Lord Jim," George sometimes calls him), had worked on for a year. She was named after a local Indian demideity. She had a diesel auxiliary and would later be rigged as a hermaphrodite brig. Her career began ominously. On the day before the launch, George labored hard for eight hours in last preparations, crawling around in the bilges, where the air was bad. He was dizzy from the stuffiness and the effort. Stepping between the dock and the ship, carrying two seventy-pound pails of ballast—steel punchings—he fell. His free fall to the water was arrested by a bolt, which passed through his arm. He hung there, impaled. The people tried to lift him off, but slipped in his blood and dropped him back on the bolt. Finally they freed him. He spent the night in plastic surgery, then at six the next morning left the hospital, not wanting *D'Sonoqua* to sail without him.

A big storm hit the boat as she left Vancouver Harbor. Because there were as yet no hatches, she immediately began taking water. "It was exciting," George recalls. "They were exciting times." *D'Sonoqua* rocked and rolled, and the five rock-and-roll musicians became instantly seasick. They remained so for the rest of the voyage.

"We thought the musicians would help fix the boat up," George says, "but it turned out they were pretty incapable of doing that. They were good guys. They weren't getting paid or anything. They were drinking and just being musicians. They even had a couple of groupies with them—fifteen-year-old girls. They drank and smoked a lot of weed and took LSD."

George, still weak from his injury, did not indulge. Nor did he get seasick, in spite of his wounds.

"We didn't know where we were going. We thought we were going to Pender Harbor. It turned out we were going all the way to Alert Bay. There were no bunks, no masts, no sails, no running water. The drinking water was in drums on deck. The fuel was paid for, and not much else. We ran out of fuel on the way back from Nanaimo. We drifted around for a few hours, then the ferry saw us and called the Coast Guard.

"We put on a dance at Alert Bay to try to make some money for fuel on the way back. We'd spent all our money on alcohol. But the dance got screwed up. The Indians were having their own dances and they had bought up all the halls. The chief let us use the tribal-council house, but by then it was too late, and in the end we played for free. The Indians enjoyed it. Indian kids really like rock and roll.

"So do whales. The musicians liked the whales, and the whales really responded. You play music, and killer whales start jumping all around your boat. It was good rock and roll."

In his written account George describes how, anchored off Hanson Island in Blackfish Sound, he first encountered killer whales:

A warm August night, with eleven people on board, all asleep but myself, as I had anchor watch on deck. In the utter quiet of calm water and still air I could hear the varied and sonorous breathings of all those below decks, and in the distance the blowings of a sizable pod of whales. As I listened intently they approached over the space of many minutes to glide silently next to our hull, unnoticed except by the faint rippling of water meeting their fins. Their slow and subdued breathing rose from the waters around me, matching that of my sleeping shipmates even to the occasional sniffle or snore. After an unperceived period of time they silently departed, leaving me unsure of the meaning of this visit except that I felt ever different after the touch of their powerful spirit.

After returning the musicians to Vancouver, George put to sea again.

D'Sonoqua and I continued on together for the following two years, spending the first winter in Quatsino Sound, where we selected our masts from the same choice groves of straight-grained spruce as did Captain Cook many years before us. We cut these trees when the sap was low, and combed the whole of this still seagoing community for rigging and canvas to set from our seasoning spars.

Squaring away before an April breeze, we rounded Cape Scott and through the breakers of Nahwitti Bar returned to British Columbia's inside waters, to try our hand at coastal trade. Supplying goods and groceries out of Vancouver, we made our living upon the water, and embarked on all manner of ventures that chance placed in our way.

—— 11 ——

Asteroids

Between Mars and Jupiter lies a large gap where one or two planets, perhaps even three, are thought to have orbited. The planets collided, or suffered some other serious accident, for the gap is now filled with fragments. These are the asteroids. There are many thousands of them, of which sixteen hundred have been tracked, each in its private orbit around the sun. They appear through telescopes as starlike points of light, hence the name. Astronomers have learned a lot about asteroids by analyzing their light. Asteroids spin, and the variations in the sunlight they reflect reveal their shapes. The smaller asteroids are irregular, the larger ones spherical. On big asteroids, gravity is respectable—nearly that of the moon. The asteroid Ceres is 480 miles in diameter. Pallas is 300 miles wide, Vesta 240, Juno 120. Icarus is a boulder one mile in diameter. Eros, in outline the size and shape of Manhattan, tumbles through space like a dead cigar.

"There's very good news from the asteroids," reports Freeman Dyson. "It appears that a large fraction of them, including the big ones, are actually very rich in H_2O. Nobody imagined that. They thought they were just big rocks."

Water obsesses Freeman. In his mental wanderings across the deserts of space, he worries about it like a Bedouin.

Freeman grows older, and the comets begin to seem farther away to him. At the same time the news from the asteroids improves. Lately he has made a focal adjustment of the imagination, turning his attention from comets to asteroids.

"A comet is a symbol for me of a place where you really get away," he says. "A comet is way out. That's where you can go and get lost. And that's one of the reasons for going into space—if you really want to get lost, so nobody will ever see you again. You'd really be on your own. A bunch of people who'd like to do that, then a comet is probably the place.

"Whereas the asteroids are much closer in. They're more conventional. It's easier to get to an asteroid than to Mars, because the gravity is lower and landing is easier. Certainly the asteroids are much more practical, right now. If we start space colonies in, say, the next twenty years, I would put my money on the asteroids."

Dyson was anticipated in this by Antoine de Saint-Exupéry and his *The Little Prince*. When the time comes to offer the asteroids to colonists, in fact, the illustrations for the prospectus could be lifted from that book. The drawing Saint-Exupéry called "The Baobabs," showing a tiny planetoid dwarfed by its baobab trees, looks very much like one of Dyson's worlds, dwarfed by its hundred-mile-high, genetically engineered orchard. Saint-Exupéry was, it is true, less optimistic about extraterrestrial agriculture than Dyson. "Now there were some terrible seeds on the planet that was the home of the Little Prince," he wrote of Asteroid B-612, "and these were the seeds of the baobab. The soil of the planet was infested with them. A baobab is something you will never, never be able to get rid of if you attend to it too late. It spreads over the entire planet. It bores clear through with its roots. And if the planet is too small, and the baobabs are too many, they split it in pieces." Neither was Saint-Exupéry as optimistic about the ennobling effects of life on the asteroids. In search of answers, his Little Prince visits a number of asteroids, and the inhabitants of each display one or another of the old human flaws.

But these doubts can be edited from the prospectus. Life in the asteroid belt will never be rendered more invitingly than in the drawings of the Little Prince moving his chair several steps westward on B-612 so he can continue to watch the sunset, or cleaning out his volcanoes, or conversing with the rose he keeps under glass at night.

Freeman Dyson and the Little Prince are a lot alike. Freeman has the large solemn eyes and the love for great questions. Freeman has a measure of the same sort of innocence. It is not hard, for me at least, to imagine the physicist in the prince's cape, wandering between Mars and Jupiter, in the vast gap where the planets crashed. I can see him hopping amongst the debris of that ancient judgment day, looking for the answers, for water, for a home.

—— 12 ——
Inside Passage

The tree house is not home to George Dyson. He thinks of his Douglas fir as the anteroom of a much larger dwelling. The entire Inside Passage province, the nine hundred miles of protected waters from the southern end of Vancouver Island to Glacier Bay in Alaska, is George's place. He would like to build rooms here and there all along that coast.

Few coastlines on Earth are so convoluted. If you could unravel all George's promontories and indentations and lay them end to end, they would run out nearly forever. There is no conclusion to the gulfs, bays, coves, straits, sounds, canals, channels, passes, passages, inlets, arms, entrances, or surprises around the corner. The coast contains, in other words, a universe. There are several Aegeans worth of islands. Ulysses never had so many archipelagos to wander in. Aeneas met no stranger people, nor did Captain Cook, nor Flash Gordon. There is the Island of the People Who Sing to Whales. There is the Island of the Indians Who Bury Their Dead Under Singer Sewing Machines. There are logging camps and fishing villages. Hidden away in deep inlets are communes of bearded men and long-haired women. Monasteries of strange religious sects stand inland in the mountains. "On *D'Sonoqua*," says George, "I learned to move in that whole society of people."

"Our friend wants a steak!" a logger demanded, his burly arm around George's slender shoulders.

The cook protested that he had no more steaks.

"That's all right," said George, who seldom ate meat now. "I don't want a steak."

"*You want a steak*," said the logger. "The cook ran out of steaks, that's his own fucking fault. He better find a steak. If he doesn't find a steak, we aren't working tomorrow."

Late one night on Denman Island, some kids from the village staggered down to the wharf.

"They were drinking," says George, "making a lot of noise, throwing their bottles down into *D'Sonoqua*. That was their drinking place. They always came down to the wharf to drink. It's the kind of thing where I just turn over and try to go back to sleep. Or if there's too much noise, I get up and read. It was their wharf. We were the strangers there. But one guy on our boat got really pissed. 'You kids get the hell out of here so I can get some sleep.' They just cursed him, so he went down and got the old Winchester we kept on the ship—it was empty—and he came up and waved it at them. It was the wrong thing to do. Those guys hunted deer for their families on that island. They went home and got their guns. They set up behind their cars and shot up the boat. They didn't actually hit it, but they did real good. They came real close. Ping! Zip! We lay low. Then some lady came down in a nightgown. She was really mad. 'Johnny! Jim! Stop that and come home!' She was somebody's mother. So they stopped shooting and they all went home."

D'Sonoqua contracted with the Indian village of Church House, on Raza Island, to deliver groceries. The Indians of Raza Island once had been consummate canoebuilders, but they no longer made canoes. They bought speedboats and big outboards and booze with

COAST OF
BRITISH COLUMBIA
AND
SOUTHERN ALASKA

N

BRADY GLACIER

Juneau

CHICHAGOF
ISLAND

ALASKA

Angoon

ADMIRALTY ISLAND

Sitka

KUPREANOF ISLAND

Petersburg

BARANOF
ISLAND

ALEXANDER ARCHIPELAGO

PRINCE
OF WALES
ISLAND

DIXON ENTRANCE

Masset

Prince Rupert

GRAHAM
ISLAND

BRITISH COLUMBIA

QUEEN CHARLOTTE ISLANDS

HECATE STRAIT

MORESBY
ISLAND

QUEEN CHARLOTTE
SOUND

QUEEN
CHARLOTTE
STRAIT

PACIFIC

OCEAN

Alert Bay

STRAIT OF
GEORGIA

VANCOUVER ISLAND

Vancouver

| 0 | MILES | 200 |
| 0 | KM | 200 |

WASHINGTON, U.S.

their government allotment. They wore the liners from hard hats as headbands. Hard-hat liners were the craze at the time. "We had to get there a day or two after the welfare checks came," says George, "or they would have spent all the money."

Sailing the Inside Passage, George met the people who would become his models, insofar as George has models. Besides Dr. Spong, the psychologist who became a student, then champion, of killer whales, he met Michael Berry, a marine biologist who became a fisherman and jack-of-all-trades, and Jim Land, who scavenges the alleys of Vancouver's Chinatown for the beautiful handmade crates that come to Canada from Communist China, and who, with the empties, has built himself a palace. He met an old woman who subsisted on crows and potatoes—an interesting dietary experiment, in George's opinion.

He met a young man who made his own wooden shoes and lived in a hammock. Few humans have dwelt more lightly and immaculately on this Earth than the young man of the hammock. He had been a librarian and a logger once, but all that had fallen away. He had simplified. He now slept everywhere in his hammock—in forests, in greasy freightyards—it didn't matter, for he levitated above all inconvenience. His toothbrush and other articles had their places on his hammock line. His whole life was suspended between two points. He was a Houdini of self-containment. He was not much older than George. Remembering him, George shakes his head with envy.

One of the nicer things about this society was how easily it was left behind. When George and Jim Bates tired of people, they simply weighed anchor, sailed around the point, and found themselves alone in the wilderness. (Passing Lasqueti Island recently, George nodded toward it. "They've got beautiful ladies on that island," he said. "Healthy. Cook their own bread." It was a nice encapsulation of most of what he wants from the world of people. But he did not want it right then, and he did not go ashore.)

George's universe has a center.

The Queen Charlotte Islands, according to his aquaintances who have visited, are a northern Eden. The Queen Charlottes lie at the midpoint of the Inside Passage, and are the most seaward of its archipelagos. They are a quintessence of the Northwest, a promised land of virgin forest, game, and shellfish. It was on the Queen Charlottes, say the Tlingit Indians, that Raven taught humans to build canoes. At first, according to the Tlingits, the early humans were afraid to climb into Raven's prototype. "The canoe is not dangerous," he assured them. "People will seldom drown." *D'Sonoqua* never had business in the islands, and George has never visited, but from the day he first learned of them, he has thought of building a vessel that would take him there. In the Queen Charlottes, he has heard, there is an Indian girl who daily swims a mile out into the ocean, and a mile back. *Two miles* in the frigid North Pacific! He would like to see if she is true.

British Columbia's coast range is a nine-hundred-mile fold in the Earth's crust. Vancouver Island and the Queen Charlottes are parts of a parallel seaward fold, most of it submerged. Both folds—the entire Inside Passage province—were covered by the Cordilleran ice sheet, which in grinding its way over George's country carved the final touches upon it. The glaciers were enormous, and so are the land and seascapes they left behind. The fiords are deep and labyrinthine. The landforms are all out of scale, belonging on a larger planet. The peninsulas between the fiords are big, steep, and dark, like negatives of the vanished tongues of ice. The darkness is less geology than botany. A dense forest of Douglas fir, cedar, Sitka spruce, and hemlock has sprung up after the thaw. As the forest colonized above waterline, the Pacific and its seaweeds were colonizing below, and today the two influences make for a jarring disconformity. Above waterline a traveler sees subboreal forest; when the tide is running, he might be on any northern river, or, when the tide is slack, on any northern lake. But below waterline he watches kelp lean with the current; from time to time a seal surfaces, or the fin of a porpoise. He's not on any northern river or lake. The water is salt. The lower boughs of the hemlocks are trimmed straight by the high tide. The river is the Pacific, and it flows both ways.

The Inside Passage is a country shaped by water. Water is responsible for its character, just as wind is responsible for the butte country of the Southwest, or meteors for the surface of the moon. Water, in one form or another, did all the work. Glacial ice carved the country steep. Heavy rainfall dark-greened it. Fog grooved the needles of the conifers and tipped the guard hairs of the wolves. Cold stream currents thickened the pelts of the mink and otter, fattened the grizzlies, streamlined and silvered the flanks of the trout, chambered the salmon's indomitable, homeward-leaping heart. The high annual precipitation sends the Douglas firs up two hundred feet and more, broadens their boles to seventeen, furrows their bark, and then, after a millennium or so, undermines their roots, topples and sends them out to the Pacific, which soaks and rolls and deposits them, smooth, barkless, and colossal, in the beach windrows whose chips feed George's fire at night.

Most of the Inside Passage lies under water, in one or another of its forms. The Pacific insinuates from the west, and year-round snow covers the summits to the east. The dry land between is seldom truly dry. Parts of the coast receive more than two hundred inches of rain a year. Streams run everywhere. Rivers rise at every opportunity and after a few turns become mighty, running clear when their source is snow, milky when their source is glacier. The glacial milk is ground-up continent in suspension, for inland the ice continues its whittling. The Ice Age is not over in George's country, and continues to enlarge it for him.

The skies of the Inside Passage belong above a more vaporous planet, like Venus. The waters rule up there, as they rule below, marching in different densities to different drummers. The sun seldom burns through the leaden overcast. Clouds boil up from the cold cauldron of the North Pacific, white against the high gray. Fogs flow tidally in and out the inlets. Mist mystifies the forest. Vapors heighten the headlands. White lenticular clouds cap the foothills. The gray inverted sea of cloud decapitates the peaks.

George, unlike his father, never has to look for water. George has to look for shelter from it.

The aborigines were water people. They built their villages on the shore, usually at the mouths of rivers. They hunted land animals—deer, elk, goats, and bear—and they were good at it, but it was more like sport than work with them. Their real business was the sea.

The Northwest Coast culture divided into seven language families. From south to north the people spoke Salish, Bella Coola, Nootka, Kwakiutl, Tsimshian, Haida, and Tlingit. These linguistic groups divided into dozens of tribes, and all were sea people: whalers, shell gatherers, fishermen. Their civilization developed in isolation, shut off by the sea in front and by the mountain wall behind. Their few foreign influences came along the coast, primarily down it, for they borrowed most from the hunting technology of the Eskimos to the north. Unlike the Eskimos, they conducted true wars—campaigns intended to exterminate their neighbors or at least to move them elsewhere. True warfare was rare among Native Americans. The wars here were probably fought for living space. The land between mountains and sea was so slim and steep that village sites were hard to find. The armies wore armor of animal hide or wood, and wooden helmets carved with terrifying faces.

The artists of the Northwest Coast were the finest in the Americas.

"To their taste or design in working figures upon their garments, corresponds their fondness for carving, in everything they make of wood," wrote Captain Cook. "Nothing is without a kind of freeze-work, or the figure of some animal upon it." This Northwestern decoration, strong, animistic, stylized, polychromatic, was several centuries ahead of its time. Rediscovered in the 1900s by men like Picasso, it had a delayed influence on the art of the world. The Indians achieved it without agriculture. Agriculture is the invention that is supposed to let a people lay in the food reserves that permit the idle periods that allow experimentation with art, and the coastal Indians practiced no agriculture at all, except for planting a little tobacco. It was the sea that allowed them to break the old rule. The coastal waters were as rich as any field. Shellfish were easy to gather in great numbers along the Inside Passage. The coastal women shucked clams and mussels instead of peas, and over the centuries their patient fingers built huge shell middens. (In a rainy climate where intentional art in wood decays, the middens endure, great banal monuments standing everywhere along the shore. They make good soil for berries, and George Dyson likes to forage them, his fingers stained purple or red.) There were also the big salmon runs on the coastal rivers. Salmon was the Northwestern maize. The Indians smoked or dried the fish in great quantities, gathered bushels of clams, then turned to their art.

They were fine basketmakers. They made ingenious fishhooks and harpoons. They wove excellent blankets from the wool of mountain goats, and one group, the Salish, raised a breed of woolly dogs that they sheared to make hair garments. They knew how to make moccasins but preferred, like George Dyson, to go barefoot. The Inside Passage is a good country for that. The rainfall carpets the forest understory with moss, and the beach stones make a pleasant cobbling underfoot. When you wear shoes there, George explains, it is not from fear of cuts or stubbed toes, but to circumvent that force which leads you to step in something unpleasant just before bed.

The Indians made seagoing canoes. These were dugouts carved from cedar logs, the hulls sculpted, painted, and rubbed regularly with oil to keep them from cracking. War canoes were sometimes sixty feet long and could carry eighty warriors. They were given names—Halibut Canoe, Gull Canoe, Crane Canoe. The prows of some were equipped with tall shields fenestrated for archers—aboriginal landing craft. In their war canoes, one group, the Nootka, hunted whales.

At the University of British Columbia there is a new art museum devoted almost entirely to the material culture of the Northwest

Coast. George's sister Katrina works there as a receptionist. I visited the museum once with George, and after we had chatted with his sister, he led me briskly through the place.

One bright, high-ceilinged hall, all glass and pale-gray concrete, is forested with totem poles. The poles are huge. On each, the massive heads of demigods, semihumans, eagles, bears, and killer whales succeed one another up to the roof. The painted eyes have weathered away. Wooden eyeballs stare blind and splintery at the concrete, or gaze out the glass. The poles face this way and that, like guests at an unsuccessful cocktail party. To my mind, the sterile concrete and glass made a fine setting for the weathered wood, and I would have liked to linger, but George rushed me along. We walked beneath Raven's outsized beak and made our exit from the totem forest.

We passed storage chests carved in geometrical designs and inlaid with mother-of-pearl. We passed bowls, food dishes, ladles, rattles, daggers, halibut clubs, headdresses, wool blankets, togas; none of it unadorned, as Captain Cook had observed. George hardly glanced around him. At his pace, Northwestern art passed as a blur. I was left only with the impression of being watched. The Northwestern artists liked to fill all available space, and they filled it most often with formalized eyes: eyes in the middle of an animal's chest, eyes marking its joints, eyes looking out from the least representational of the geometric designs.

We passed a wall of masks. They grimaced and leered at me. The masks, I thought, had most to say about the people. The old Northwestern Indians would have liked Boris Karloff movies. A pantheon of demons gibbered against the black felt of the display. They were carved with great imagination and humor. They jumped time and the culture gap to scare me in the twentieth century. There were clownish masks too, full of a more raucous humor. There was sharp parody in the few masks depicting white men. The black backdrop was a fine idea, I thought, especially for the demon masks and death's heads. They seemed to be materializing in the darkness of the aboriginal unconscious. I would have liked to study them longer. But George had moved ahead, and I followed.

We came to the canoes.

The success of Northwestern art, I had decided, was in the grace of its curves, and that grace reached apogee in the canoes. Looking at the canoes, I wondered where that Northwestern curve came from. What had inspired it? Was it the glacier-shaped curve of the fiord headlands? Was it the curve of the lens clouds, or the dorsal curve of a fleeing whale? Or could it have derived from the canoe lines themselves? Maybe all Northwestern art began in that pragmatic solution to the problem posed by the waves. It was a happy solution, certainly, both in form and function. The designers of the clipper ships had thought so, and had let it influence them in lofting their bow lines.

The finest lines, for me, were those turned by the Haida, the inhabitants of the Queen Charlottes, where canoes began in myth. The leaf-bladed Haida paddle is surely one of the classic shapes devised by man. It has all the inevitability of the leaf-bladed African spear, or, for that matter, of the leaf. But George walked past. He finished the museum almost at a dead run.

"You liked it?" he asked me at the door, surprised. He shook his head. He didn't like the museum at all, he confided. It made him nervous. He hated the glass and concrete. He preferred finding his totem poles under blueberry bushes, overgrown where they had fallen.

"Doesn't it seem like a graveyard to you?" he asked. "A bunch of rich white people get this stuff and bring it here. As if it was dead."

—— 13 ——

The Promise of Our Destiny

"We can hope to survive in a world bristling with hydrogen bombs for a few centuries, if we are lucky," Freeman Dyson has written. "But I believe we have small chance of surviving ten thousand years if we stay stuck to this planet. We are too many eggs in too small a basket.

"The emigration into distant parts of the solar system of a substantial number of people would make our species as a whole invulnerable. A nuclear holocaust on Earth would still be an unspeakable tragedy, and might still wipe out ninety-nine percent of our numbers. But the one percent who had dispersed themselves could not be wiped out simultaneously by any man-made catastrophe, and they would remain to carry on the promise of our destiny.

"This vision of comet-hopping emigrants, streaming onward like the covered wagons on the Santa Fe Trail, is perhaps absurdly romantic or fanciful. Maybe it will never happen the way I imagine it. But I am convinced that something more or less along these lines will ultimately happen. Space is huge enough, so that somewhere in its vastness there will always be a place for rebels and outlaws. Near to the sun, space will belong to big governments and computerized industries. Outside, the open frontier will beckon as it has beckoned before, to persecuted minorities escaping from oppression, to religious fanatics escaping from their neighbors, to recalcitrant teen-agers escaping from their parents, to lovers of solitude escaping from crowds. Perhaps most important of all for man's future, there will be groups of people setting out to find a place where they can be free from prying eyes, free to experiment with the creation of radically new types of human beings, surpassing us in mental capacities as we surpass the apes."

—— 14 ——

The Promise of Our Destiny
(Another Opinion)

According to the Tlingits, the Creator tried to make human beings out of a rock and out of a leaf at the same time. The rock was slow, while the leaf was very quick. Therefore human beings came from the leaf. The Creator showed a leaf to the first human beings, and told them, "See this leaf. You are to be like it. When it falls off the branch and rots, there is nothing left of it." That is why there is death in the world. If men had come from the rock there would be no death.

"We are unfortunate in not having been made from rock," people used to say, as they grew old. "Being made from a leaf, we must die."

—— 15 ——

Orion

The idea of a bomb-propelled spaceship began with Stanislaw Ulam, the inventor of the hydrogen bomb. He and Cornelius Everett worked the notion out in a rough way at Los Alamos in 1955. It was taken over by Theodore Taylor, a former colleague of Ulam's at Los Alamos. Taylor was a physicist who had spent much of his career designing bombs, and who wished that he hadn't. His gift was for the concrete. He did with Ulam's spaceship what he had done previously with a succession of bombs; he rendered an abstract notion practical.

"Ulam is very much a man of my own type," says Freeman Dyson. "Basically a mathematician. He's more like me than like Ted Taylor. Ulam and I never stick with anything very long. Ted does. Ted got hold of the idea and made it a lot better. Ted designed it, understood how to do it in detail. He could organize. He got the project going, as Ulam could never have done."

It was Taylor who gave the project its name. "I just picked it out of the sky," he says of Orion.

Taylor, like Dyson a former student of Hans Bethe's, met with their old teacher in 1956 in San Diego at a conference on atomic energy. Also on hand was Edward Teller, Alvin Weinberg, Marshall Rosenbluth, and other nuclear heavyweights. The conference was organized by Frederic de Hoffmann, a former Los Alamos physicist who now headed General Atomic, a new division of General Dynamics Corporation. Secrecy had just been lifted from nuclear reactors, and de Hoffmann wanted a free discussion on what might be done with them. Edward Teller had one idea. He believed that what the world needed was a reactor so safe it was "not just foolproof, but Ph.D.-proof." Taylor and Dyson liked the idea, and they joined the safe-reactor team. They found they worked well together. They collaborated in the design of a small nuclear reactor called TRIGA, its purpose the production of medical isotopes. That was how they spent their summer vacations. Then they went their separate ways, Freeman back to Princeton, Taylor to work at General Atomic.

In winter of 1957, Taylor called Dyson in Princeton and explained Ulam's new idea. Taylor wanted to build a ship that would blast them into space with atomic bombs. This did not for a moment sound crazy to Freeman.

"It sounded good. It didn't frighten me. The immediate reaction of everybody is that it will blow the ship to pieces. I wasn't bothered by that. The thing made sense on a technical level. It sounded like what we'd all been waiting for. This was an alternative to chemical rocketry that could work."

Freeman has little enthusiasm for chemical rockets. In a rocket, velocity is severely limited by the heat-tolerance of the engine alloys. In a chemical rocket, temperature limitations hold the velocity of the ejected gas to about four kilometers per second. In a nuclear rocket the limit is about eight kilometers per second. A nuclear-powered rocket remains an inviting idea, however, in that nuclear fuel is the most compact energy source known, with a million times the energy of any chemical fuel. A lot of high-velocity human thought has gone into nuclear engines and possible ways to circumvent their temperature limitations. "Gas-core" systems would cheat by insulating the engine with a gas that, upon being heated, becomes the propellant. "Nuclear-electric" systems would use a nuclear reactor to generate electromagnetic energy and produce a jet of ions—the plasma-drive that powers much of science fiction. Plasma-drive has yet to power a real engine, but it's a promising idea, and someday Freeman would like to give some time to it. "There's no problem in plasma drive, except in the energy source," he says. "It's one of the things I'd like to build—a nuclear-electric engine for a spaceship." A plasma-drive engine would be sharply limited in its thrust. The ship would accelerate slowly, and thus would be most valuable in long-range, unmanned voyages.

Unmanned voyages do not particularly excite Freeman Dyson. The voyages that Ted Taylor was planning *did* excite him. Taylor's manned spaceship would move its crew and equipment rapidly around the solar system. It presented fewer problems to be worked out than other systems presented, Freeman thought, and he believed these could be resolved in his lifetime. In spring of 1958 he took a leave of absence from the Institute for Advanced Studies, moved his family to California, and began work on Orion. In July 1958 he wrote this manifesto:

From my childhood it has been my conviction that men would reach the planets in my lifetime, and that I should help in the enterprise. If I try to rationalize this conviction, I suppose it rests on two beliefs, one scientific and one political.

1. There are more things in heaven and earth than are dreamed of in our present-day science. And we shall only find out what they are if we go out and look for them.

2. It is in the long run essential to the growth of any new and high civilization that small groups of men can escape from their neighbours and from their governments, to go and live as they please in the wilderness. A truly isolated, small, and creative society will never again be possible on this planet.

To these two articles of faith I have now to add a third.

3. We have for the first time imagined a way to use the huge stockpiles of our bombs for better purpose than for murdering people. My purpose, and my belief, is that the bombs which killed and maimed at Hiroshima and Nagasaki shall one day open the skies to man.

The Orion spaceship would escape temperature limitations by fleeing the heat. The time during which each bomb blast interacted with Orion's pusher plate would be reduced to a millisecond or less. The explosions would transfer their momentum to the spacecraft—blow it away—before the heat could penetrate. Common sense has the spaceship *blowing away, all right*, but common sense is wrong. In explaining their idea to doubters, the Orion men used the coal-on-the-rug analogy. A hot coal pops from the fire onto the rug. If you convey it carefully between thumb and forefinger back to the fireplace, you scream. If you flick it into the fireplace, you get away free. The bombs would flick Orion through space. Aluminum and steel can withstand surface temperatures of more than 80,000° K. for short periods, losing only a thin epithelium of metal to ablation. An external-combustion engine like Orion's can operate at those temperatures, whereas the internal-combustion engines of rockets are limited to propellant temperatures of around 4,000° K.

Ablation in Orion could be stopped entirely, the Orion men discovered, if the pusher plate was greased between detonations.

The pusher plate would move in jerks every half second. The plate would be made of aluminum. It would be lens-shaped and very heavy, about a third of the weight of the vehicle. It would be connected to the ship by pneumatic shock-absorbers, which would even out the ride, leaving it lurchy but not unpleasant. Greased like a channel swimmer, Orion would frog-kick through the void.

The shock absorbers were crucial, clearly.

"Above the pusher plate," explains Ted Taylor, "there was a set of flexible gas-filled doughnuts about three feet high, sort of like a stack of tires. Then came a set of aluminum cylinders about twenty feet high, filled with compressed nitrogen, and they worked like pistons. Those really smoothed out the shock. The peak acceleration of the ship proper was about three or four Gs, which is lower than what the people in Apollo got.

"We had two ways of running the shock absorbers. One was in what we called the 'dissipative mode.' There, the shock absorbers compress and then expand, reverberating dissipatively until they stop. That meant a bouncy ride—you get kicked up to about three or four Gs every second, then down again. We were willing to bet that everyone would get violently seasick.

"But there was another way of doing it, and this was what we finally settled on. It was to drive the shock absorbers in synchronism, the result of which was that the acceleration of the ship proper was steady, at about a G and a half or two Gs. That would have been quite comfortable. It took some careful timing and got a little bit tricky, but it seemed to be worth it."

Orion would move so fast that few of the detonations would occur in the atmosphere. Somewhere out past the ionosphere, Orion would hang a right and head for Saturn. The atmospheric detonations would add an increment to the fallout from the current bomb testing, but not a big one. Orion's saving grace was that the spaceship, unlike the testing, was at least going somewhere. The Orion men guessed that pure fusion bombs would be invented by the time they were ready to depart, so they didn't worry much about sprinkling plutonium over the planet they were leaving behind.

They didn't worry, either, about space travel's small niceties. No one bothered to calculate how much shielding they would need from cosmic rays. Orion would have to be such a thick hunk of metal, what with atomic bombs going off regularly a hundred feet away, and gamma rays pounding its abdomen, that a few wandering cosmic rays would not be a problem. The Orion men did not waste time designing interior accommodations. Orion in its enormous power could haul such excesses of freight that no cleverness was necessary in planning staterooms and storage. The crew would not need to recycle their urine, for they could afford to carry hundreds of tons of water. They would simply vent their wastes into space. They would not have to squeeze bland meals from tubes, for they could carry whole sides of beef in Orion's freezers.

Freeman became Orion's chief theoretician, and he shared with Ted Taylor the responsibility for the overview. His special area, insofar as any of the Orion men had special areas, was the physics of the explosions. He and Taylor spent much of their time thinking about that. The shock wave alone was not enough to drive the ship, they knew. The bombs had to be packaged with some sort of propellant—material that would vaporize and strike the pusher plate.

"If the bomb explodes in all directions equally, you've wasted most of the propellant," says Freeman. "To make it efficient it was important that all the debris go forward and backward. Half of it was supposed to hit the ship, and half was supposed to fly out backward. That's the most efficient arrangement. To achieve it you have to design the bomb-propellant arrangement very carefully.

"For bigger ships, using existing stockpiles of weapons would have worked. Just put enough propellant around, and it didn't matter that the charge was not shaped. That was characteristic of everything we did. It was always easier if you made the thing big enough.

"You can use anything you like as propellant. Water was clearly very good. That was another reason it was very important to go to a place with water. From Earth, the propellant most likely was paraffin wax. One thing that would not work was rock. That's why the moon looked bad. In a way, it was easier to go on long trips to Mars and Saturn. Rocks would have increased the ablation problem. It wasn't clear that rocks would vaporize. You didn't want bits of rock punching holes in your pusher plate.

"I think we all had conventional ideas about where to go. The moon certainly was first. We wanted to know if there was water there. That's important if you're serious. I've been discouraged by the lack of water found. But there's still a chance to find it. On the north or south pole, you might find ice in some dark cave.

"Second was Mars. We would look for the same thing—water.

We wanted to go to the north pole of Mars. There it's really certain that there's ice. We would have built a permanent base on the north pole of Mars.

"Third was the rings of Saturn. Both for practical and for aesthetic reasons. We all wanted to have a look at those. We thought, then, that they were a fog of ice crystals. Radar now suggests big chunks of ice at least a few feet in size. We would have stopped and collected some. That's one of the beauties of Orion—it can refuel. For each hundred pounds of bomb, you need nine hundred pounds of propellant, and ice will do fine."

Dyson and Taylor planned to be on Mars by 1964, on Saturn by 1970.

Taylor wanted a few rocks from Mars on his mantelpiece. He hoped Orion would make Martian rocks so common on Earth that you could just leave them lying around. Freeman wanted to know why Saturn's moon Iapetus was black on one side and white on the other.

Taylor and Dyson did most of the mental space traveling for the Orion team. Their cerebral voyages were peculiar: boyish in enthusiasm, but not in detail. They spent little time imagining themselves clunking around in weighted boots. They imagined instead the worlds they would see, and the phenomena. They went as disembodied intellects, or as wandering eyes.

Freeman was especially eager to visit the satellites of the outer planets. A lot of interesting real estate orbits out there. Jupiter's moon Ganymede is larger than the planet Mercury, and three of Ganymede's sisters are larger than our moon. The moons of Jupiter and Saturn, Freeman thought, would be good spots from which to observe those enormous worlds.

Powerful gravitational forces made landing on the big planets themselves difficult, but the same forces would be a help in landing on their satellites. Freeman explained this in a paper he wrote for General Atomic, GAMD-1012, "The Accessibility of the Outer Planets to a High-Thrust Nuclear Spaceship." In it he calculated that an Orion ship, operating with an exhaust velocity of thirty kilometers per second, could make a round trip to the satellites of Jupiter in two years, and to the satellites of Saturn in three, with takeoff and landing at both ends. It would accomplish this by making use of gravity and of Orion's remarkable capacity to decelerate quickly.

On a trip to Jupiter's moon Callisto, for example, Orion would rumble off Earth on a course parallel to Earth's orbital velocity, on a day when such a course put it into a hyperbolic orbit that would intercept Jupiter. The spaceship would expend a great load of bombs in the vicinity of Earth, then sail in silence on the long voyage to Jupiter. As Orion grazed Jupiter at sixty-seven kilometers per second, it would retrofire a salvo of bombs, decelerating at a rate of seven kilometers per second and allowing itself to be captured by the planet's gravitational field. Because Jupiter's radius is seventy-one thousand kilometers, only about one thousand seconds would be available for the maneuver. For a low-thrust spaceship like a nuclear-electric rocket, this is not nearly time enough. For Orion, it's a piece of cake. Once captured by Jupiter, Orion has a free ride. Its elliptical orbit is chosen to bring the ship tangentially to Callisto's orbit. A final velocity change would be necessary at Callisto, but a small one, for the gravity there is slight. With a last, polite clearing of its mighty throat, Orion would settle on Callisto's surface.

Freeman was most interested in the inner satellites of the outer planets. The inner moons of Jupiter and Saturn would give the best views of those beautiful, frigid, poisonous spheres. Mimas, Saturn's innermost moon, is only 115,000 miles from the planet's surface. Seen from Mimas, Saturn would fill much of the sky. Orion's crew could watch Saturn's atmospheric bands rotate at their different speeds. They could study the thin tropic of shadow cast by Saturn's rings. From one of Jupiter's inner moons, they could watch that planet's rapid spin, the centrifugal force bulging the equator and flattening the poles. They could watch the Jovian Red Spot change color from its salmon red to its pale green.

Freeman figured the velocity increments necessary for trips to various moons and he set down the results in tables. "The inner satellites," he summarized, "which are much the most interesting for observing the planets, were substantially harder to reach than the outer satellites. Fortunately, the help available from refueling is most certain where it is most needed, namely at the inner satellites."

Happy coincidence. If Orion could refuel, everything became easier. For propellant, Orion could use ice, ammonia, or hydrocarbons, and "these substances are certainly to be found on Mimas, which has density .52 and is probably composed mainly of ice or snow." (The density of water is 1.) "The mass of Jupiter 5 is unknown, but it is likely to have a density and composition similar to those of Mimas. The big intermediate satellites, Callisto and Titan, have densities 1.7 and 2.1. For comparison, the earth's moon, which is of comparable size and is made of rock, has density 3.3. It is, therefore, almost certain that Callisto and Titan have thick outer layers of ice which would be available as propellant. In addition, we could, if necessary, convert the methane in Titan's atmosphere into propellant."

Freeman had wanted to visit Iapetus and learn why it is black on one side and white on the other. Unfortunately, that satellite is both outer—the eighth moon of Saturn's nine—and dense. At density 5.5 it is probably composed of metal or rock. "It may or may not have a thin outer layer of ice," wrote Freeman. That was giving Iapetus, considerably denser than our own waterless moon, the benefit of the doubt.

"In conclusion, we may say that a high-thrust propulsion system would be peculiarly well suited to take maximum advantage of celestial mechanics. Using the outer planets as hitching-posts, we could make round trips to their satellites with over-all velocity increments which are surprisingly small. The probability that we could refuel with propellant on the satellites would make such trips hardly more formidable than voyages to Mars or Venus."

Maybe so, but not everyone on the Orion team thought that way. Brian Dunne, who was in charge of hardware for the project, was not planning his visits to Tethys, Hyperion, and Europa. "I was dealing with more prosaic things," says Dunne, "like getting experimental teams together, keeping people from getting blown up, keeping progress reports coming. And I would see these GAMD reports on voyages to the outer planets. Those guys were so far out.

"I think Orion will eventually become a great human endeavor. But my feeling is that the thing will come to pass in the 2020 era, or 2050. I discussed it with Taylor, and he was adamant that it should be now, and here, and in our time, and that *he* wanted to go. And so did Dyson. They were both intoxicated with the idea of taking flights past Saturn's rings."

During coffee breaks in the project, Dunne and Carlo Riparbelli, one of Orion's engineers, liked to discuss Taylor and Dyson. One day Riparbelli threw up his hands, shook his head in wonder, rolled his eyes, and laughed. "They're just worlds apart from us, Brian, you have to accept that." Dunne had to agree. It was literally true.

"Freeman and Ted Taylor were extraordinarily complementary," says Dunne. "Ted was tremendously visual. He could see neutrons banging around like billiard balls. He had this intuitive feeling about what was going on. But he lacked the ability to put anything down in precise mathematical terms. In fact, he was just a terrible mathematician. I knew him well—I was a classmate of his at Cal Tech—and he was certainly not outstanding. His talent began to flower much later. With Freeman ... those two ... Freeman with that Mozartian mind that's ... well, that's phenomenal. It's just phenomenal. Taylor had a lot of ideas, and some of them were really outlandish. Freeman would sort out the concepts that were right, and build them up. It was a special, unusual friendship. They would look into each other's eyes—there was lots of electricity. I always hated to interrupt."

Taylor himself is not sure that "complementary" is the right word. "Freeman understood a vast number of things that I had no inkling about," he says. "The reverse was not true. He understood everything I said, if it made sense. If it didn't make sense, he'd point out why it didn't. And in a very warm and friendly way.

"Freeman's gift? It's cosmic. He is able to see more interconnections between more things than almost anybody. He sees the interrelationships, whether it's in some microscopic physical process or in a big complicated machine like Orion. He has been, from the time he was in his teens, capable of understanding essentially anything that he's interested in. He's the most intelligent person I know. I've always believed that if he'd decided to plunge himself permanently into conceiving things that got built, starting with Orion and continuing through the twenty years that have gone by, the whole world would have been different."

When Taylor doodled his ideas, he doodled in sketches. Freeman doodled in formulae. Freeman did his thinking at his desk, walking around—everywhere. One of the things he thought about a lot was the opacity of the gases generated by Orion's explosions. A Freeman Dyson thought on opacity looks like this:

$$\overline{K} \leq \frac{h}{kT \, S^2} \int \Sigma(\nu) \, d\nu = \frac{h}{kT} \, \frac{\pi e^2}{mc} \, \frac{Z}{AM} \, \frac{1}{S^2}$$

"He had an office next to mine," remembers Dunne. "I was reluctant to come in and bother him because he was, you know, so eminent. You felt there was something fairly precious there. You didn't want to disturb it with small talk or trivia.

"One day I went next door to ask him something. He was sitting there writing on a yellow pad with his number-two pencil. Most people have antennae up. They realize you're in the room. But not Freeman. I stood there for a few minutes. I didn't want to interrupt. Then he saw me. He jumped four inches out of the chair. He was in another world. It was startling.

"In our business we talk about the signal-to-noise ratio. There's always background noise from the things you've got to do, things to remember. The things you've got to pick up from the supermarket. It all interferes. When the noise level gets up near the signal strength, you're unable to carry on much of our kind of work. Freeman's mind has a fantastic signal-to-noise ratio.

"He'd write GAMD reports in an afternoon. He'd do them

straight out, single spaced, with the equations and everything, and I don't think I ever saw him use an eraser. Five, six, seven pages, and he'd hand them to the secretary and be off for the weekend. It would take me about ten drafts to get anything done. The first draft to get the English right, the second for the spelling, the third for the equations, the fourth to get the sense of it. Freeman was unnerving.

"When he first came, I think he was suffering from nervous exhaustion. He was going through a divorce. He was having trouble with his eyes—irritation of the optic nerve, I think. He used to wear these surplus Air Force goggles and put filters in them, because his eyes were so sensitive to the light. Any time he wasn't indoors or working, he had these Air Force goggles on. They were just like Snoopy goggles." Dunne laughed at the memory. "Freeman was a strange bird to begin with. With these goggles on, people would look twice and thrice. They could not feature this, whether he was a man from Mars or what.

"In 1958, when he first came to La Jolla, Freeman wanted to visit Tijuana. He went down with some friends. He was shopping in this market, in all the chaos of Tijuana, when a mad dog came into the store. Of all the people it had to set upon, it picked Freeman. It bit him in the leg, then dashed out into the street. I guess they never caught it. Freeman had to undergo the Pasteur treatment, but he didn't miss a day's work. He would appear on the job perspiring and obviously in terrific discomfort, but seemingly unaffected in his output. He would be writing away, or talking, or lecturing. There's a lot of iron in Freeman. He's so slight, you might consider him on the frail side, but he's got a lot of stamina, a lot of iron. And absolutely fantastic concentration."

Freeman and his colleagues worked furiously, in the knowledge that they had little time. Soon the government would decide whether its spaceships would be chemical or nuclear, and the Orion men had to be ready with a workable design. "It was a race between us and von Braun," says Freeman, "though we never achieved parity."

Freeman was so busy with the spaceship that he was unable to attend sessions of the sailplane club he had joined on moving to La Jolla. Katrina, who was now fourteen, went as his substitute. In the clubhouse she learned to drink coffee and smoke cigarettes. She learned to fly sailplanes. While Freeman was navigating the void in his imagination, his stepdaughter, cigarette dangling from lip, soared in real life above Earth.

George was then five. On arriving in La Jolla he had planted parsley, as was his custom. He was attending La Jolla Country Day School, a posh institution whose scholars heard lectures from people like Dr. Suess. (Did Dr. Suess influence George's direction? The tree house, certainly, is architecture in the Suess style.) "The school had no windows facing the ocean," George remembers. "The ocean would have been too interesting. But the bathroom had a window. There were two things that came by there—submarines and gray whales. Somebody would go to the bathroom and see a submarine or a whale, and the word would get around. The next guy would raise his hand. Pretty soon everybody was going to the bathroom.

"La Jolla was a magic time. I was little, but I knew something big was going on. My father was always looking at the stars, pointing out the constellations for us. It was like he was in love. There was an old brass telescope in his desk. It was great. You couldn't see a thing with it."

Much of the La Jolla stargazing took place in Ted Taylor's backyard.

"We used to look at the moons of Jupiter," remembers Taylor. "We used a cheap cast-off telescope I had bought from a colleague's son, who was about fourteen. It was a black cardboard reflector tube. We'd look at these things and talk about them, usually with Freeman telling me what was there."

Taylor remembers George underfoot, but he remembers only vaguely. "I have a general impression of a darting kid with very bright eyes. But we didn't spend much time together as families. Freeman and I spent a lot of time together. We sort of wandered off by ourselves and got excited."

"Taylor," says Brian Dunne, "used to tell me how smart Freeman was. For many months I just did not accept this, because Taylor had a lot of enthusiasm for people, much of it misplaced. I had had dealings with lots of very eminent theorists, and I'd found huge gaps in their knowledge of things, particularly experimental problems. How to put something together that works. After a while you get this funny experimentalist-theorist antipathy.

"When I realized he really is a fine engineer, I was astounded. He knows electrical engineering, mechanical engineering, structural. That's unnerving, in a theoretical physicist with the eminence that he enjoys. His contributions to quantum electrodynamics are classics. They are beautiful pieces of work—poetry in physics, if you will. To see the same man do an analysis of the pusher-plate motion, and the shock-absorber motion, putting in the damping coefficients, and the strengths and stresses, and getting it all right, that's unnerving.

"A theoretical physicist is supposed to be very impractical. He's not supposed to know the limitations of materials, and the limitations of people in the way they construct things. Getting the proper balance in a design is an art form. To balance the design of a reactor, or a space vehicle, or an aircraft, *or a canoe*, to get the balance right, is an art form and a talent. You just don't expect to see this spectrum of talents in one person.

"Freeman doesn't have the *handbuchderphysik*, the last-word sort of German precision. He doesn't have the French quality of slap-dash, a point here well taken, but the rest of it wrong. He doesn't have the stiff British restraint. It's a style he's developed that's all his own."

What Freeman contributed most, according to Dunne, was an elevated sort of common sense. It was an invaluable trait, apparently, in the company that Orion had gathered. "He had this ability to cut through things with an enormous understanding. I remember once I took in a streak-camera record. I was very proud of it. It was one of the first records we got of an explosive simulation device for measuring ablation. We had enormous speeds on the thing." A streak camera, Dunne explained to me, has a rotating mirror powered by a gas turbine. The light enters though a slit, hits the mirror as it spins, and reflects to write a distance-time plot of luminous phenomena. It was very useful in plasma physics, he assured me. The writing speeds were enormous because of the lever arm of the mirror. It went as fast as a centimeter per microsecond. "We got carried away and we raced this turbine, really revved it up. Freeman glanced at it and looked up. He said, 'Oh, that's quite interesting. I see, yes. But perhaps you shouldn't run the rotor quite so fast.'"

Remembering, Dunne grinned at the brilliance of this.

I didn't get it.

"Well," Dunne explained. "Bing! Freeman had cut right through. He was exactly right, because to get a good measurement, you need something on about a forty-five-degree angle, like a graph. I had this thing tipped up so that it was impossible to measure the angle. Bing! Just like that. Instant perception."

Occasionally Freeman tired of his role as editor of crazy ideas. He rebelled and proposed some of his own.

"I remember some nice designs," he says. "I wrote one called 'The Bolo and the Squid.' We were fed up with shock absorbers. They weren't very elegant. So I proposed these two. The bolo was a ship on a long string—the pusher plate separated from the main body by a long cable. The squid was a slightly more practical version."

In the bolo, explosions under the pusher plate whipped the ship through space with a mosquito-wiggler motion. In the squid, the pusher plate became the top, not the bottom, of the spacecraft. Six cables attached the plate to the rest of the ship. The squid's bombs would detonate within the great birdcage formed by the six cables. With each explosion, the cables would straighten as the pusher plate jumped forward. Then, as the pusher plate lost momentum, the ship would catch up, and the cables would bunch again. The ship's motion in the blackness of space would have been eerily like that of a squid in the blackness of the abyss.

"Ted liked it very much," says Freeman. "It was worthless, of course."

"I would say it was a period of great warmth in Freeman's life," says Brian Dunne. "There was the camaraderie. For some reason, the chemistry of all those people was just right. I never saw anything go so fast, technically and creatively. Freeman got caught up in the enthusiasm. Maybe it was the dissolving of the individual ego into the team. The society he was used to is quite competitive. There's a lot of academic rivalry, and backbiting, and priority claims. There's publish or perish. There's not all that much emotional nourishment. In the climate we had at General Atomic, there was a tremendous amount of emotional nourishment."

Freeman concurs. "That was the year in my life that I learned the most," he says. "That was the joy. We had no experts. There *are* no experts in this kind of thing. *We* had to become the experts. It was very much a free-for-all. We all had different skills, but we weren't tied down to particular jobs. Everybody did everything, even to moving bricks around. There were no personality clashes, at least in the time that I was there. It began with a lot of hope. We had the common goal. We had some good minds, high-powered but not famous. There was a lot of excitement in having good minds playing with an idea in the same room. I've never quite had the same experience since.

"Ted was our leader. He was slow, and that was good. He would have us go over something again and again before deciding on it. Bert Freeman was our computer man and very important. He was the most specialized. He was amazing. He worked tremendously hard and late. He didn't seem to need any sleep or recreation or anything. Brian Dunne was responsible for hardware, and there was quite a bit of it to be designed for this thing—pieces of shock absorbers, pieces of pusher plates, and so forth. Jerry Astl was our explosives expert. He was always completely happy if he had high explosives in his hands. He was Czech. He had learned to handle high explosives by derailing German trains. He was an artist in the sabotage of trains."

One Saturday afternoon in 1959, Brian Dunne and Jerry Astl, laden with explosives, went down to Point Loma, a steep-sided, brush-covered peninsula near San Diego. ("No, he wasn't a train derailer," Dunne says of Astl. "He was an airplane saboteur. He worked in a German-run Czech factory that made German bombers. Jerry was on the crew that made the wings. He took hacksaw blades and cut through the wing structure on a whole series of planes.") On Point Loma, which the engineer and the saboteur now climbed, stood a tower that had been used for quarter-scale static-motor tests for the Atlas rocket.

"The tower was encrusted with rusted junk that the Atlas people had left," Dunne recalls. "We took about two hundred pounds of composition C-4 explosive and Primacord, and we strung the tower like a Christmas tree. We blasted that thing. There was the most tremendous roar you ever heard, and rust and dust filled the air, and all the junk came crashing down. We went up and cut off a few surviving odds and ends with explosive. It was a wonderful day of demolition."

The tower was now ready for model testing.

The Orion men had decided that as an antidote to skepticism they would need to build a working model. Freeman suggested a small Orion with a pusher plate one meter in diameter, a dimension easy to remember and easy to scale. Dunne, who was the man in charge of model testing, liked that idea. Carlo Riparbelli proposed that the bombs be held on top, then swung down on strings and detonated somehow with light beams. This was the sort of idea that drove Dunne to distraction. He insisted that the bombs be ejected through a hole in the center of the pusher plate, and with Freeman's support he got his way.

Dunne conducted a series of static, single-shot tests with the Orion model tethered to the tower. He learned how the pusher plate had to be shaped so as not to be dented, and how far each charge had to be shot before detonation. Finally he was ready for multiple shots.

"Freeman came down when we were doing one of these multiple shots. The charges kept coming out of the thing, *kabam, kabam, kabam,* and the model just sat there. It didn't move. It was pretty heavy, with this fiberglass dome on it. Freeman made a very sly remark I'll always remember. He said, 'I believe we should suspend these tests unless we can achieve over one-G acceleration.' "

Dunne chuckled at the slyness of that.

I didn't get it.

"It was a pregnant thought," he insisted. "We had to get the model up in the air, but I hadn't seen that. Sometimes when you're closely involved, the obvious eludes you."

Dunne pared the model down to barest essentials. He removed the fiberglass dome, the upper shock absorber, and a skirt. The result was an Orion so stripped-down they called it "Hot Rod." On a succession of Saturdays, a succession of hot rods roared majestically skyward and blew apart.

Ted Taylor invited Richard Courant, one of the world's great mathematicians and an expert on shock waves, to witness one of the tests. That day the model disintegrated a short distance above the ground. As they came out of the bunker afterward, Taylor walked on ahead, and Courant was heard to mutter, in his strong accent, "Zis is not nuts. Zis is supernuts."

As Orion floated in hundreds of pieces back to Earth, Freeman wondered what the Saturday-afternoon sailors made of it all. The blue Pacific below Point Loma was dotted with white sails, and the sun scintillated on the water. Freeman walked the clifftop, in the smell of chaparral and flowering cactus, searching for fragments. When he found these he stuck them in his pocket.

"It was the chanciest thing I've ever undertaken," Dunne admits. "To this day I don't understand what propelled us to take such risks. It was very dangerous. We were using primitive explosives and techniques. We worked with two-pound charges, five or six of them. They were like grenades, encased in aluminum canisters. If one of those goes off prematurely, you've wiped out the whole crew. The Primacord fuses were sensitive to sparks. You can't use steel knives to cut them, you have to use bronze knives. We had no good detonators, just blasting caps. When I look back on it, I know there must have been some kind of wild intoxication."

On November 12, 1959, came the big test. Scientists came to Point Loma from all over. As they gathered, Brian Dunne saw the potential for a catastrophe. An errant Orion could put a real dent in the American scientific community. Jerry Astl would not stay behind the barricade, but kept popping his head out, and Dunne was afraid a fragment would clip him.

Orion rested in what they called "the tub," a short-barreled cannon that would fire it into the air. Five movie cameras on the hilltop started grinding, recording the event. The countdown ended, there was a roar, and Orion vanished in smoke. Through the slit windows of the blockhouse, the crew inside could not see what was happening, except that Orion was no longer in the tub. They listened and counted explosions. There were six—a sweet, successful sound. The crowd on the hill, and all five cameras, saw Orion rise heavenward on a column of fire.

---- 16 ----

Baidarka

Haida paddlers stroked with such power, George Dyson has heard, that they could, with much churning of the surface, lift their war canoes entirely out of the water. "Then they slapped them down on the surface," he says. "It was like burning rubber on the highway." George is impressed, but he is drawn temperamentally to craft of less splash. The dugouts of the Northwest Coast were fine boats, but a canoe of a more silent and seaworthy design sometimes glided down into the Inside Passage.

Northwest of Glacier Bay in Alaska, where the Inside Passage ends, Eskimo country begins, and the dugout gives way to the skin boat. The Eskimos, and their cousins the Aleuts, were a rude people, compared to the sculptors and carpenters of the Inside Passage, but they were better seamen. They had no interconnected system of inland fiords, no bulwark of seaward archipelagos, to protect them from the North Pacific. They ventured into that moody, storm-breeding sea in canoes so light they could be carried under one arm. Made of animal skin stretched over wood frames, Eskimo boats were simple, easy to repair, shock-resistant, beautiful, and fast. Eskimo *umiaks*, large open vessels, carried tremendous loads and as many as forty people. Eskimo *kayaks*, slender and nearly weightless, were the finest hunting canoes in history. Skin boats made the Eskimo culture circumpolar, extending its reach over the northernmost coasts of Asia, America, and Greenland. The oars of the umiaks and the double-bladed paddles of the kayaks chopped down vast distances, allowing Eskimos to exchange ideas, designs, and genes all around the top of the world. A Greenland Eskimo could follow, haltingly, the speech of an Eskimo from western Alaska. It was not that way in the dugout country. When a Tsimshian addressed a Nootka, he might as well have been speaking Chinese, or Kwakiutl.

Other peoples have experimented with skin boats. In Europe the Celts built them. The Irish went to sea in a sort of umiak as recently as Elizabethan times, and they still paddle the cowhide *curragh* on lakes. Next to the kayak, this curragh, oval, dumpy, and slow, is a sorry performance.

Kayak design varied. In the Gulf of Alaska, where big storm waves came up suddenly, the kayaks were built strong and seaworthy. In northern Alaska, where offshore pack ice narrowed the reach, and where the hunters had to navigate thin leads in the ice, kayaks were built light, slim, and low-sided. Materials varied. The Greenland Eskimos covered their kayaks with seal skin, the Canadian Eskimos with caribou skin, the Aleuts with sea-lion skin. The Alaskan Eskimos used bearded seal when they could get it, and walrus when they couldn't. For frames, most Eskimos used wood, but not the caribou Eskimos of the central Arctic. No trees grew on their tundra. What scraps they had were driftwood, and they were ignorant of its origin. They believed that trees grew like kelp in undersea forests, which storms uprooted and washed ashore. They made their kayak skeletons by reassembling in a somewhat changed order the skeletons of whales.

For the frame of his first canoe, George picked aluminum. For the skin he picked fiberglass.

"In my travels and experience with heavy craft requiring the use of sails or machinery," he has written, "I soon realized that much of the British Columbia coastline was either inaccessible or posed extreme danger to such vessels. Most of British Columbia's vast system of open coast and intricate tidal waterways is outside the limits of what is considered a safe path for modern travel and can be viewed only briefly and at a distance through such means."

After *D'Sonoqua,* George had worked on a number of big boats requiring the use of sail or machinery. He remembered some fondly, but had no desire to build or own one. He was bothered not just by their breadth of beam and the depth they drew, but by their financial encumbrances. Several of George's friends owned boats and tried to scratch out livings with them, and all these friends were in trouble with the bank.

In Vancouver with George I visited one such friend, a man named Dave. Dave was a former dope smuggler who had gone straight. He was now master of the *Barbara B.,* a tiny cargo vessel. We found *Barbara B.* moored in the shadow of one of the city's bridges. The light was dim, the air was cavelike, and the traffic shook the bridge high above us. (George Dyson's Vancouver is like that—shadowy and out of the way. He seems to transact most of his business under freeways or on decaying wharves.) Dave, the captain, was a bald man with a full black beard, which the uncertainties of the dope game and the boat business had rimed with gray. He had been on the receiving end of his old smuggling operation when he fell in love with the vessels bringing in his contraband. *Barbara B.* was his first command. He had got her with only five hundred dollars and some fast talk at the bank. He greeted George full of good news. He had a new partner up in Union Bay, he said. The partner was a wheeler-dealer, a hustler, an expert at juggling A and B fishing licenses, that sort of thing, but the man had a heart of gold. The new partner wanted to serve the communities up there, and *Barbara B.* was going to be the ship. They were going to process fresh fish—salmon, cod, halibut, crabs, prawns, everything—and send it down to Vancouver on *Barbara B.* Dave was going to steam north soon to scout out the place. There was, believe it or not, George (said Dave), a machine shop up there. Or so Dave had heard. The potatoes in Union Bay, Dave understood, cost less than in Vancouver. That was a very good sign, Dave thought.

Dave's mate was a stocky, red-bearded man in overalls and no shirt. He kept his meaty arms folded in front of him. He looked surly and said nothing. He did not look bright. I wondered if he was Dave's enforcer from the old days. He seemed to watch us with suspicion.

We drank herb tea in the low-ceilinged, handmade galley, over a table surfaced with a chart of the British Columbia coast. Then we said good-bye. George and I walked down the plank and away from the boat. I had noticed that George did not seem to share Dave's enthusiasm. "Sounds pretty encouraging," I ventured. George made an unintelligible sound. I asked if *Barbara B.* wasn't a good boat. Yes, she was a good boat, he answered—she had a big hold—but she was in trouble with the bank. It was in watching people like Dave, George said, that he had decided he wanted no part of the big-boat business.

"It was the use of the light seagoing canoe," he writes, "which once enabled people to live and travel throughout this coastline, instead of in the present pattern of centralization at the few areas offering facilities for modern transport and communication. I could see that this presently extinct manner of travel was the one which offered me a chance for the closer contact I sought to establish with this coast, and I began to accumulate all available information on canoe travel throughout the world's history.

"The canoe must be fast in order to deal with strong tidal currents and to make the greatest use of this coast's limited periods of predictable and favorable conditions for crossing long stretches of open water. It must be as light as possible in order to be easily propelled in the water and carried safely ashore in the many areas where no anchorage or shelter for heavy craft exists. If it is inherently stable without ballast or keel it may survive heavy weather at sea by being tossed harmlessly out of the way of large breaking waves, avoiding the heavy-keeled craft's habit of remaining tragically fixed at the advance of a destructive mass of water. If an open canoe is given the freeboard necessary to remain safe in unskilled hands and rough waters it will possess so much windage as to require much extra effort against the least breeze, so it is advantageous to lower the freeboard and achieve safety by decking the canoe and seating the paddlers in individual manholes. The low profile and center of gravity of such a decked canoe can be stabilized with very little beam, and an exceptionally narrow, efficient, and easily driven craft results. The fine lines of such a craft pass easily through and among rough waters, and safe travel in these conditions is possible, along with the ability to land on open beaches through heavy surf. The little sail needed to drive such a craft when winds permit can be carried without need for ballast or fixed rigging, and easily hoisted or stowed as desired.

"It was necessary for me to consider all possible materials and methods, and make the compromises which occur between ideal design and practical technique. The form I had in mind had much in common with those developed by the Aleuts and Eskimos, and I studied their adaptable and efficient pattern of construction involving a light flexible frame covered with a tough waterproof skin. It was this combination of independently flexible frame and skin which enabled their otherwise light and frail craft to withstand the stresses of the stormy, shallow, and ice-filled northern seas.

"Their boats were pieced together from bone, driftwood, and animal hides and were greatly limited by this in their size, strength, and durability. By adapting their highly evolved methods to presently available and superior materials I arrived at a workable system. Aluminum tubing is lashed strongly but flexibly together to

74

form a frame, which is covered with a waterproof and durable skin of laminated glass-reinforced poly resin. This produces a stronger, lighter, and more easily fabricated hull than any existing process known to boatbuilding, although it is similar to some present methods of building aircraft."

George's first fiberglass kayak was sixteen feet long, modeled on a kayak from Nunivak Island. He first tried to cover the frame with a green fabric, but he couldn't get the material taut. The Eskimos had sewn their skins on raw and wet and let them shrink tight, but the green fabric would not behave that way. When it failed, George settled on fiberglass. He copied the kayak's lines directly from *The Bark Canoes and Skin Boats of North America,* by Chapelle and Adney. This book is George's bible. The authors had begun it from concern with the speed at which skin boats decay in museums. "The purpose of the study," wrote Chapelle, "was to measure the skin boats and to make scale drawings that would permit the construction of a replica exact in details of appearance, form, construction, and also in working behavior." George did so, following the Nunivak Eskimos in everything but materials. His kayak is figure 184 come to life.

The Nunivak kayak had a single large manhole in which a passenger sat with his back to the paddler's. George's version proved tippy, and today he is embarrassed by it. He continues to use it for short errands, though, and its skin shows not a single dent from a career of rough use on stony beaches.

George looked around for a better model.

The best of the old kayaks, according to Chapelle, were those of the Alaskans and the Greenlanders. Kayaks from Asia and the Canadian Arctic were not nearly so good. Of the two superior genera of kayaks, Greenland's needle-tipped boats were decked with more elaborate equipment than Alaska's, but the quality of the basic design was about the same. Alaska was closer to George, so his attention turned there. The best of the Alaskan kayaks were made by the Aleuts, he learned. The Aleuts handled their kayaks better than anyone in the world.

The Aleuts were master kayakers out of necessity. The Aleutian Islands have one of the dreariest climates on Earth. When gales are not whipping the islands, dense fogs are smothering them softly. The Aleutians seldom see direct sunlight. In all the chain, there are only two stands of trees, small groves of Sitka spruce planted by white men a century and a half ago, still stunted today. Before these sad little plantations, the wind howled over the islands without a single obstruction. Aleutian birds hug the ground. Aleutian insects have lain so low for so long that the wings of some species have atrophied. Aleutian people lived in communal lodges buried for warmth in the tundra.

The caribou Eskimos of the Canadian Arctic were treeless and windswept too, but they had caribou. The Aleuts, aside from a few edible plants, nesting birds, and bird eggs, had only a cruel sea. They went out into it with an arsenal: sinew-backed bows, bone-tipped arrows, dart throwers, spear throwers, bolos, harpoons, bird spears, and lances. They brought back seals, sea lions, sea otter, sea cows, whales, ducks, geese, loons, murres, cormorants. They fished for halibut and cod with 150-fathom lines braided from the stalks of giant kelp. They caught flounder with small hooks of shell.

The artistic dugout-builders of the Inside Passage hated to leave sight of land, and they ventured over the horizon only when a harpooned whale towed them there, or when a storm blew them. The Aleut kayakers paddled over the horizon regularly, and on purpose. They made casual trips to the Kamchatka Peninsula in Asia. It may be, in fact, that the Aleut racial divergence from the Eskimo is because of intermarriage with Kamchatka natives. The Aleuts may not have been highbrow, but they were cosmopolitan.

The Aleuts' sea-otter hunts were cooperative. From four to twenty kayaks, some with one manhole, some with two, fanned out in a semicircle. When a hunter saw an otter surfacing for air, he pointed with his paddle, and the kayaks converged on the spot. When the otter surfaced again, it was greeted by a barrage of stone darts. These were cast with the added leverage of a throwing board, and each was connected by a line to a seal-bladder float, which impeded the wounded otter's escape and marked its position. The kayaks kept pace easily with the fleeing float. The pursuit added interest to the otter's oxygen debt, and it had to come to the surface to pay off. When it did, the kayaks were gathered in a tight circle around the float, and the throwing boards were cocked once again.

The otter were hunted also in two-man kayaks with bow and arrow. One man was the archer, the other carried a long pole fitted at the end with crosspieces, like a brush, with which he fished out the arrows. The archer might miss, but would succeed in driving the otter underwater before it could draw a full breath. The hunters followed the tiring otter by watching the bubbles.

The Aleuts killed their whales with poisoned lances. First they prepared their souls, through the arduous ritual that always preceded Native American whaling, then they smeared their lances with a deadly extract from the roots of monkshood, a dark-cowled flower common in the Aleutians. At least two canoes went out. If one was smashed by flukes, the other could come to the rescue. The hunters approached the whale cautiously from the rear. They threw their lances, blew on their hands in superstition, and paddled like hell in the other direction. The poison killed the whale in a few days, and if the hunters were lucky the body drifted ashore.

In Aleut kayaks, the rims of the manholes were fitted with waterproof skirts of intestine, which the paddler drew tight around his chest and tied in a bow. In addition, he wore an intestine parka with drawstrings at the neck and sleeves. When he had knotted his last drawstring, the hunter was truly embarked. Man and kayak became a watertight unit, a sea centaur. If a wave flipped the kayak, the paddler knew how to right it. He had techniques for retrieving a paddle lost while he was upside down under water, then righting the canoe with it. He even had a technique for righting the canoe with no paddle at all. Today, Greenland Eskimos practice ten different rolls designed to meet ten different contingencies at sea, and it is likely that the Aleuts were as well drilled and as acrobatic. They, like the Greenlanders, were expert at rolling deliberately to duck the force of a breaking wave. They played in the surf like sea lions.

The Aleuts could repair serious damage to a kayak without coming ashore. Just as porpoises come to the aid of wounded or sick pod members, supporting them at the surface with blowholes above the water, so two healthy kayaks would float side by side while the sick one was lifted from the sea and laid lengthwise across their decks, where the damage could be mended.

The Aleut's boots had soles of sea-lion flipper and uppers of sea-lion esophagus. Under his intestine rain parka was a second parka of sea-lion hide. He could no longer call his epidermis his own. He imitated the structure of sea mammals in building his boats. Paddling, his heart beat within a framework of artificial ribs inspired by those creatures. He fed on fish. He was as easy in the water as the animals he borrowed designs and materials from. His ease was not instinctive; it had to be taught him by his elders, but so it is for most of the other warm-blooded animals that have returned to the ocean. It is hard to devise a definition for sea mammal that does not make the Aleut a specimen. When the naturalist Georg Steller, who accompanied Vitus Bering to Alaska in 1741, saw his first Aleut, a man kayak-shaped below the waist, sea-lioned and bird-feathered above, with sun-darkened face and bone in nose, the naturalist was seeing a new species.

Russian fur-hunters followed Bering to the Aleutians, searching for fur seal and sea otter. They named the Aleut umiak the *baidar.* The kayak they called by the diminutive, *baidarka.*

George built his second fiberglass canoe, a baidarka, in 1972.

When his Nunivak Island canoe is pulled up on the beach beside its Aleut successor, it looks like a toy. George's proficiency with design and materials took a leap, clearly. Missing are two or three steps in between. "Design of canoe—product of intuition and analysis," he wrote, in one of the notes to himself that he collects in a cardboard box on his table.

Chapelle had written that probably none of the Aleut baidarkas had exceeded thirty feet in length. George's baidarka is thirty-one feet long. It has three manholes, instead of two, and it has two sails. In spite of these additions, it remains in the mainline of Eskimo-Aleut tradition. The various kayaks are a single circumpolar idea, clothed differently. Where the Aleuts covered theirs with sea-lion skin, and the northern Alaskans with bearded seal, George used fiberglass.

Aleut boats were waterproofed by soaking the seams with blubber. George's baidarka is waterproofed by polyester resin. He likes to think, though, that the Eskimos and Aleuts might have used resin too, and he is not alone in thinking so. "Pitch was used at one time in curragh building," writes Chapelle, "and it would be unwise to assume that the oil treatment used by the Eskimo was their only method." The Aleuts were experimentalists, continually fooling around with their designs, and it is hard to believe they didn't at least give resin a try, especially the mainland Aleuts, who had trees to draw pitch from. A vegetable gum or a resin, Chapelle notes, would have much improved the waterproofing, though it might have made the kayak less flexible.

The preparation of the skins for an Aleut baidarka was hard and smelly work. The skins were piled and sweated until the hair came loose, then soaked in urine, scraped of fat, and sewn together. The holes in the hide were punched with bone awls. The sewing needles were made from small bones in the wings of gulls. The thread was sinew. The boat had to be re-oiled after a week in the water, and after several years of use the skin had to be replaced entirely.

The application of fiberglass to George's baidarka was hard and smelly work, too. The fumes from the cans of resin were headier and more dangerous than those that rose from the urine tubs, but the fiberglass did not have to be re-oiled weekly nor replaced every few years. It was far tougher than skin. It lost a bit in flexibility and was not so light. George could not tuck his baidarka under his arm and walk up the beach with it, as the Aleuts had done with their boats.

A supreme virtue of fiberglass, from George's point of view, was that he had to kill no sea lions, bearded seals, walrus, or caribou to get it. It is now harder to find those creatures than it was in Aleut days, and it is less legal to slay them, and George is short on bloodlust anyway.

George's materials are space-age, but his baidarka remains an Aleut canoe. The white-water kayaks made of fiberglass or molded plastic that are sold in stores are not Aleut or Eskimo canoes, having departed from the organic analogy—independent skeleton within a waterproof epidermis. Their forerunner is not the sea lion, but the beer can.

"Fiberglass is used normally as a structural member, ' says George. "Not in my canoe. My canoe is not really a fiberglass boat. It's a boat with a waterproof membrane of fiberglass. The strength of the fiberglass is tensile, in the fibers. Fiberglass fails when compressive stress is exerted on it. In my canoe, fiberglass takes the tensile loads and aluminum takes the compressive loads."

The Aleuts lashed their frames together with sinew or twisted gut. George uses nylon. In Aleut baidarkas, the skirts of intestine were laced at the bottom to the manhole rim, and fitted at the top with drawstrings. In George's the skirts are bright-yellow nylon, elasticized at top and bottom. The Aleuts went to sea with repair kits of animal fat that they smeared over leaky seams. George goes to sea with a repair kit of fiber patches, resin, and catalyst. The Aleuts brought hollow bones for sucking water from their bilges. George brings a sponge. The Aleuts lashed their harpoons, lances, and fishing gear to their decks. George does the same—less in imitation than in surrender to inevitability, for when you spend much of your time in a baidarka, tying things on deck comes naturally. George's cod-jigger, his extra paddles, his coiled stern and bow lines, his toothbrush, all have their places on the deck, lashed there with 110-pound-test nylon cord. In convenient spots on deck, small sandwiches of Velcro hold extra lengths of cord, ready for emergencies.

George's Gunter lug sails are certainly a departure from Eskimo and Aleut tradition. It is not certain, though, that *sails* are a departure. Eskimos may or may not have used sails before contact with white men. The Aleuts are known to have joined two baidarkas to make a catamaran, then raise sail, but it is uncertain whether this idea was home-grown or picked up somewhere in their wide travels. George's sails are no big deal. His forty square feet of canvas move the baidarka as fast as he wants to go. When there is no wind, George takes down both masts and sticks them in a manhole.

George did add one sure innovation, a rudder. It is controlled by a set of reins that runs the length of the baidarka on either side of the manholes. A crewman in any one of the three holes can gee or haw the canoe by tugging on the reins. The rudder, interestingly, is the one part of the canoe that gives George cause to worry. It has not benefited from the long evolution—biological almost in its slowness and conservatism—that has shaped the rest of the craft. The rudder is the baidarka's one moving part. He thinks a lot about how to refine it.

The three-hole baidarka that George chose as his model is the kayak with the strongest claim to a history in the Inside Passage. An armada of three-man baidarkas once swept through in search of furs. The three holes seem to have been a Russian suggestion, though some Aleut may have originated the idea, before regretting it. Because of its doubtful origin, Chapelle and Adney did not include a blueprint. In building his boat George had to extrapolate from drawings of the two-man baidarka.

"I've looked everywhere," he says, "and I haven't seen a single drawing, or diagram, or reconstruction of the boats the Russians used, but they were three-man canoes. The Russians had fleets of two hundred or more of them.

"The Russians were outlaws. They had been thrown out in the different revolutions and they moved east across Siberia. You had to be tough to cross Siberia on foot. You couldn't be just an ordinary man. Most of those who reached the Pacific died on the coast. Only a few made it across the ocean, the toughest of the toughest. A lot of them had been rich people before they were thrown out. They were into the money thing. The trip was to go and find a tribe of Aleuts to enslave. Then you went off with them to kill fur seals. The Russian sat in the middle, paddled by his slaves in front and back. Because that's what they were—slaves."

At first the Aleuts, in their wooden armor, fought the Russians with bows and lances. Putting aside old feuds, they united against the fur hunters and succeeded in killing a few, but the reprisals were always more terrible. In the end the Aleuts, defeated, became half-willing accomplices, joining the Russians on fur-hunting expeditions far beyond the Aleutians. Nothing was left them but that bleak adventure. Aleut men between the ages of eighteen and fifty were subject to the draft. The lucky ones were allowed to work on shares, keeping half their catch. They hunted sea otter on Kodiak Island and were attacked by the Eskimos there. They hunted Prince William Sound and were attacked by those Eskimos, too.

In 1799 a fleet of five hundred baidarkas under the command of Baranof entered the Inside Passage. They paddled deep into the Alexander Archipelago to found the settlement of Sitka, which would become the capital of Russian America. The Aleuts and their Russian masters were attacked at every opportunity by the Tlingits, the warlike people who guarded the top of the Inside Passage. Hundreds of Aleuts were killed when the Tlingits sacked Old Sitka in 1802.

Baranof and his Aleut hunters conducted a kind of *blitzkrieg* against the sea otter of the Inside Passage. Five or six hundred baidarkas formed a skirmish line miles in length, moving as fast as seven miles per hour. Encountering otter, the line divided into hunting groups of six to eight boats. They cleaned out the otter, re-formed, and swept on.

In time the baidarka fleets reached California. In San Francisco Bay, early in the nineteenth century, the sea otter were so thick and fearless that sailors clubbed them with oars. The arctic boats entered the Golden Gate and temperate waters, paddled by men weary of the world, surely, having seen so much more of it than they had planned. The Aleuts cleaned out the otter, turned, and at last began to work their way home.

Before the Russians came to the Aleutians, the islands had been one of the most densely populated regions of aboriginal America. The sea around was wild but rich, and Aleut one- and two-man baidarkas won a good living from it, supporting a population of from fifteen to twenty thousand. After forty years of Russian fur hunting in three-man baidarkas, the Aleuts were reduced to two thousand. Steller's sea cow had vanished from the face of the Earth, and the sea otter was on the verge of extinction.

It was not from any admiration of this savage history that George picked the three-man baidarka. It was that he, like the Russians, needed better carrying capacity. Theirs was for furs, his for the supplies that would make his baidarka a traveling canoe. In George idealism and pragmatism mix unpredictably. He was untroubled by the ghosts of Aleut slaves in the manholes front and back of him.

In April 1972, George's baidarka had its first real test. *D'Sonoqua* carried George and his canoe north up the Inside Passage as far as Yuculta Rapids, and there let him off. At sunset, with the tide full, the moon full and rising, George set off alone. He was scared. "It's supposed to be against all the rules," he says, "going through Yuculta Rapids at full tide."

The rapids are a notorious narrows between Sonora Island and the mainland. Sheer, forested foothills shoulder together there, pinching off the channel. Three thousand feet above, the dark green of the foothills ends, snowline begins, and higher still rise tall white peaks.

The rapids come upon you like the rapids of a river. First there's the sibilance, distant and ominous. Then the roar. Then your last preparations, and then that becalmed, full-empty, suspended moment in which you wait for the current to seize you. The first riffles advance, not slow, not fast, then the canoe's bow passes over the lip and swings into the stream. Speed picks up. Quickly you're moving fast, as if somewhere ahead a drain plug has been jerked. In Yuculta Rapids the canoe, accelerating, exhilarating, no way to turn around or get off, races down to where the silver river, and everything on it, disappears into the dark mountain. Instead of vanishing into some tunnel, the current at the last moment turns hard left, divides, and sweeps through two gaps in the foothills. The river runs smooth, disguising its speed and turbulence. The canoe spins inexplicably this way and that, as if its needle tip were magnetized by water friction. Eddies pass the canoe along to tide rips, which entrust it to whirlpools, which deposit it in brief, slick, circular oases of calm. George dervished downstream. The moon shone on the turbulence, and killer whales and porpoises hunted around him. The cetaceans like the rapids because the fishing at the meeting of the currents is good. The baidarka swam as easily, almost, as the sea mammals. George knew where the bad whirlpools were, and he pulled away with his double paddle. His fear departed. He had reached the midpoint of the rapids when it got dark. He hauled out on a moss-covered rock and spent the night there, excited, sleeping hardly at all.

For the next two days he worked his way against the wind through Cordero Channel, then Wellbore Channel, and then past Whirlpool Rapids. When he reached Johnstone Strait, where the narrow passages open up, the wind changed. A strong southeaster blew up the strait. The wind ran against the tide, setting up big breaking waves. George raised his sails for the first time. "I was scared to death," he says. "I didn't know what my boat would do in these big waves. Everyone had told me I'd never survive some of those places." But everyone was wrong. The baidarka covered forty miles that morning. It was, George concedes, a great moment. "At that point, I knew I had a canoe to travel in. Until the sails worked, it was just a big kayak."

Then the unforeseen happened.

The baidarka built up so much speed that the bow came out of the water. The vessel planed.

"I didn't expect it to fly. It never entered my head that it would take off and plane. It's frightening, when it takes off. The sudden speed. You have a sense of fear from the speed, like motorcycle racing or something."

So much of the hull came out of the water that the canoe was difficult to steer. George crouched like a jockey in his paddling hole, hands tugging on the steering reins, eyes on the straining sails, waiting for something to snap. Nothing did.

"It was like water-skiing. At times it was entirely out of the water. Well, that's an exaggeration. Half of it was out of the water. I hadn't planned on that. I had no idea it would fly."

------ 17 ------

Oatmeal

High above Point Loma, the parachute popped open, and Orion floated back to Earth, landing in front of the blockhouse. The Orion men celebrated with champagne.

"Everything worked," says Brian Dunne. "It was one of those moments in your life where you've stretched yourself as far as you can, and it comes off right. It was fantastically exciting. You know what it was like? It was like painting a free-form picture. You suspend part of your analytical machinery. You're thinking with your subconscious. It's done by feel. And it came out right."

" 'A product of intuition and analysis,' " I suggested.

"Yes, that's a good way to put it."

The success of the model program kept Orion alive, but the project was now struggling. It had begun officially in July 1958, just after Sputnik— "The one time possible to sell such a project," according to Freeman Dyson. That time was brief, and rapidly came to a close.

"The first year," says Ted Taylor, "was one of accelerating excitement and assurance that we were really involved in busting the door into space wide open, not as Freeman put it, just looking through the keyhole. Then we started running into difficulties. A lot of people started gnawing away at it. They couldn't destroy it, because it really did seem to make sense. But it began to drag."

In summer of 1959, Werner von Braun won his race with Taylor. The United States government decided that chemical rockets, not nuclear, would power its space program. Orion was turned over to the Air Force. "The Air Force didn't really want it," says Freeman. "We didn't want them, either. It was a marriage of convenience." The Orion men knew from the beginning that there was no way to make a weapon of the spaceship, and after a while the Air Force began to suspect it too.

A squad from La Jolla flew to New Mexico to give the Air Force Weapons Lab a progress report. Unaccustomed to giving presentations, the Orion men were nervous. There was an airline strike on, and they had to travel by a roundabout route. They arrived tardy and tired.

"The next morning at breakfast," remembers Brian Dunne, "Dr. Harris Meyer was there, the barrel-chested director of the laboratory, a kind of giant scoutmaster type. He's eating an inch-thick steak, with three eggs on top of it, and hash-brown potatoes and coffee. The whole works. A gigantic breakfast. Taylor's telling bawdy stories, Meyer is laughing his head off as he's consuming this huge protein breakfast. Freeman steps in, with this quiet British 'Good morning.' The waitress asks him what he wants, and he says, 'Oh, I think I'll have some oatmeal. And some tea.' So he had his oatmeal and tea.

"We got on the bus and went out to the auditorium. There were four or five hundred people there. I got up and gave a presentation on some of the experiments, and the others gave presentations.

"We got into this big discussion on opacity. Opacity was one of the key considerations in Orion. Whether the pusher plate ablated depended on the opacity of these very hot gases as they piled up on it. If the gas wasn't opaque enough, the radiation would go in and boil off the plate. The whole concept lived or died on opacity. The people at Los Alamos were very big on opacity, because in H-bomb technology opacity is the key thing, too. They were very, very strong in that field. The critics of Orion seized on it, and strove to put the matter to rest. Harris Meyer was one of them. He had this booming, authoritative voice. He thought he had the whole floor.

"Freeman got up in the audience, and in this clear, piping voice just whittled them down. It was the most beautiful piece of dignified, scientific oratory I've ever heard. 'This follows from that, and therefore, and so on,' and so on, and on and on. And all this on oatmeal and tea, and no sleep. The place was silent. Because it was a phenomenon. He turned slowly around as he did it, so everyone would get the full benefit of his remarks, and then he very politely sat down."

But this oratory was just a rearguard action. The life was going out of the project. Orion's historical passage was to be as meteoric as its interplanetary departure would have been. The spaceship burned very bright for a moment, then was gone. Good technical work was done after 1959, but not by men who believed they were personally going to space. The limited-test-ban treaty of 1963, in stopping nuclear explosions in the atmosphere and space, put Orion on the ropes. A final no by NASA killed any remaining hope. The project officially ended in spring of 1965.

"I was there the day it died," says Freeman. "It stopped at five o'clock. We were tidying up, writing final reports. We talked about old times. What was so dramatic was that it wasn't dramatic. It was just a bunch of people sitting there watching the clock." In his desk drawer at Princeton, Freeman placed a bag of aluminum fragments from the tests at Point Loma. He keeps it there still, shards of the dream, proof that he was not just dreaming.

Sir George Dyson, in his *The Progress of Music*, had written, long before, without intending it, a kind of epitaph for Orion, a prophetic appreciation of his son's involvement with the space-craft. The metaphor was musical. The subject was a great composer.

"By a supreme act of faith," Sir George wrote, "he deliberately devoted the best years of his life to the inception and gradual completion of a work of colossal proportions, a work covering the whole range of his ideas, philosophic, poetic, and musical, and a work which he, the practical operatic producer, of all men well knew to be absolutely beyond the available means of any theatre then existing in the world. There is in music no parallel to *The Ring*. There is no parallel to it in any other art. If an architect were to spend half his life designing a huge and elaborate building which was not only unauthorized and unwanted, but for which the very materials did not at the time exist anywhere in the world, that would be a fair parallel to Wagner's chosen task."

The difference is that Freeman did not devote half his life to Orion, just one or two of his best years, and that the spaceship, unlike *The Ring*, never flew. Had Orion left the ground, though, it would have done so with much crashing of cymbals. Pounding through space, Orion would have made Wagnerian music.

Homo, Lupus, Leviathan

"In trying to slip quietly around on the waters of this planet," writes the second George Dyson in one of his unpublished accounts, "you take a slender form that the wind and waves won't notice; you blend into the interface of water and air by cunningly adopting their lightness and quickness of movement; with small wings and little strain you move with the wind."

Exploring British Columbia in his baidarka, George relearned the things the Aleuts had known for centuries. Most of that knowledge had passed from human experience, but each day in the baidarka revived a little more of it.

"I was free to seek the safety and comfort of solid ground wherever the slightest open beach or protected cove permitted the landing of my canoe, yet was also free to travel long distances in comfort, speed, and freedom from concern for mechanical systems.

"A canoe traveling silently through fog, darkness, or storm needs no radar or attention to navigational equipment to perceive and avoid danger, but only the alert human senses. One can smell the proximity of the coast, hear dangerous breakers in a storm, or echoes from projecting rocks on a black and quiet night, and feel by the movement of the sea the character and position of one's invisible surroundings in thick weather. I required no machinery or fuel to go where I wished but only the use of wind, tide, and paddle. My food and fuel was that provided lavishly by my surroundings: a rich variety of seafood cooked over fires of abundant driftwood. I had a close relationship with all the many forms of life inhabiting this area, and grew to know the conditions of tide, weather, and seasonal migration affecting them. My canoe was as much on shore as in the water, and it was this capability

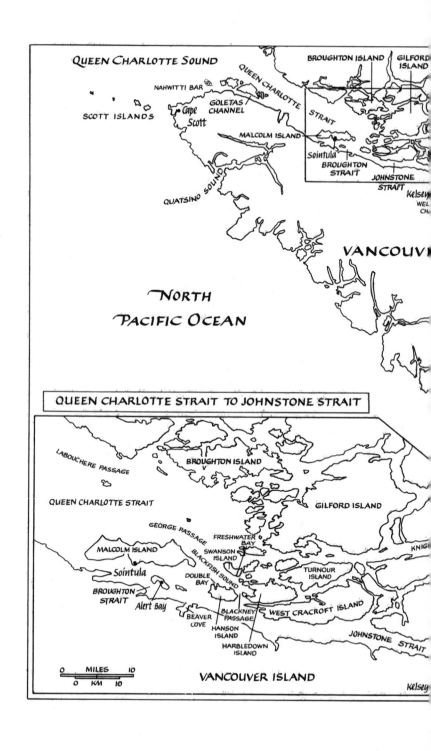

QUEEN CHARLOTTE SOUND

NAHWITTI BAR

QUEEN CHARLOTTE

BROUGHTON ISLAND

GILFORD
ISLAND

SCOTT ISLANDS

GOLETAS
CHANNEL

Cape
Scott

STRAIT

MALCOLM ISLAND

Sointula

BROUGHTON
STRAIT

JOHNSTONE
STRAIT

Kelsey

WEL
CH

QUATSINO SOUND

VANCOUV

NORTH

PACIFIC OCEAN

QUEEN CHARLOTTE STRAIT TO JOHNSTONE STRAIT

LABOUCHERE PASSAGE

BROUGHTON ISLAND

QUEEN CHARLOTTE STRAIT

GILFORD ISLAND

GEORGE PASSAGE

FRESHWATER
BAY

MALCOLM ISLAND

SWANSON
ISLAND

KNIGH

Sointula

BLACKFISH SOUND

DOUBLE
BAY

TURNOUR
ISLAND

BROUGHTON
STRAIT

Alert Bay

BEAVER
COVE

BLACKNEY
PASSAGE

WEST CRACROFT ISLAND

HANSON
ISLAND

JOHNSTONE STRAIT

HARBLEDOWN
ISLAND

MILES   10

KM   10

VANCOUVER ISLAND

Kelsey

VANCOUVER ISLAND

MILES
0   50
0   KM   50

N

KNIGHT INLET

WICKE ND

CORDERO CHANNEL

SONORA ISLAND
RAZA ISLAND

URLOW LANDS

QUADRA ISLAND

BRITISH   COLUMBIA

SLAND

DENMAN ISLAND

TEXADA ISLAND

LASQUETI ISLAND

INDIAN ARM

Belcarra Park
Vancouver

A   N   A   D   A

STRAIT OF GEORGIA

Nanaimo

NORTH PENDER ISLAND

NLET

Victoria

JUAN DE FUCA STRAIT

HARDWICKE ISLAND

WASHINGTON

UNITED STATES

palacios

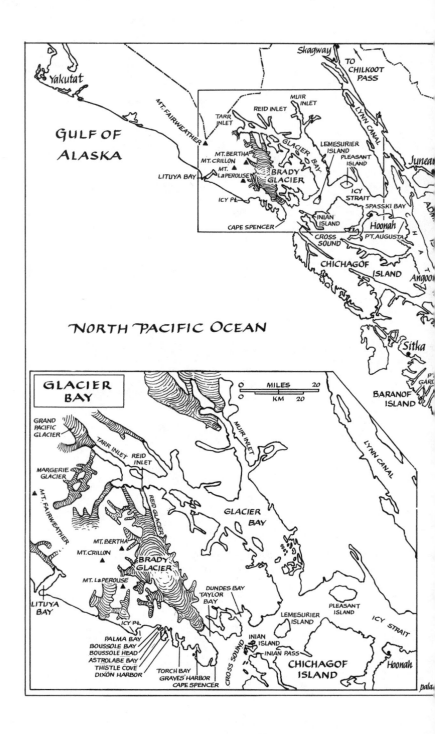

GULF OF
ALASKA

NORTH PACIFIC OCEAN

Skagway
TO
CHILKOOT
PASS

Yakutat

MT. FAIRWEATHER

MUIR
INLET

TARR
INLET

REID INLET

GLACIER BAY

LEMESURIER
ISLAND

PLEASANT
ISLAND

LYNN CANAL

Juneau

MT. BERTHA
MT. CRILLON

MT.
LaPEROUSE

BRADY
GLACIER

LITUYA BAY

ICY PT.

ICY
STRAIT

SPASSKI BAY

CAPE SPENCER

INIAN
ISLAND

CROSS
SOUND

Hoonah

PT. AUGUSTA

CHICHAGOF

ISLAND

Angoon

Sitka

PT.
GARI

BARANOF
ISLAND

GLACIER
BAY

MILES   20

KM   20

MUIR INLET

GRAND
PACIFIC
GLACIER

TARR INLET

REID
INLET

LYNN CANAL

MARGERIE
GLACIER

MT. FAIRWEATHER

REID GLACIER

GLACIER
BAY

MT. BERTHA

MT. CRILLON

BRADY
GLACIER

MT. LaPEROUSE

DUNDES BAY
TAYLOR
BAY

PLEASANT
ISLAND

LITUYA
BAY

ICY PT.

LEMESURIER
ISLAND

ICY STRAIT

PALMA BAY
BOUSSOLE BAY
BOUSSOLE HEAD
ASTROLABE BAY
THISTLE COVE
DIXON HARBOR

TORCH BAY
GRAVES HARBOR
CAPE SPENCER

INIAN
ISLAND

INIAN PASS

CROSS SOUND

CHICHAGOF
ISLAND

Hoonah

pala

ALEXANDER
ARCHIPELAGO

MILES 50
KM 50

N

BRITISH COLUMBIA

CANADA

TRACY ARM

STEPHENS PASSAGE

FREDERICK SOUND

Kake

Petersburg

KUPREANOF ISLAND

ROCKY PASSAGE

KUIU ISLAND

SUMNER STRAIT

PT. BAKER

ALASKA
U.S.

CLARENCE STRAIT

PRINCE
OF WALES
ISLAND

Ketchikan

HECATE STRAIT

Prince
Rupert

DIXON ENTRANCE

which permitted study of the meeting of ocean and continent from both viewpoints."

The baidarka carried George deeper into solitude. Sometimes he found paddlers to accompany him, but often he did not. Alone in his canoe, he heard voices in the waves. Sailors have heard that murmuring for as long as men have gone to sea, imagining it, in the old days, to be the plaint of all the seamen who ever drowned. George heard whole sentences. The sentences were disappointing. "It's never, 'Beauty is the secret of the Universe,' " he complains. "It's, 'Hey Joe, pass the butter.' "

The baidarka brought him that grudging appreciation of civilization that comes with travel in the wilderness. Once, after some days alone, George found a waterlogged newspaper on the beach. Its news of civilized goings-on was old, but George was greedy for it. He peeled off the pages and read them one by one.

He never thought of himself as an adventurer. For George the baidarka is just transportation. He operates almost entirely without cash, and the canoe is his way of seeing a lot of country without spending a penny. The point of his trips has never been the risk. George is more impressed by the business-as-usual feats of the Aleuts, and of those old sourdoughs who traveled from Seattle to Juneau in rowboats, than by the adventures of wealthy young sailors on vacation. He is awed by the deeds of the old-timers. He believes we live in an age of lesser men.

In summer of 1973, George spent a week investigating the inlets and islands north of Hanson Island. At the end of that week, the wind turned against him and began to blow briskly from the north. Paddling against a wind, even a mild one, is hard work in a baidarka, so George came about, raised sail, and in a single long day traveled eighty miles back to Hanson Island.

The next day he sat in the pub at Alert Bay, an Indian town near Hanson. He was passing time, waiting for the mail, when a man in cowboy boots and cowboy hat sat beside him. The uniform was peculiar. In George's northern woods, cork boots and wool caps are more the style. George, curious and loosened a little by beer, struck up a conversation. The cowboy, he learned, was from Colorado and was named Carol Martin. On comparing notes, Martin and George realized that they had met before, when Martin was a hunting guide in the Rockies and George a pot washer there. Martin now was waiting too—not for mail, but for a diesel part for his tugboat. The tug, said Martin, was towing a barge. The barge, he claimed, was full of hay, cows, and horses bound for Alaska. When he got his diesel part, he planned to charter a float plane and fly back to his ailing tug, then resume his expedition north. George did not believe the part about hay, cows, and horses—no one would barge such a zoo up the Inside Passage to Alaska—but he was alert, like all his brothers who scuffle for a living on British Columbia's waterways, at the chance to turn a buck. *D'Sonoqua* had just arrived from the south, and George offered to charter her to Martin at a price that would beat the bush pilot's. Martin agreed.

Martin's story was all true, it turned out. He and his hay, horses, and cows were headed for Juneau, where he planned to start a new ranch and a new life. He needed someone who knew about boats, and he invited George to come along.

George thought about it. Juneau, he knew, was somewhere near Glacier Bay. And Glacier Bay's deep inlets were the very last of the Inside Passage. The bay was thus the roof of his nine-hundred-mile house. It's a poor tenant who has never checked his shingles. George agreed to go. He travels so lightly that no arrangements or good-byes were necessary. He just hauled his baidarka up on the barge.

"It was a weird change," he says. "One day I'm in my canoe going south. The next day I'm heading north in a barge full of animals. I'm doing the *chores*. I've never done chores before. I had to feed and water the animals. Forty-five gallons for the horses and cows between them. The barge was beautiful, though. It was Colorado. You'd walk around and smell the hay."

One hundred ten feet long, forty feet wide, the barge carried three cows, four horses, twenty-five tons of hay, six thousand gallons of water, a pick-up truck, a sixty-foot house trailer, enough lumber for a house, and tons of food and gear. It was Martin's Ark, containing everything he would need to start fresh. It was a whole settlement, yet it was pulled by a minitug. George had seen this sort of configuration before. In the forgiving waters of the Inside Passage, barges are often comically overloaded. George has intercepted them in his baidarka on the strength of his arm. He has camped on points of land and watched them pass him cheerily on the flood tide, then pass again on the ebb, going backward. But Martin's set-up was an extreme case. "The tug was meant for pulling a couple of logs around a harbor," George says, "and here it was towing a hundred-foot barge. 'Underpowered' isn't even the word. It could hardly move against the tide. We made four knots in a dead calm. It's the old story—you can move the Queen Mary with an outboard, but you can't move her very fast. For me it was interesting, because I had to use all the skill I'd learned with my canoe. We had to play the tides and winds.

"There was no radiophone. A tugboat going between Seattle and Alaska with no radiophone? That's unheard of. There was no compass, either. No radar. There was no winch for the towline. Instead, we hitched the line to the truck and drove back and forth on the barge. We lost the reverse gear in Prince Rupert. *We had no reverse gear.* It's a hassle with no reverse gear, bringing a hundred-foot barge into a town somewhere."

Coming in for a landing, they had to aim the barge at the dock, cut the tug away, and pray that the speed and trajectory were right. The dock was supposed to capture the barge much as Jupiter would have captured Orion, but George had no computer to figure the angles. "That's how we shook up the cannery," he confesses.

Gliding into the dock at Petersburg, the barge rammed the cannery building. The windows filled instantly with the frightened faces of cannery workers. George still winces when he remembers. "Nobody has seen anything like it since. People still talk about it on the coast. It was the most haywire operation I've ever been a part of."

Carol Martin was skipper. George was mate and navigator. The original deckhands were Joe Martin, Carol's nine-year-old son, and a hitchhiker from Tucson whom Martin had picked up in the States. In Kelsey Bay they absorbed a third deckhand, a wild man from the

Yukon named Eric. "Eric," says George, "was returning to the Yukon from Vancouver in this monster canoe. It was a twenty-foot homemade thing—just hopeless. It was like a whale—it had to be buoyed up by water. It couldn't stand the force of gravity. When we lifted it from the water, things started to snap and break. Eric was the ultimate clumsy guy. Couldn't hammer a nail straight, and lazy, but he could steer a straight course and he was a great guy."

Captain Martin knew nothing about boats. He knew a little about engines, which was a good thing, for George was no help in that department. "I never touched the engine," George states proudly. "I've done some work on engines of various kinds. I could be a good mechanic. But once you start fooling with engines you get good at it, and you're always fixing engines."

Martin had left Colorado because it was becoming too crowded for him. Alaska, he thought, should have sufficient elbow room. Outraged by the freight prices to Alaska, he had bought his own tug and barge in Tacoma, and had sent his wife and younger children ahead to Juneau. On the rainy days of the voyage north, Captain Martin was gloomy, anxious to reach Juneau and reunite with his family. On sunny days, though, he saw no reason to rush. He lay back and enjoyed the country as it crept by. "That'd be a good place for a farm," he would observe, pointing to some clearing in the forest, or, pointing high, "Look at those goats up there! What hunting we'd have!" On the bright days, the skipper seemed to forget his family, and the expedition dallied. George would drive the livestock down to the beach to graze; nautical one moment, his life was pastoral the next. There were one or two especially beautiful spots where he thought the barge might put out its roots and stay for good. "There was enough food and stuff on the barge to keep ten people alive for two years," George says. "All kinds of guns, equipment, and everything. There was a huge freezer full of meat. I had to eat it—there was nothing else. We ate straight meat, like mountain men. It was good meat, though, elk and stuff like that."

Then the rain would return, the idyl would end, and the expedition would lurch forward.

When they went ashore at the small towns along the route, the barge's crew made a strange procession. There was Carol Martin in his cowboy clothes, and Yukon Eric, who never wore shoes and whose feet were callused and cracked, and the hitchhiker from Tucson, tall, lean, wondering how he got into this, and George, in his trapper-hippie dress, and Joe Martin, nine years old, who stood watch like a man and went ashore for liberty like the rest of them.

The towns themselves were strange. George's life often has a dreamlike quality, as he recounts it, and the Alaskan towns he saw were dream towns. "Petersburg was a town of women. We went into the bar, and three-fourths of the people were beautiful co-eds from Oregon and places like that. They were working in the cannery for the summer. Their boyfriends were out in boats until Friday." The barge men were content just to look at the girls. Having seen their fill, they left the bar, and, stepping outside, they were set upon by three figures in hideous, hook-beaked masks. Fortified by beer, George and his mates stood their ground. At this the three masks emitted sounds of disappointment. The masks came off, and beneath were the faces of three beautiful teen-age girls. (In George's stories, all girls are beautiful.) The girls explained that they were underage, and that the masks were disguises to get them into the bar. George wishes, now, that he and his friends had been more suitably frightened. "But we didn't know Petersburg," he says. "We thought it was normal."

He told the girls about the barge and its three cows, four horses, and twenty-five tons of hay. The girls didn't believe it for a moment. Southeast Alaska is a poor country for horses, and hardly any live there. But the girls were interested. They were of a horsey age, yet had lived horseless lives. When George invited them down to see his four, they accepted. For George, a twenty-year-old whose austere and nomadic life had been practically girlless, this was not a bad line—"Come down to the barge and see my horses"—but he did not follow up. The girls petted the livestock, talked for a while, then said good-bye.

The expedition continued north.

It paused in an Indian village whose children had never seen horses. When invited to tour the barge, the Indian kids made wide circles around those monstrous animals. Peeking in the freezer, they saw the great quantities of meat there, and assumed that this was horse feed. It was a reasonable deduction—the only land animal they knew of comparable size was the grizzly. Finally they got their courage up and crowded around the corral. Those in back pushed forward, those in front strained back. When a horse stamped or whinnied, everyone scattered. Then they reassembled and waited to be frightened again.

The expedition made precarious progress. "We nearly lost everything several times. It was like a thrilling nonstop adventure all the way every day. A couple of times we almost sank the tug." The near-sinkings came when the engine failed or when the helmsman made some miscalculation. They would turn to see the barge coming up from behind, massive and inexorable, like fate. There were plenty of lifeboats, fortunately, and George never feared for his life. Martin had a big speedboat, Eric had his monster canoe, and George had his baidarka. Loyal as a ship's rat, George kept the baidarka loaded with all his possessions, ready to depart on a moment's notice.

The tug departed one anchorage in heavy fog. They were scarcely underway when the fog thickened and locked them in its whiteness. They lost track of where they were. George could make out no auditory landfalls, as he might have in his canoe, for the fog muted sound and the tug's engine made a white noise as opaque as the weather. Then, dead ahead, loomed an iceberg. They remembered the *Titanic*, but they made for the berg. "We figured," says George, "that it was less likely to get into trouble than we were." Someone recalled that seven-eighths of an iceberg is underwater, so the bottom beneath this one must be deep. Whatever their fate, they would not go aground. They circled the iceberg, waiting for the fog to lift. George saw himself from a remove, and the view amused him. Here he was, George Dyson, in a barge full of horses, cows, and twenty-five tons of hay, towed by a little tug in circles around an iceberg.

The fog lifted, and the expedition resumed.

One day a cow fell overboard. Carol Martin chased it in the tug, twirling a lariat, full of happy memories of Colorado. He lassoed the cow from deck, and they hauled it aboard.

Another day the hitchhiker from Tucson fell off the tug. He caught himself on the towline and clambered back, but was so shaken by the experience that he went below and wasn't seen again until Juneau.

The expedition meandered, circling its icebergs and chasing its cows, but the general drift was northwest. The mountains that bordered the straits got taller and snowier. The tug was retracing, thousands of years afterward, the course the glaciers had taken as they receded. George was following the ice to the mountain fortresses where it retreats no more. In Glacier Bay and other lairs at the head of the Inside Passage, the glaciers estivate, moving tentatively forward some years, then inching back, awaiting another ice age.

The weather grew chillier.

Yukon Eric broke down and bought himself a pair of huge tennis shoes, capitulating to the increasing cold, to all the wicked projections on the deck of a tug, and to that tendency to step in something just before bed. He had to buy tennis shoes because his old boots no longer fit. This often happens, George has observed, when you go without shoes for too long. Callus enlarges your feet by a shoe size or two. Eric looked less wild now, but more clownish.

As the cold deepened, George built himself a nest.

"I had my little apartment in the hay. It was twenty-five tons of hay. That's a lot of hay. When I fed the horses I would keep burrowing back into it. I hollowed out a room. It was Alaskan weather outside, but it was warm and dry inside. A candle would keep it at ninety degrees. It was usually about eighty degrees anyway, because of the spontaneous combustion—I mean, decomposition—of the hay."

On the misty reaches of Queen Charlotte Sound and Clarence Strait, in a chamber deep within a migrating mountain of hay, George's hidden candle burned.

"Sometimes we would sit in the truck—me and Eric and sometimes Little Joe—and we would play the truck radio. We'd pick up country music bouncing over the mountains from Alberta. That made us crazy. We couldn't see over the sides of the barge from the truck, so we didn't know where we were. With the smell of the hay, and the country music, we thought we were in Colorado."

Carol Martin had brought his piano. (He was not entering the wilderness to abandon civilization, and he had stocked as many of its props as he could.) George had no training on the piano, but occasionally he went into the house trailer, sat at the piano bench, rubbed his cold hands, and laid his fingers on the keys. On the frigid currents of Frederick Sound and Stephens Passage, in the company of minke whales and icebergs, passing murrelets, which ducked under or beat away over the surface, and bull-necked Steller sea lions, which gave the barge brief, whiskery sniffs and stares, and bald eagles, which laughed crazily, the grandson of Sir George Dyson picked out experimental tunes.

Two days from Juneau, they encountered a stiff headwind, and in twelve hours of struggle against it, they burned up the last of their fuel. The tug puttered to a stop at the mouth of Tracy Arm, where the fiord walls are steep. There was no suitable bottom, and they dragged anchor for a while. Then, with all their cable out, one of the points took hold. They discussed their options. They were off any normal lane of navigation, so that help from another vessel was unlikely. George could sail his baidarka back toward Petersburg for help, but there was no guarantee the barge would still be there when he returned. Unable to think of anything, the barge men, immune by now to worry, just went to sleep. They woke to a bump in the darkness of early morning. A giant tug had tied up to the barge. Its improbable presence here was the result of an old accident. Two years earlier, to the day, some logs had broken from a boom to drift into Tracy Arm, and the tug had come to retrieve them before the two years elapsed and the logs entered public domain. The tug captain invited George and the others aboard, and they followed him up to the wheelhouse. George's friends were too embarrassed, at first, to mention their difficulty. "It was a beautiful wheelhouse," explains George. "There was a big brass compass. Huge throttles and brass dials. Everything was so *solid.*" Finally, just before leaving the wheelhouse, Carol Martin forced himself to admit that he was out of diesel fuel, and the tug captain happily filled him up.

At last they reached Juneau. The hitchhiker from Tucson made an ashen appearance, walked shakily from the tug, and wired home for money. Carol and Joe Martin had a happy reunion with their family. Eric continued homeward to the Yukon. George paused in Juneau for a month and a half, building stalls for Martin's animals and otherwise helping his boss. He lived in his apartment in the hay, which he and the horses were continually enlarging. When there was nothing left to do, he decided to resume his northwestern journey.

The weather was bad toward Glacier Bay, so he thought he would go instead up Lynn Canal to Skagway, put his baidarka on the little train that switchbacks over Chilkoot Pass, then take the baidarka off on the other side and run a couple of thousand miles down the Yukon to the Bering Sea. When I asked, long afterward, what he would have done once he reached the Bering Sea, George was vague. He would have improvised.

Fortunately the weather cleared in the direction of Glacier Bay, and he reverted to his old plan. He lifted the baidarka off the tug, its mother ship. With his double-bladed paddle he pushed off. The barge fell quickly behind, like the spent booster stage of a rocket. It had done its job, bringing him this far. In the blue sliver of his baidarka he pressed on alone.

The country at the top of the Inside Passage is so big that it seemed impossible at first to make progress against it. After a day of sailing and paddling, the white mountains of the Fairweather Range appeared just as distant as when he started. The narrow wake trailing his stern might have been an illusion. Then, grudgingly, the mountains grew larger. The weather remained clear and calm, unusual for late September. There was no following wind when George reached Icy Strait, and he was grateful. The absence of wind meant he would have to paddle across, but he would encounter none of the steep chop for which the strait is famous. The name "Icy Strait" on the chart had chilled him, but the real strait was not so bad. From dawn to dusk he worked his way over, in the company of humpback whales, who were grazing on the krill. Toward evening the tide turned against him, and he covered the last stretch paddling hard. He made for the first convenient beach, jumped out in his gum boots, and pulled the baidarka high. He had come a hundred miles from Juneau. He had reached Glacier Bay.

Above the strand grew a meadow of beach grass, and behind the grass stood a dark forest of young spruces. The trees were small: the glacial ice had been here just two hundred years before, and the spruces, the climax species, had only recently taken their place in the plant succession. It was new earth. At the edge of the tall grass, George unrolled his bag. He lay back, feeling tired and virtuous. He was alone in the big land. The moon was rising from the forest behind him and it illuminated a white peak across the water.

The moon rose full, and as it cleared the spruce tops it was greeted by a sudden howling. George sat up in bed. Wolves had come down silently from the forest and had infiltrated the beach grass. It seemed to George that the sound went straight to the center of his being. It passed through the center and out the other side, traveling over Icy Strait toward the moonlit mountain.

All his sensibilities quickened. Now and again, when the wolves stopped for a moment, George heard each grass blade rustling, each wave lapping. Waiting for the wolves to resume, he heard the blowing of humpback whales as they swung in close to shore.

The wolves were ending their song when, from the sea, the whales answered it. George swears that this is true. The whale music was, he says, like whistling, trumpeting, and singing combined. It resembled no work of man he knew, but it blended perfectly with the chorus of the wolves. The forest's mournful ululations mingled with the brass winds and wood winds of the deep. The Earth was singing to its moon, and the sea was harmonizing.

George sat silent in the middle of the music, yet did not feel left out. It seemed to him that the two worlds, land and sea, were coming together in him. This morning he had padded, like the wolves, in bare feet on the mossy forest floor, and this afternoon he had paddled Icy Strait, like the humpback whales. A triumvirate, they praised the moon: lupus, George, leviathan.

—— 19 ——

Inletkeeper

Two hundred years before, Glacier Bay had not existed. When longboats from H.M.S. *Discovery* reached its mouth in 1794, they found just an incipience, an indentation in the shore terminated by a blue-white wall of ice. Glacier Bay was very little bay and lots of glacier. The water around the longboats was full of bergs, for the ice front had begun the great recession that would expose the bay, and it was calving prolifically into the waters of Icy Strait. In the years since, the ice has receded with dramatic speed, in a glacial sense, and in places its termini now lie sixty-five miles inland of the terminus that the *Discovery*'s men saw.

When the ice made room for them, the Tlingits came to sojourn in Glacier Bay, establishing summer sealing camps near the ice front, where the seals were most plentiful. They called the bay *Sitt-eeta-ghaee,* "Bay from where the ice receded." Departing in a rush, the ice left the Tlingits new waterways, a dendritic system of berg-filled coves and inlets, and it left them new land, a moonscape of bare boulders and gravel fans, untarnished at first by life. Nowhere in recent times has ice retreated so rapidly, and seldom are geological processes, or the principles of succession in plant communities, so clearly laid out. The birth of the new landscapes was spectacular and noisy. In the daytime the Tlingits saw great monoliths of ice break from the glaciers' faces and crash into the bay, and at night they heard the thunder. Then the glaciers withdrew around several corners. The last echo died away, and the lifeless new country was silent. Not a leaf rustled. Not an insect chirped.

The innermost recess of Glacier Bay, the arm in which the ice has receded farthest, is Tarr Inlet. Not long ago in Tarr Inlet, the ice withdrew all the way to another country. Its regress went like this: In 1892 the terminus of the Grand Pacific Glacier, which occupies Tarr Inlet, was sixteen miles from the Canadian border. In 1907 the terminus was only three miles away. By 1925 the Grand Pacific, no longer so grand, had shrunk a mile inside Canada. Then came an advance, and by 1966 the terminus had moved a quarter mile beyond the boundary line.

In 1973, when George Dyson paddled into Glacier Bay, the glacier was retreating again, or so he was told. The terminus lay once more within Canada. It was possible to paddle into a tiny harbor of very cold Canadian water, climb out, and set foot on Canadian soil—Canadian rock, rather, for soil had not had time to form.

George decided to build a house of stone at the head of Tarr Inlet. Stone it would have to be, for no wood grew for miles around. Somewhere near the ice wall, George figured, there had to be a moraine suitable to set a house on. A bare moraine in that lunar landscape struck the son of Freeman Dyson as a perfect place to build.

"A solitude of newborn rocks, dim, dreary, mysterious," wrote an early explorer, and most of the literature reads like that. The freshly deglaciated terrain of Glacier Bay has been described by various visitors as austere, chaotic, enormous, silent, cold, gloomy, brooding, wild, harsh, strange, fantastic, wonderful, desolate, primeval. Nearly every writer has at least once called it a moonscape. "The creation was all new," wrote Charles Hallock in 1885, "and the glacier was still at work gradually preparing it for the abode of organic life. Darkness only was needed to relegate us to the primordium of chaos." George had read all that, but he wasn't deterred. His walls would be built of primordium. His window would frame the chaos.

The house in Tarr Inlet would be a room in the attic of his

greater house, that nine-hundred-mile mansion of fiordland between Vancouver Island and Glacier Bay. It would be a summer room, from which he would commute by canoe to his winter rooms in lower British Columbia. It would be a refuge within a refuge within a refuge. A stone hut, on a corner of peaceful Canada, within a U.S. national monument. Tarr Inlet would become George's personal Tibet, encircled by headwaters of ice and by some of the tallest, snowiest, most impassable mountains in Canada. The peaks guaranteed that he would not be bothered by overland visitors. And in the inlet itself there was pan ice until May. Few boats could enter as early or as easily as his baidarka. He would thread his way through the bergs, pushing aside the smaller ones, trying to anticipate which of the larger ones might roll. The baidarka would make musical progress, for icebergs continually creak and sigh. George would be respectful of the twenty-foot tides. He would be careful not to upset, for in the thirty-eight-degree water he would not live long.

He planned to fish for his protein and to bring his staples in by canoe. Glacial till won't support a garden, and he guessed he would have to do without one.

There once had been a garden in Reid Inlet, two inlets to the south, seventeen miles from where George wanted to build. In the 1940s, Joe Ibach, the most famous of Glacier Bay's characters, had brought in some topsoil by barge, and he and his wife Muz had planted the garden that fed them while they worked their Reid Inlet gold claim. Besides vegetables, the Ibachs had planted flowers, strawberries, and three spruce trees. Today the Ibach cabin is in ruins, but the spruces grow tall—three lonely exceptions to the laws of the plant succession on deglaciated ground. George had only his baidarka for transport, however. He couldn't do as the Ibachs had—they dug their soil from Lemesurier Island, at the mouth of Glacier Bay, seventy miles away, the nearest convenient place. George could not, from a canoeload of soil, grow enough potatoes to replace all the calories he would burn up in paddling the soil seventy miles. A garden was not possible within his canoe economy.

Tarr Inlet still resounds to the thunder of nativity that is silent throughout most of Glacier Bay. The sides of the Grand Pacific terminus are presently stagnant and dirty, but the middle portion is active and drops small pieces of blue-white ice, and Margerie Glacier, which enters the inlet from the side, drops big pillars and monuments of ice. The noise would fill George's nights, as it had filled the Tlingits'.

The Grand Pacific Glacier was beginning to advance again, George understood. This did not trouble him. He was prepared for changes in glacial weather. He knew that a glacier keeps its own counsel, moving forward or back according to principles that no one understands, on schedules that no one can anticipate. He knew that a glacier's slow, cold respiration is notoriously arrhythmic, that glaciers are given to turning over suddenly in their sleep. ("My son's daughter, be very careful. You might come down on me," the Tlingits had reminded their glaciers. The glaciers had not always heeded.) But if the Grand Pacific moved down to evict him, George would simply leave. He would pack up without argument. He needed only to pile his things in his canoe. He saw nothing precarious in perching there on the brink of an ice age.

"Wouldn't there be better places, from the standpoint of food?" I once asked.

"*Food?*" he said. "There's plenty of food of the other kind up there. That's where all the big mountains come out of—the climbing country. Food would be no problem. It would be a place where my climbing friends could come. I'd call them and ask if they wanted to stay at my house for a summer of climbing. I'd tell them to bring some food."

"You'd be sort of the innkeeper of Tarr Inlet," I suggested. "The inletkeeper."

"I guess so. I'd like that."

But it was too late in the season for George to begin his house. He stored his baidarka under a building at the National Park headquarters at Glacier Bay, and he worked his way south to Vancouver on a tiny salmon seiner. He retired to his tree house and spent the winter working on plans for canoes.

20

Cook

The next April, when the low spring rates were still in effect, George rode the ferry up to Alaska, sleeping steerage on deck. On reaching Glacier Bay, he was pleased to find that the baidarka had survived the winter without a scratch. He had only to sponge out the bottom a little, and she was seaworthy. He was ready to begin the house in Tarr Inlet.

This was not to be. His life took another of its sudden turns. The staff at Glacier Bay National Monument had become fascinated by the baidarka and wanted to find some way to use it as a research vessel. They offered George a job as cook and baidarka-driver for a scientific expedition. George needed money for his canoe projects, and he knew that access to Tarr Inlet would depend on good relations with the U.S. Park Service, so he accepted.

The summer's research was to take place in Torch Bay, a small fiord on the outer coast of Glacier Bay Monument. George set out for the bay in the baidarka. He carried a passenger, a ranger whom he was supposed to drop off on the way.

Leaving Cross Sound for the open ocean, George and the ranger encountered bad weather and had to wait at Cape Spencer for two days. The ranger was a reckless type, anxious to continue, and his urgings finally got on George's nerves, overcoming his normal caution. As soon as the storm had abated somewhat, they pushed off, negotiating surf heavier than George liked. They rounded the cape, entering the Gulf of Alaska. George dropped the ranger off at his lonely post in Graves Harbor. Alone again in the baidarka, George paddled north to Torch Bay.

The bay was a deep, L-shaped, glacier-carved notch in the coast. The ridges containing it were from two to three thousand feet high, and they rose sheer from the water. They were covered with snow, spruce, and hemlock. Recessed high in the headwall was a cirque, which spilled a tall waterfall into the fiord.

As he entered the bay's mouth, George had come nearly to the end of the canoe country. Above Torch Bay there were three more small fiords, then the coastline straightened. From a spot called Icy Point, the coast ran on northwestward, linear and harborless.

George was joined in Torch Bay by Ned Gillette, a mountaineer and cross-country ski instructor. Gillette was to be camp manager. He motored to the bay in a rubber Perelli raft that he had used in an expedition to Patagonia. Together the two men set up camp, organizing the gear and supplies that the Park Service had sent in by ship. For the next two and a half months, Torch Bay was to be their home.

As nearly as they could tell, they were the bay's first human inhabitants. The only sign of man they could find was the sawed-off stump of a small Sitka spruce. They guessed that a fisherman with a broken trolling pole had come ashore to cut a new one. They found nothing else—not an initial on a tree, not a cartridge casing, not an arrowhead, not a thing. It was George's belief that no Indians had ever lived in the bay, for he could find no trace of shell mounds.

They erected the camp tents high on the beach meadow, under the mildly curious gaze of black bears. The bears did not act like bears who had ever seen humans. They were not leery, like bears who have been shot at by fishermen, or mannerless, like the camp bears of national parks. On a given morning, there were usually two or three of them grazing on the beach grass, finishing up their spring foraging. The two men and the three bears shared the tidal meadow. Everyone respected the space of everyone else.

The laboratories were two eight-by-ten-foot wall tents. The cook tent was a ten-by-fifteen. Ned and George laid the plywood tent floors on foundations of driftwood they gathered from the bay's rocky shore. To the supporting post at the rear of the cook tent, George nailed two crosspieces, and from them he hung his pots and pans. He built a big, chest-high table, his working surface, then a tall cook's chair to reach it, then a picnic table for the scientists. Ned, who liked mashed potatoes, carved George a potato masher from a chunk of red cedar, using the grain so well that the result looked like sculpture. George hammered in another nail and hung the masher alongside his pots and pans.

George pitched his tent on a steep, thirty-foot knoll above the beach meadow. A fallen log served as his ladder to the summit. The branches were his rungs. From his back door, the view inland was intimate and shadowy, for the knoll's forest of young spruces shut out most of the light. A few rays threaded the canopy, fell onto the moss of the forest floor, and smoldered there greenly. From his front door the view was wide and bright. He looked through the last of the knoll's spruces, one of which guyed up his tent, down to the waters of the fiord and across to the fiord wall. It was a scene from a Japanese screen. The conifers on the far slope were bonsaied naturally by the high latitude and the steepness of the slopes. George's double-walled tent was the mountain temple. He had picked, with an infallible sense he has, the best campsite in Torch Bay. He could look directly down on his baidarka, which rested on the tussocks of the beach meadow. He kept it tethered, his sea horse, to an alder at the base of the knoll.

To prevent a proliferation of paths in the meadow, Ned and George flagged with red ribbons a single trail from the tents to the water. They were determined to leave the wilderness of Torch Bay as untrampled as when they found it. Their trail would concentrate the traffic in scientists, they hoped, and in two or three years the grass would reclaim it.

George climbed two widely separated spruces, raising between them the wire that served as radio antenna. Torch Bay radio, KB661, began its operation. Inside the tent, on top of the transmitter, they placed the .357 Magnum revolver that the Park Service had given them. The Magnum was for brown bears. In this season, late spring, the big bears were supposed to be foraging at higher elevations, but later in the year, when the late-summer salmon run began, they would make their appearance in the low country. At that time the black bears would respectfully move out, and the scientists would have to be careful. The Alaska brown bear is the largest and most powerful carnivore on Earth.

There are two schools of thought on brown bears and guns. Some Northerners think that because of the great strength and unpredictability of *Ursus horribilis*, it is foolish not to carry a gun. Others think that because of the perfectly predictable ferocity of brown bears when wounded, it is dangerous to carry one. George was of the latter school. He knew little about guns and didn't want to know more. He preferred traveling the forest unencumbered and alert, with his senses his only armament. The .357 on the radio made him nervous.

When George and Ned arrived at Torch Bay, snow still covered the upper tidal meadow. The fiddle ferns were just beginning to curl above the surface of exposed patches of ground. George collected and boiled them as greens. By the time the first scientist was about to arrive, two weeks later, the snow had melted hundreds of feet up the hillside, and the ferns were six inches to a foot high, already a little bitter. In their comings and goings, George and Ned had already worn their flagged trail down to the earth.

As they awaited the scientists, George was wondering how he got into this. He watched spring advance in Torch Bay, and he thought about springtime in other places he knew. He thought of Tarr Inlet, and wondered how the break-up was proceeding there. He was impatient, after only two weeks, at being so long in one place.

It is just as well, though, that George was in Torch Bay and not building his stone house in Tarr Inlet. His plans for Tarr Inlet were based on a misapprehension. The Grand Pacific Glacier had not withdrawn past the Canadian border, as he had been led to believe. It has not withdrawn today, and Canada remains under ice. The border of his adopted country would have given him a cold reception.

When, later in the summer, George learned the truth—that his stone house would have to wait another year, or another decade— he was not distressed. George is mostly a conceptual settler. The *idea* of building in Tarr Inlet was the important thing; it was not vital to actually pile up the stones.

21

Ramblings

I flew to Torch Bay with the first scientist. He was a stocky, bearded young ornithologist named Sam Patten, Jr., and he was accompanied by his wife Renee. Our Cessna floatplane left inner Glacier Bay, flew across a low range of mountains, then over the vast icefield of the Brady Glacier, the largest in Glacier Bay Monument. Our wings made a tiny shadow on the whiteness. From our height above the Brady, we saw the monument's outer coast, our destination, and beyond it the Gulf of Alaska. The coast was just a mountainous green fringe, ruffled by fiords, that edged the glacier's whiteness. The fiords cut in almost to the ice. Then the shadow of our wings left the glacier and we were flying over the green fringe. It was a rainy, high-latitude green. The landforms seemed too large, out of scale. The terrain freest of snow was the seaward ridges that separated the fiords. Steep and spruce-covered, they ended in bluff headlands. The headlands were coming up fast. We passed above a tarn half-full of pan ice. The land rose a little. Then the spruces of the ridge below us suddenly dropped away into the gorge of Torch Bay. We saw the camp tents beneath.

I spotted the baidarka. George had dragged it up on the beach meadow and had tied it to the alder at the base of his knoll. It was the most colorful thing in camp, its deck bright blue, its three hatch-covers bright yellow.

Torch Bay was a deep, beautiful little fiord. In the headwall was the snow-filled cirque spilling its tall waterfall into the fiord. An old hanging glacier, long gone, had carved the cirque handsomely. Cirque and waterfall were lovely, cool, and vertical.

We landed and taxied toward a wooden barge anchored off-shore. The barge was named S. S. *Urschleim,* and on it the camp food was stored out of reach of the bears. George and Ned rowed out in a dory to meet us. We shook hands all around. Helping us unload, George and Ned laughed oddly and inordinately at small things. They made jokes we couldn't follow. Ned apologized, explaining that they had been in Torch Bay too long without seeing other people. They were a little crazy, he said, from eating too much halibut. George had caught a thirty-five-pound halibut on a setline near shore, with only the two of them to eat it. For the past five days they had been eating halibut three times a day.

George's face was brown. There had been nearly two weeks of sun in Torch Bay—rare weather for Southeast Alaska. I searched his dark features for a hint of the Briton in his ancestry. I could not detect it. His Nootka beard was still sparse and downy. His nose was as heroically large and crooked as Red Cloud's or Geronimo's. His hair reached halfway to his shoulders.

Today was overcast and cool. Beneath his ragged sweater and combat pants, George wore Army-surplus long woolen underwear, tops and bottoms. The sweater hung from the two bony points of his shoulders. His combat pants had big pockets, full of things. On his head was an L. L. Bean waterproof hat. He was barefoot in spite of the cool. His feet were long, with the metatarsals near the surface. They looked prehensile.

Sam Patten, the ornithologist, studied the long, heronlike bones in George's feet with professional interest. The toes were gripping a seat slat as if it were a branch. "Aren't your feet cold?" Sam asked.

"I've still got my winter blood," George answered. "Your body gets used to the cold—your metabolism. You eat a lot of food and burn it off all day. It keeps you warm. And I think the spruce tea helps keep your blood right. We had to cut down some little spruce trees where the cook tent is. We've been drinking tea from the needles."

The next morning we decided to climb the small, three-thousand-foot peak that was the highpoint of the ridge above camp. Neither George nor Ned had found time for that before.

We crossed the beach meadow first and entered the spruce forest. None of the spruces were mammoth trees, for the land had not been deglaciated long enough. Wherever there were no tree trunks, or streams, or small patches of devil's club, there was moss. It lay everywhere in drifts. It covered now, in spring, everything that snow would cover in winter. After ten minutes of walking we left the shade of the spruces and started up a steep-sloping meadow dominated by mountain hemlock. The sun came through more freely, for the foliage of the hemlocks was airy and sea-pruned. Fat, spring-green spears of skunk cabbage were pushing up through the darker green of the meadow. We reached the base of the waterfall and climbed alongside it up toward the cirque. The thunder of the falls dampened our conversation. We passed the lip of the waterfall, entering the demibowl of the cirque. The stream flowed horizontally again, and we rested beside it. The cirque's lower elevations had been free of snow for a week or so, and the willows were still springing up from the weight of winter. Not all of them realized yet that they were free. The higher walls of the cirque were still snowy.

George pointed, and in the willows above we saw three mountain goats. They had seen us first and were loping straight upward, heading for the cirque's high rim. They were as white as gulls and as high above us. They moved effortlessly and without panic. Twice they paused and stood in profile to look back at us. They were noble-looking animals, bearded and close-built, with torsos like weightlifters'. They left the willow-covered slope and plunged up a slope of snow, but the new surface did not slow them or alter their muscular rhythm. We lost them in the snow's whiteness.

George told us he wanted to gather the fleece for a sweater. The goats left strands of it here and there, he said, and in the course of the summer he thought he could find enough. We rose and headed upward like the goats, though much more slowly. We sweated in the spring sunshine.

The goats reappeared just below the top of the cirque. There hadn't been time enough for them to get that high, but there they were. George watched them through his spyglass, which was one half of a broken pair of binoculars, and the rest of us took turns with Sam Patten's field glasses. The goats were contouring the cirque, covering so much ground, in their effortless way, that we had to laugh—goats climb so fast and people so slow. They bounded across the steep snow slope with an exaggerated, rocking-horse motion. They seemed to like feeling their muscles work. They were yeti-hearted. Above them was nothing but a final cornice and the blue of the sky. The sky was clear except for the fleece of a single cloud.

When we humans reached the snow, I went on ahead, kicking steps. George stayed behind with his rope, belaying Renee Patten as she climbed the steep places. I reached the ridge before the others and followed it up toward the summit. Spring was well advanced on the ridgeline, and patches of alpine meadow alternated with patches of snow. The low-growing mosses and lichens of the meadow were as tightly woven as the goats that grazed there, but not so soft—certain of the tiny alpine plants were prickly. I came to a spot where a mountain goat, in lying to rest, had carded itself on the meadow. It had left behind a long strip of fleece. The fleece was warm in my hand and it smelled good and clean. At first it was odorless, then I tried harder and caught a faint pungence of alpine moss and just a hint of animal. I put the fleece in my pocket. I had decided to collect enough for a mountain-goat sweater of my own. Continuing up the ridge, I came to more places where goats had rested—they seemed to prefer small depressions where they could lie out of the wind. I stripped the fleece from the burr of the meadow and added it to the ball in my pocket.

I saw several rock ptarmigan, still in their winter plumage. Perching on rocks, they held perfectly motionless. They might have been *real* rock ptarmigan, ptarmigan made from actual rocks, like those ptarmigan carved by Eskimos from soapstone. They let me come very close. Now and then a male launched himself into display flight. He buzzed out furiously, set his wings suddenly, and croaked. It was happening below me. I had climbed above the flight of the ptarmigan.

Reaching the summit before the others, I felt like stout Cortez on a peak in Darien. Except that our situations were reversed. At my back was the Pacific, before me was an Atlantic of ice—the Brady Glacier. The high isthmus between, on a prominence of which I now stood stoutly, was slim.

The view from the summit was much the same as yesterday's view from the plane, but with a world of difference. From the window of a flying vehicle, the scene below is just a scene. Under your own two feet, it becomes real. A few steps through a country establish its scale and proportion. Its slow life becomes sensible through the soles of your boots. You begin to read the geology correctly, feeling the old uplift and the past movement of the glaciers.

I thought of Freeman Dyson. Would the same subtleties of terrain be sensible, I wondered, through an astronaut's weighted boots? Was it the earth of Earth that Anteus required under his feet for strength, or would the soil of some other planet do?

There was not a cloud left in the sky. To the west was the broad Pacific, its horizon bending with the curve of the planet. The fiords were the ocean's fingers, clutching the continent. Up and down the coast, from elevations like this one, ridges descended, became peninsulas, and plunged steeply in. When I looked seaward, the ridges seemed big; then I looked north and saw the real peaks, LaPerouse and Crillon and Bertha, constructed all of black rock, ice falls, and hanging glaciers.

To the north and east was the ice field of the Brady Glacier. There was something scary about the field. There was a vagueness to it. The peaks that bordered the field made hard lines against the sky, their rock and snow substantial, their angles cleanly etched. But the horizon of the ice field itself was blurred and miasmal. The ice looked like a sea of heavy gas in which the peaks had crystallized before rising. If I had encountered such a sea on another planet, I would have taken the long way around.

The others caught up with me. We ate lunch on the summit, then lay like goats in depressions out of the wind. We zipped up our parkas, stuck our hands in our pockets, and slept. The wan spring sunlight was warm on our faces. Dozing, I felt the breeze stir in my beginning beard. I settled deeper into the wind shadow.

Sometimes the wind blew from the west, a sea wind; sometimes from the east, a glacier wind.

Early the next morning, back at sea level, we dressed in our raingear and climbed into the dory. Sam Patten wanted to visit a kittiwake colony in a headland two fiords north of Torch Bay. The trip would take most of the morning, so we had eaten with first light.

Pumping out the dory, George banged his nose on the upstroke with the pump handle. "My nose, it's too big," he complained. "It gets in the way." He had broken it, he told us, in a Vancouver car accident three years before. For a long time he hadn't known it was broken. "It shows you how much I look in the mirror. One day I did look, finally, and I said, 'Hey, something's wrong! It's crooked!' Nobody in Vancouver had noticed."

The ocean was calm. The coast was misty, and at first we were cold, then the sun broke through feebly and warmed us a little. As we left Torch Bay, we began to see seabirds, and soon they were everywhere. A V of ducks low on the water, going north. A gang of glaucous-wing gulls much higher, going east. In between, a squadron of puffins, with bodies like bumblebees and beaks like parrots, going south. Pelagic cormorants were everywhere, fleeing us at every angle. Murres. Bonaparte gulls. There was a single bird here, a double over there, four birds yonder. In the course of the morning's trip we counted fifteen bald eagles. They hung about the headlands, sitting watchful in the tops of spruces or soaring high above. They were as chesty and close-built as yesterday's mountain goats.

When a mature bald eagle sits in a spruce, its big white head poises above the broad white triangle of its tail. In between, the bird is as dark as the spruce, and seen from a distance it makes two white spots in the forest. At first we exclaimed and pointed at each eagle, but after ten birds or so, our excitement began to feel foolish. The exclamations died in our throats, and our arms stuck to our sides. It seemed strange not to exclaim at an eagle.

We reached Boussole Head, the grim, ship-shaped, 640-foot rock where the kittiwakes nested. The walls of the rock were perpendicular or overhanging. The stunted trees on top grew close to the edge, some leaning over. Kittiwakes, Sam explained, always choose such cliffs to nest on, protected from raiding land animals by the sheer walls. Because they are accustomed to these inaccessible places, kittiwakes have developed little of the aggressive nest-defending behavior of other gulls; and because they are not aggressive, they like inaccessible places. It's hard to know which came first, the kittiwake or the cliff. In their nesting preferences kittiwakes had a lot in common with George Dyson, I thought.

We drifted beneath the cliff, looking up at the kittiwakes as they looked down on us. The gulls screamed and lifted their wings, but few left their ledges. The button on Sam's hand-counter clicked like a machine gun. George stood at the tiller of the outboard engine, steering as close as possible to the cliff. The engine was turning over just fast enough for the boat to keep up its way. The boat was a fine old Down East dory, painted red. In it, George, in his raincoat and rainpants, with his L. L. Bean hat pulled back like a sou'wester over the nape of his neck, was a figure from Winslow Homer. The swell surged against the cliff, peacefully but heavily. Small rocks were foaming all around, and I was a little nervous. If we should overturn, there was no place on the kittiwake's sheer cliff where we could climb out. George watched both the birds and the surge. His eyes were alert and calm.

At the end of Boussole Head, the surf had cut a natural arch ninety feet high. As we rounded the tip from the south, the arch slowly opened up for us. Through it we saw the double peak of Mount LaPerouse on the mainland behind. The snow and ice of LaPerouse were blue with distance. The arch of dark rock framed the bright Himalayan scene beyond. For a moment we forgot the birds. Sam's hand-counter stopped clicking.

The largest of Boussole Head's four kittiwake subcolonies lived in a cave at the base of the arch. We peered in and saw ranks and ranks of birds, ghostly white in the darkness. The *kittiwake kittiwake* of the kittiwakes started up as they saw us, and the echo crescendoed off the damp inner walls. In the dark, each gull was holding to some crevice imperceptible to us. A white arrow of birdlime pointed to each bird. Sam told us that few species of gull could afford to flag their nests so conspicuously.

At first the kittiwakes in the cave were content to scream at us. Then a change of mind rushed like a wind through the colony. First a few, and in the next instant most of the rest, left their perches. They came at us like albino bats, but much faster, on trim seabird wings. They left the cave, divided, and flew around us. As they passed out under the arch, the contrasts suddenly reversed. The white birds went dark against the ethereal icefall of the mountain beyond.

"Geez," said Sam. "Geez, what a neat colony."

George made five passes along the cliff, and with each pass Sam counted the birds in each subcolony. He would average his five totals for a rough estimate of the colony's size. At the end of the final pass, George surprised us by twisting up the throttle and heading toward the arch. The waves were choppy and confused underneath it, and there wasn't much clearance, but we made it through easily enough. George turned and passed back through the arch, then we headed homeward. He looked glum. "Now I've done the two things I wanted here," he said. "I've climbed the mountain and I've gone through the arch."

Nearing home, in a spot twenty yards from where the surf broke mildly over a cluster of offshore rocks, George cut the dory's outboard, and we drifted.

"What is it?" someone asked.

"Listen," said George.

With the motor off, it was very quiet. We heard the slap of the waves against the hull, and the whispery rush of the surf curling over the rocks. We heard the working birds in the distance, and the low endless roar the ocean makes in meeting the continent. No one spoke. I looked around our circle and saw everyone listening by himself. Each of us looked off in his own direction. Each was alone with the sea's sounds in his head. This, I thought, was how the world always sounded, in a baidarka. Then George yanked on the starter cord, and we were on our way again.

22

Mouse Woman

The Cessna returned, bringing two intertidal ecologists. There were now seven of us in Torch Bay, and another tent went up in the meadow. George did not feel crowded yet, but he began to worry. "Can you imagine what this place will be like with twenty people in it?" he asked me. I tried to imagine. It didn't seem so awful.

The intertidal ecologists, who were both graduate students, were hard workers, and George likes cooking for people who work hard. When he cooks for people who just sit around, it hurts his own sense of worth. He explained this pointedly several times, and we took it as a warning.

"The cook has a lot of power, and I intend to use it," George confided once to Ned and me. It was a funny line or a disquieting one, I wasn't sure which. We discussed George, outside the kingdom of his cook tent, and we agreed that his occasional moods and rudenesses were a result of his solitary life. He would be better when he was more around people. Besides, cooks are notoriously ill-tempered. They get away with it if they are good, and George was a good cook. One accepts a lot of arrogance from someone who for dessert one night bakes four different kinds of pie.

One morning, as we finished a breakfast of George's sourdough pancakes, we saw a wolf on the far shore. The wolf was rounding the head of the bay, coming toward us, and we followed his progress through binoculars. It was the first time any of us had seen a wolf in the wild.

The wolf headed straight for George's knoll. He reached the baidarka but was not alarmed by it. He did not seem to connect it with anything human. Then he scented us. His head came up and he froze. He stared at us for a full minute, his muzzle black and his eyes yellow. He looked nothing like a dog. I remember thinking he looked like a man in a mask. He was embarrassed, I'm convinced, at having stumbled so blindly upon human beings. Then he turned and walked with exaggerated dignity into the forest behind George's knoll.

When the wolf was gone, Sam Patten turned to his wife. "You'll never see a wild wolf so close again," he told her. I was inclined to believe him, but that very afternoon, from the dory, as Sam and Renee drifted along the shore of Torch Bay's southern arm, they saw a second wolf. This one was younger and lighter colored. It was hunting something in the beach grass. It saw Sam and Renee in the dory, but seemed to pay them no attention. It stuck its nose back in the grass, intent on whatever it had trapped there.

We never saw wolves again. It was a sad little lesson. Torch Bay to us still looked like perfect wilderness, but for the wolves it was tainted, and they moved on to another country.

That night in the cook tent, after we had discussed the wolves and had compared notes on the other animals we were seeing, our conversation turned to school. Sam Patten told us about the oral examination for his master's, which he had passed just before coming to Alaska. The orals were an ordeal, he said. In two hours or so, men aged five years. "They probe with their little knives," Sam said. "Poke, poke, poke. 'Aha, here's an area he's weak in!' And then they really stick it in. You'd like to stand up and tell them what you think of them, but you can't. You're coming to them, after all. It's a rite of passage.

"One guy asked me what was the most important bird in the history of embryology. I didn't know." Sam grimaced, reliving the moment.

"The chicken?" I guessed.

Sam gave me a long look and nodded without smiling. "Yes. The chicken. But I was expecting something more . . . I didn't know what he was talking about."

"It was a joke question?" I asked.

"That's right. Exactly. It was a joke question."

"Why?" said George.

"Why what?"

"Why would anyone want to do any of it?"

George smiled a faint, superior smile.

The next time the Cessna returned it brought Jeff Skaflestad, a high-school boy from Hoonah, the nearest village. Jeff was to help around camp and to serve as assistant to the expedition's small-mammalogist, who had not yet arrived. We were now eight. Torch Bay was filling fast, but George did not as yet feel pinched. George liked Jeff, and that helped. Jeff was part Tlingit Indian. He was one of that category George calls "real people." Fishermen and loggers and tugboat captains and Indians are real people. Scientists and writers are not so real. Jeff did make George a bit nervous by carrying everywhere, slung over his shoulder, a .300 Magnum rifle with telescopic sight. Like most of the real people of Southeast Alaska, Jeff believed it was foolish to travel in brown-bear country unarmed.

Then we learned by radio that the Cessna was returning once more, bringing the small-mammalogist. (The mammalogist was not herself small. She was nearly six feet tall, in fact. It was the voles and shrews she was studying that were tiny.) We would soon be nine in Torch Bay, and George began to feel Malthusian pressures. He decided in advance that he would not like the small-mammalogist. He disliked the prospect of having mice killed and skinned around him, or he sensed that with the addition of this ninth person his range would be exceeding its carrying capacity, or both. He called her Mouse Woman. He wondered aloud what it would be like when Mouse Woman came with her hundreds of mousetraps. How would it be, he asked rhetorically, to walk down a game trail in this pristine wilderness and come upon traplines of Victor mousetraps?

"They aren't Victor mousetraps," said Jeff, who had assisted Mouse Woman the previous summer in the fiord to the north.

"They're some other kind. They're bigger, like rattraps."

Jeff told us of his mousetrapping experience—how you skinned the little animals, measured their organs, things like that.

"Can you identify the different species?" I asked.

"Sure. There's *Microtus longicaudus*, *Microtus clethriones*, and *Sorex something or other*. One's brown, one's gray, and one's a shrew."

"Did you learn how to skin them?"

"Naw. My hands are too big. I just fuck them up."

Jeff told us how he and Mouse Woman set up her double trapline. They laid down two parallel lines, with traps set a measured distance apart, baited with peanut butter and bacon fat.

Peanut butter, I thought. I glanced at George. Peanut butter is probably his favorite food. I tried to read his reaction to this new information on the trickery of Mouse Woman, but his face, for now, was unreadable.

"Don't the traps ruin the mice?" asked one of the intertidal men. "I mean, at home a Victor mousetrap sometimes catches them on the eyes, or way back on the body. Can she use the organs then?"

"Sure," said Jeff. "She still looks at the corpus luteum and stuff like that. She takes all the mice, even half-eaten."

"Really? What eats them?"

"The other mice come out and eat them alive. And sometimes you see a little trail where the mouse has dragged the trap around—bloody and everything."

"*Scientists!*" said George softly. He looked heavenward. "These people are psychotics. All in the name of the god Science. They drown animals in alcohol, torture them, put them in little bottles."

"What does she do with the skins," asked the intertidal man, in order to change the subject. He himself had spent the morning putting mollusks in little bottles.

"She sends them to the Smithsonian Institution," said Jeff.

"Really? But she must do more than that with them."

"Not necessarily," said the second intertidal man. "That's the way these mammalogists work."

"The *Smithsonian!*" said the first intertidal man.

George was not impressed. "They've built huge basements in the Smithsonian just to take that stuff," he informed us. "They have tons of it. They probably need the mouse skins to dust the glass cases." He turned to Jeff. "This Mouse Woman sounds like someone whose trip you should stay away from. You should watch out in those hills. It only takes one mouse, pushing, to start a rockslide."

Mouse Woman, then, never really had a chance with George.

Their first argument was over diet. Mouse Woman believed that her personal metabolism required some animal protein with her meals. This, George thought, was superstition. It was all in her head. He himself ate some fish, a lot of rice, vegetables, and potatoes, and very little meat. Meat was all right under certain circumstances, he explained. "If you chase one of these goats along the ridges for half a day, and finally you corner him, and shoot at him, *and you miss,* and then, in the middle of the next day you finally do kill him on some ridge ten miles from here, *then* you can eat him. You can eat the whole goat if you want." Otherwise, he said, the meat just sits in your stomach and clogs things up. It is too strong a food to fuel moderate enterprises. George made it clear he believed Mouse Woman's science to be a very moderate enterprise indeed. Mouse Woman, for her part, thought George's ideas on nutrition were half-baked.

They had another argument over toilet paper. As cook, George was ex officio our quartermaster, and one day Mouse Woman asked him how many rolls were left on the barge. (Mouse Woman was, it must be said, an excessive worrier.) George said he didn't know. He had no idea. He never set foot in the camp latrine and he never used toilet paper. He climbed up in the hills to answer his needs.

"You don't use toilet paper, George?" she asked. "What do you use?"

"What do you think leaves are for?" he replied. "They cut down a spruce forest to make toilet paper just so people can . . . They cut down a forest when there are all those nice leaves and mosses. Moss is best. Try it sometime."

The Cessna returned again, and then again, bringing two

freshwater-fish specialists, a botanist, and three glacial geologists. George began to chafe. He was feeling crowded.

One day, with the rain beating on the canvas and the Torch Bay population holding at sixteen, the scientists sat in the cook tent, waiting out the weather. One of the intertidal men was telling us about spelunking in the caves of upstate New York. George came in late, missing the first part. He hung his raincoat on the nail, sat, and listened. The intertidal man spoke of tight squeezes and exhaustion. He spoke of the claustrophobia that seizes some people, and the pervading wetness and cold of the caves, and the problem of adjusting to total darkness.

"Where are these caves?" asked George.

"In upstate New York."

"Does anybody live in them?" George wondered.

Another day, in the same tent but under a different rain cloud, another of the scientists, this time a glacial geologist, sat on the sea-rounded square of the driftwood beam we used for a bench, and described for us the dry valleys of Antarctica, where lately he had done research. The dry valleys, we learned, are oases of rudimentary soil in the desert of the antarctic ice cap. They lie there miraculous and unexpected—a little bare ground and a few low-growing mosses and lichens in a continent of ice. The geologist told us of watching clouds form, day after day, beyond the head of his valley, then seeing them dissipate before they reached it. They always dissipated. Something in the configuration of the valley's head diverted almost all precipitation, making for the dry ground. The geologist told us of the antarctic seals that, for reasons unknown, crawl to the dry valleys, sometimes as far as twenty miles inland, to die. They lie for centuries in the spots where they stopped moving, mummified by the dry, cold air that pours off the surrounding glaciers. Some of the carcasses are four thousand years old.

There was a silence as we contemplated that. George broke it.

"Does anybody live there permanently?" he asked.

By now I was familiar enough with the Dyson instinct for stark, remote, depopulate worlds to know where George's thoughts were running. In his imagination he was trying out as habitations the dry valleys of Antarctica and the caves of New York. He was thinking of moving on.

—— 23 ——

Sweathouse

When George got blue, his remedy was to go off by himself and build something. He was still combing the beach regularly, and he kept beside the cook tent a pile of driftwood and flotsam, into which he dipped whenever the scientists got on his nerves.

One day he made a crab trap. He formed the hoop from an alder sapling, forcing it slowly into a circle, trimming the outside with his hand ax wherever the sapling offered resistance. He worked moodily, speaking in monosyllables when he spoke at all. I looked at his laboring arms. They were lean. With George, exercise goes less to build muscle than to ramify an impressive network of veins, which deliver plenty of blood to what muscle he's got. When the alder hoop was completed, George took some old netting he had found tangled in the beach rocks, and this he tied taut across the hoop.

Before going any further, George decided to test the bottom for crabs. He baited the hoop with fish heads and we lowered it. A few hours later we raised it, and it came up heavier. As the hoop rose from the murk, we saw a spot of color in it—orange. It was a big spot. The color took shape, but not the shape George wanted. His catch was a many-rayed starfish, enormous, bigger than the hoop. It waved its arms at us, a Beast from Five Fathoms. George dumped it and we watched it settle, waving, to the bottom. He did not try again. Where dwelt such a creature, he figured, there were unlikely to be crabs. He left the trap unfinished, but the enterprise had succeeded in occupying him for a while.

Another afternoon, when both the weather and his mood were

bleak, George decided to make himself a new spare paddle. His old spare, tied to the deck of the baidarka for the trip to Torch Bay, had been smashed by a wave.

George knew where to find the perfect tree for his paddle shaft. The fiord to the north of us, Dixon Harbor, had an arm called Thistle Cove, and on the hillside above this cove grew a yellow-cedar sapling, very straight and slim. George had noted the cedar a month before, when he first visited the cove, and he had filed it away in his memory. I went with him to find it again.

We followed a wolf trail for a quarter mile from the cove's shore, then headed cross country. We walked uphill through a meadow-land broken by stands of cedar and mountain hemlock. George cast about for the tree, but had trouble finding it. We came upon several cedars that grew pretty straight, but George passed them by.

"Won't that one do?" I asked, finally.

"When you cut down a living tree, you make sure it's right," he said.

At last we found it, a sapling about three inches in diameter. George put his eye to the trunk and sighted up. Satisfied, he unsheathed his knife. It was a razor-sharp Russel, with a blade of Canadian steel. The first stroke exposed yellow wood. This was a yellow cedar, all right, not a red cedar, the wood of which is inferior. George felled the sapling, carving his downcuts two-handed, the palm of his left hand bearing down on the blade tip. He hacked his upcuts with his right hand alone. As he bent over the fallen tree, trimming off the branches, he happened to look back at the stump. He noticed how conspicuously the whittled yellow cone caught the light in the forest. I had noticed too. It was startling how, in this wilderness, an act of man called attention to itself. "They'll think beavers did it," George said, but he did not sound convinced, and with reason—there were no beavers in this country. He took some mud and smeared the stump with it, trying to dull the brightness of the yellow. He stood off and studied the result. He was not satisfied. He added more mud as a foundation and on top pressed several handfulls of moss.

We dragged the tree through the forest and down to the cove. Back home at Torch Bay, George carved the sapling into a shaft. He made the double blades from plywood, epoxied them to the shaft, and hung the new paddle from the roof of a lab tent, where the epoxy cured in the heat of a Coleman lantern.

One evening the wind rose, starting whitecaps on Torch Bay. They were the first real waves we had seen in the fiord. The sky lowered and a bank of fog cut off the fiord walls halfway up. The spruces climbed in ragged ranks into the fog. The higher they went, the more substance they lost in it. They mounted venerable and ghostly, like ancestors going over. The highest spruces were just the ghosts of ghosts, and we couldn't be sure of them.

We were all depressed by the weather. We had a premature dusk, at ten in the evening. On clear days, the sky did not go dark until around midnight, but lately in Torch Bay we had seen few clear days. In the cook tent Sam and I read paperbacks, and Ned, Renee, and the intertidal men played hearts. They invited George to join them, but he declined. He is not much of a cardplayer. He went out into the wind without saying anything, and no one saw him again that night.

The next morning we woke to see a wigwam on the far shore. In the course of the wild, wet night, George had built himself a sweathouse. For privacy he had placed it a half mile away, on the stone beach beneath the favorite meadow of the black bears. It was a teepee of beachcombed plastic draped over a tripod of driftwood poles. The circumference was weighted down with rocks. George had spent the night there. He heated stones in a fire outside, brought them in, closed the flap behind him, and emptied a bucket of seawater over them. The water exploded as steam. When he was as hot as he could stand, he ran out and jumped into the frigid fiord. He had repeated this process all night long. It was his shock therapy.

We watched with field glasses as the morning's first black bear encountered the sweathouse. The bear smelled the smoke from George's fire, stopped its grazing, and walked over to investigate.

Through our binoculars the scene was foreshortened, and the bear appeared to be standing at the sweathouse door, waiting for its turn inside. We were a little nervous. Jeff Skaflestad, watching through the telescopic sight of his rifle, boasted that he could save George's life with a single shot from this range. It would have been some shot. Just then George emerged naked from the sweathouse.

If any of us hoped for some comic gesture of surprise or alarm from George—and I'm afraid we all did—he disappointed us. He simply glanced at the bear and walked past. The bear watched the steaming human hop over the beach stones toward the fiord. George has long arms, and hopping over barnacled beach stones he carries them like a gibbon, uncertain exactly what to do with them. He jumped in. The bear lost interest and went back to its grazing.

—— 24 ——

Rum

One rainy night the intertidal men broke out their bottle of 151-proof rum, and soon the cook tent was much cheerier.

Rum is a nautical drink, and George approves of it. He has a general affinity for alcohol, in truth, and he has to make an effort to stay away from it. Alcohol makes another George of George. Tonight it loosened his tongue considerably. It gave the scientists their first peek at his interior nature. He told us about his family.

"Family is important. I need to know where they're at. I feel I should start where my father left off. Where his work is in physics, mine will be in the physics of the natural energy of places like this." But it was tough, he said, because all the family history was back in England. He wished he knew more about his grandfather, Sir George Dyson. "He wrote a book called *Fiddling While Rome Burns*. During World War I he wrote a manual on how to make hand grenades. It's still in print! That's fantastic—the Black

Panthers or somebody could be using it. It shows you how to make bombs and stuff out of nothing."

George told us that he had four younger half-sisters. He had not seen them for years. He wanted to get them in his canoe before it was too late—before New Jersey captured their spirits irrevocably. He had not seen his father, either. His father did not seem to want to see him, George said, and that was puzzling. He thought sometimes he glimpsed the reason—it went back before his own birth, he suspected—but he didn't know for sure. His father was a riddle to him. He told us that Freeman once had sent him, without explanation, a copy of *Slaughterhouse-Five*, Kurt Vonnegut's account of the firebombing of Dresden. Why on Earth, he asked the cook tent, had Freeman sent that? *I* had an idea why Freeman, the former RAF mathematician, had sent it, and I guessed that George did too. This bafflement over *Slaughterhouse-Five* was, I decided, rum-rhetorical and not so complete as George pretended.

He stood, tottered a little, and admitted that he was drunk. So were we all. The scientists folded first. One by one they went off to bed, pushing the flap aside and stepping out into the rain. Finally only George, Ned, and I were left.

We three had spent a lot of time in wild places, and now, with the scientists gone, our conversation turned to that. We discussed the virtues of solitude and wilderness against those of bustle and the city. We agreed that there was a lot to be said for both. We discussed the old dilemma of the bachelor: Freedom or the Girl?

"I'd like nothing better than to, you know, have children," said George. "That seems a far-out trip. But there's no way I can do that now. That's what my big canoe will be for. Maybe the big canoe . . ."

Maybe the big canoe, I thought. George had hinted before that he was planning a huge canoe. I knew that he had ordered the aluminum for it earlier this spring, but that the energy crisis of 1974 had struck before the aluminum could be delivered. Now, thanks to rum, I knew the secret purpose of the big canoe. It was for George to rear a family on.

Outside, the rain was beating on the canvas roof. The blue grouse were drumming in the spruce forest behind us. The call was both whispery and resonant, like a child hooting in a bottle. It was a sound so constant in Torch Bay that we no longer heard it, unless something reminded us to listen. George turned to me.

"Yeah, I've been getting weirder and weirder since that time you first knew me," he said. "I've been off on this trip. There's been no girls that I've, you know, sort of stayed with but one. But I know how I have to live. I have to be able to move on. My canoe. I just get in my canoe."

—— 25 ——

The Most Beautiful Thing in the World

One evening George was sniffling as he fixed dinner. He set the food out for us and left without eating anything. I found him later down by his baidarka, where he had taken off the yellow hatch-covers and was pulling his masts and sails out through the manholes. I mentioned the sniffling and asked if he was sick. No, he said, the sniffling was just a symptom of something wrong in his head. He knew what he needed—to get out for a while in his canoe.

He invited me along, and I quickly accepted. It would be my first ride in the baidarka. We seized the manhole rims and walked the canoe toward the bay. I was surprised at how easily the hull moved over the tussocks of the meadow. The canoe's length smoothed out the bumps, and the boat seemed to slide on rails into the water. The tide was high and it came right up to the grass. I waded out in my gum boots and climbed into the forward hole. George pushed off, then climbed into the middle hole.

My forward hole was the smallest of the three, and the space in the prow was confined. It took some contortions to fit my legs in

133

and get them comfortable. It occurred to me that if the canoe flipped, it would take a while to get out, yet somehow I felt perfectly safe. I had been in many small boats on the ocean without ever completely losing my uneasiness; the prospect of drowning always had been somewhere in the back of my mind. Now it was gone. I didn't know why.

We sat very low on the water, an inch or two beneath sea level. It is this closeness, believes George, and the snugness of the manhole, that banishes fear of the ocean. He may be right. I looked inside the hole. The blue fiberglass was translucent, and the daylight came through beautifully. Beside my thigh in an undulating line was a darker blue where the ocean met the day. George saw me studying the interior light. "In late summer, the water is phosphorescent, sometimes," he said. "At night this canoe glows."

From down so low on the water, the mountains above Torch Bay rose higher and nobler than they had before. The small difference in vantage changed the view markedly, and I seemed to see Torch Bay with new eyes. That was fine with me, for like George I was tired of my old eyes and the old Torch Bay. I had been here six weeks.

The canoe came to a slim point a few feet in front of me. Unless I looked straight down, I saw no canoe at all. It was a great sensation, like being seated Christlike on the water. The baidarka was not much wider than my shoulders. Leaning slightly, I could look directly down into the fiord, from three feet away. With my first glance I saw a jellyfish, my first of the season. In quick succession I saw five more, pulsing below me at different depths. I looked back to see George smiling broadly. When he saw me looking, he tried to dampen his smile, failed, and looked off instead at the mountains.

Once we got our speed up, the canoe moved quickly through the water. It did not glide magically along, as if the paddles were double-bladed wands. Somehow I had thought it might. Paddling took some work, especially for me, because I hadn't yet mastered the rhythm. The baidarka was far more steady in the water than the kayaks I had paddled—a function of its slightly greater beam and its considerably greater length. Again I had the sensation of being on rails; the canoe seemed immune to the turbulence of the waves. The canoe was quiet. There was no roar of outboard or creak of oarlocks, as when we traveled in the dory or in the expedition's rubber boats. There was only the quiet dipping of the blades.

We coasted past the bear meadow. A black bear was cropping the grass above the beach, and as we watched he broke into a run, apparently just for the hell of it. "That's the way I want to see my *brown* bears," said George. "From my canoe. Come to within ten feet of them."

The wind died before we could use it. We paddled to the middle of the fiord, shipped our paddles, and waited under limp sails for the breeze to stir again. We studied the mountains in silence.

After a while George spoke. He was unhappy with the scientists, he confided. They were just measurers and counters, in his opinion. They didn't seem to be connected in any way with the animals they were studying, or even to *like* animals. "These people aren't like the biologists I've known before. Like Paul Spong or the other people I know who study whales. The whale people aren't after degrees or anything. These people here, they could really get close to the bears, if they wanted. If they put everything else out of their heads. These bears and wolves don't know about people. They aren't programmed to run away or attack or anything. These people could be *with* the bears." He paused, then added, "I don't think I want to feed a lady who's killing mice. Sending them to *Washington*."

He told me to dip my paddle in. I did, and felt the tug of resisting water. We were moving. The breeze had come up imperceptibly and was sending us seaward. The canoe was so light that the slightest puff moved it. When I complimented George on this, he assured me that his big canoe would sail even better. It would sail close to the wind, as this baidarka, which had no keel or centerboard, could not. We rode the wind past the dogleg in Torch

Bay, and on rounding the corner we saw the open ocean. It was inviting. For a moment I thought we might just keep going.

Then the breeze died. We turned and paddled home.

As we neared shore, the water got shallower and shallower, until we were skating along on a thin pane of it. I kept expecting us to scrape, and my sympathetic nervous system locked into a flinch, but the flinch was never justified. We drew hardly any water at all. Underneath passed algae and snails and starfish in many colors. "What a boat for coral reefs!" I said.

"Icebergs," George corrected. "There's nothing in the world more beautiful than icebergs."

We paddled right up onto the beach meadow. The prow left water and hissed to a stop on grass. Between sea and land there was no discontinuity. I couldn't feel the difference, but I think I heard it—the canoe's passage through the grass was raspier. We climbed out, gripped the rims of our manholes, and hauled the baidarka up toward George's knoll. We floundered in the tussocks of the meadow while the canoe slid smoothly between us. *We* were the land creatures, yet the baidarka was more graceful here, too.

—— 26 ——

Burma-Shave

The season was winding down. We felt the first hint of autumn in the air, and saw the first autumn colors. The black bears had left Torch Bay to forage elsewhere. The bugs had come, first the mosquitos and then, much worse, the black flies. The snow, which had covered the shore when George first came, remained only in isolated patches on the highest ridges, and the whiteness of the ptarmigan had melted into the mottled reds and browns of their summer plumage. Torch Bay's fiddle ferns, which George had boiled earlier for greens, were all uncurled and standing at full height, too bitter to think of eating. The blue grouse, which had drummed ceaselessly throughout spring and summer, had finally stopped, and in their silence we now heard them.

The mountain goats had lost their whiteness. As the spring snow gave way to the wet, black earth of summer, their coats had turned dingy. Their weightlifters' bodies proved in part illusion. As the summer progressed they shed, growing steadily slenderer. The deep chests, humps, and haunches had been more fleece than muscle. Their wool now hung in strips, and on the butts of many, like ischial callosities in monkeys, were twin spots of mud where they had sat. Their nobility was unraveling. We knew them too well.

George remembered that the blueberries were soon to get ripe in British Columbia. The winds and weather were right for a run to the south. He had learned by letter that the aluminum for his big canoe had arrived the week after he left Vancouver. He was anxious to start work on that project. The air in its new coolness, the goats in their dullness, the blue grouse in their silence, the aluminum in Vancouver, all told him it was time to go.

Morale in camp was low. When the cook is in bad spirits, things go to hell, and George's spirits were terrible. Our camp manager, Ned, was unhappy too. We called a meeting in the cook tent to clear the air. Each of us in turn told the gathering what he thought was wrong.

When Ned's turn came, he was apologetic, taking the blame on himself. It was an admirable gesture. Everyone felt better.

When George's turn came, he talked longer than anyone. Something cathartic in the meeting brought him out. Normally he is a man of few words. His speech now was peculiar, rambling and disjointed. He used a number of analogies from physics that none of us understood. He would change tack in the middle of sentences, and often his words trailed off into nothing. Sometimes even a single word was aborted in midbreath. He seemed to be trying to convey something in the very haltingness of his delivery. I looked around the circle of faces in the cook tent, and they all looked puzzled, then bored. George's green eyes were wide and visionary.

Occasionally he glanced at his audience and noticed that they weren't following, but that hardly caused him to pause.

Some things were clear. George told us about his tree house in British Columbia, and about building his canoe. He explained that the entire Northwest Coast, from Vancouver Island to Glacier Bay, was his home, and that as far as he knew, Torch Bay and its neighboring fiords were the last of that protected fiordland. It was thus the northernmost extension of his place. It was a special spot. And not just for him, but for itself. He described the wildness of Torch Bay when he first came. He talked about the fearlessness of the bears, and the absence of shell middens. Then, just as he seemed to be nearing some point, he shied away. He digressed into one of his analogies from physics. As cook, he told us, he was center of camp. The scientists went out daily in their orbits to gather their data and in the evening they came back to him. If things were to be right with him, the people around him had to be moving in their orbits. He implied that they were not. The camp had lost its spin, he said, and the spin was what gave the center its energy. He was resigning and moving to a new center.

"I'm on a different level," he concluded. "I'm building a different thing. I know it's strange. But I'm an expert on this business of inner space and outer space, and how one is a manifestation of the other."

George had resigned, then, but he was in no hurry to leave Torch Bay and move to his new center. Days went by, and he made no preparations to sail.

I couldn't understand. The wind was northerly and the weather to the south was fine. The aluminum and the big canoe were awaiting him in that direction. When I asked what was keeping him—and keeping me, for I was to be his crew—his answers were irritable and mysterious. It was important, he said, to make sure the departure time was right. He consulted the *I Ching* several times a day, throwing his coins and turning to the pages they indicated. The advice, apparently, was always to stay.

I was slow in understanding, I think, because I had fallen too much into the scientific frame of mind. That was forgivable, considering the company I'd been keeping that summer. I was expecting George to make rational sense, when he was part of a different tradition. The baidarka had transported him deep into that tradition. The moments of decision for his departures were full of mystery because they were truly momentous. It was a long voyage south, in a small boat, on a big ocean. Torch Bay was terra firma, and in Torch Bay he was sure of his meals. Once he left, there was nothing to help him but himself—no radar, radio, or weather reports. There was no manual to consult in emergencies. No such manual ever existed for baidarkas, except in the heads of Aleuts. George was calling now on the old forces. He was behaving like one of those Aleut or Nootka whalers who fasted arduously, avoided women, and spoke carefully lest they offend the gods as they watched, in special huts on special promontories, for the arrival of the whales. George was improvising his own magic. The time had to be right. He was waiting for a sign.

I couldn't stand Torch Bay any longer. I hitched a dory ride with the glacial geologists around the point to Thistle Cove, and from there, alone, I walked north to Astrolabe and Boussole bays, two small fiords named for the frigates of the explorer La Pérouse. Walking, for me, meant what the sweathouse did for George. I climbed the headland that bounds Boussole Bay to the north, and I followed goat trails over the mountain to Palma Bay on the other side. I was the first on our expedition to come this far, and for two days I had Palma Bay to myself. Then I turned and walked back to Thistle Cove, where I hitched a ride homeward in the rubber Zodiac with Sam and Renee Patten.

Sam shouted, over the outboard noise, that things had changed in my absence. Professor Weisbrod, one of the organizers of the expedition, had arrived in the bay, and things were very different. I asked Sam for details, but he wouldn't tell. I would see soon enough for myself, he said.

We stepped ashore at Torch Bay, and Sam and Renee let me go

ahead. Walking up the path toward camp, I noticed nothing amiss, at first. Then I saw the first Burma-Shave sign. I looked up with a start and saw the others. They were lettered in felt pen on plywood. They stood to the right of the path, like the Burma-Shave signs on a highway. They had a cumulative message and a stupid punchline, just like the real thing.

This was the path that George and Ned had flagged so carefully through a virgin meadow just two months before. It suddenly looked as tawdry as Highway 15 outside Las Vegas. Civilization had come full cycle to Torch Bay. The intermediate stages had dispensed with themselves. The bay had passed through no Golden Age of Greece, no Renaissance. The meadow had gone straight from beach grass to Burma-Shave.

I came to the latrine tarp. At either end were signs reading HERREN and DAMEN. This was almost funny; there was only one hole inside, and everyone knew it. In front of George's cook tent was a sign reading THE SOCIAL DIRECTOR IS IN___OUT _X_. The lab tents had signs naming them after laboratory buildings at the University of Washington, Professor Weisbrod's campus. There were signs everywhere. One was printed on a board that George had been saving all summer for a paddle blade. George now had the omen he was waiting for, I thought. He had the sign. He had plenty of signs.

Sam Patten caught up with me from behind. He explained that Professor Weisbrod, sensing that morale was low, had appointed himself social director and had printed the signs to cheer the place up.

I found George inside one of the lab tents. The interior was full of the smell of epoxy and the heat of Coleman lanterns. He had just finished gluing a blade to the shaft of a new paddle, and the lanterns were burning to speed the curing. We stared at each other, incredulous. George did not have to ask if I had seen the signs—there was no way I could have avoided them. His eyes were wild, yet somehow also calm and determined. He pressed the new paddle into my hand, and said, meaningfully, "Here, Ken, try this for size."

Starship

"Freeman's last lecture, toward the end of his stay, was a marvelous thing," Brian Dunne remembers of the older Dyson's final days on the Orion Project. "He decided to take Orion to the ultimate. It was funnier than hell. First I didn't believe it. Then I did. Then I didn't. It was just so outlandish, beyond anything we had ever envisioned before. He was going to have a pusher plate that was, I think, a mile in diameter. It was going to be made out of Mylar. He would send H-bombs down the central tube. They would go out several miles and be set off. This *very* high-temperature cloud would be caught by this *giant* pusher plate. It would send us to Alpha Centauri, which is about 4.33 light-years away."

Dunne laughed, then remembered another detail, and laughed harder.

"And he was going to recycle everything. He was going to use the feces of the astronauts as propellant!"

This, then, would have been the shitstorm. Freeman wanted to elevate it from the figurative. He was going to engineer a real, atomic one.

"Was he serious?" I asked.

"No," said Dunne. Then he stopped laughing. His face went thoughtful. "Well, you never know. You can't tell with Freeman. You have to be cautious."

Dunne ruminated for a moment.

"I think in Freeman there's some kind of deep-seated sense of the future," he said. "The basic tragedy of the man is that he's just too bright for his own good. He sees into the future and he'd rather not. I think he may be looking into World War III, or seeing other things we don't. Those eyes of his—that stare."

I told Dunne that Freeman's son George had the same eyes.

"If the son's eyes are the same, that's good," Dunne said. "They say the eyes are windows of the soul. I only hope he has the same brain."

—— 28 ——

Some Kind of a Gifted Person

"While traveling in my canoe," the son had written, before leaving for Alaska,

> particularly in the inspiring periods spent offshore in the open Pacific, I was analyzing the behavior of my craft and what would be involved in scaling it up in size. To double the length would mean increasing cross-sectional area and hull surface by a factor of about eight, but the concept remained well within the realm of possibility. Twelve manholes could be staggered on both sides, leaving the center of the deck free to accommodate an uninterrupted deck beam, to give the necessary greatly increased longitudinal strength. With a length of sixty-two feet, paddling speed would increase to about ten knots, and sailing speed could easily reach twice that, when lightly loaded in favorable conditions. Three sails of a total area of about two hundred and fifty square feet would be fitted and easily adjusted to any situation. This craft could carry up to twelve people and several tons of cargo or equipment in safety and a high degree of comfort through all waters, and

give these people the contact with themselves and their surroundings which I had experienced in my recent travels.

George had decided to build the Queen Mary of kayaks. A superbaidarka. He applied for a grant from the Canadian government, and the government sent back a form.

Give any personal data, such as educational background and experience, which you feel may be pertinent to your application.

I have lived on the coast of British Columbia since the age of seventeen, at which time I began my experience in boatbuilding by assisting in the construction of an auxiliary sailing vessel of twenty-one tons. I spent two years on this boat engaged in chartering and trade and so acquired my first knowledge of the British Columbia coast and its inhabitants. Since then I have worked on and operated vessels of many types in these waters. I am educated in my knowledge of marine design, boatbuilding, and coastal navigation through a combination of study, experience, and experiment.

Give a brief outline of any work closely related to your project which has been done by others.

The past inhabitants of this coast developed the art and skills of seagoing canoe travel to a degree unmatched anywhere in the world. Using the readily available virgin cedar and generations of woodworking experience, they built large dugout craft of sophisticated design, which when combined with these peoples' strength and seamanship enabled swift and reliable travel throughout the Pacific coast. I know of no work other than my own which seeks to adapt this once widespread manner of life and travel to presently available skills and materials.

George was asked to attach letters of appraisal (Lettres d'Appré-ciation). He did so. One was from Bob Hunter, a columnist with the Vancouver *Sun*. "I think," wrote Hunter, "that George is some kind of a gifted person, whose method of expression is different in kind from the usual type of artist, but which is essentially artistic. He may be a genius. Certainly, he deserves my support."

George was not quite certain why this sixty-foot kayak was necessary. Sometimes he thought he would outfit the big canoe with hydrophones and charter it to his friend Paul Spong and to other students of whales. Dr. Spong and the other cetologists would be able to approach their whales rapidly and silently, yet with a lot of electronic listening equipment. Other times George thought he would make a living by selling plans of the canoe. Sometimes the canoe's purpose was to allow him to start a family. (His thirty-foot baidarka was too small for a woman to set up housekeeping in, and so was his tree house.) Other times the canoe was to take him to the Queen Charlottes, where he would find out about that Haida girl who swims two miles every day in the Pacific. Sometimes it was to take him to Hawaii or the Marquesas.

In his application, George settled upon a purpose that was large and socially significant. He was going to revive canoe travel in British Columbia. He saw a future in which great, cheap, seagoing canoes carried passengers and freight around the coast, as they had two hundred years before. His vision was, of course, crazy.

Freeman Dyson has expressed some thoughts on craziness. In a *Scientific American* article called "Innovation in Physics," he began by quoting Niels Bohr. Bohr had been in attendance at a lecture in which Wolfgang Pauli proposed a new theory of elementary particles. Pauli came under heavy criticism, which Bohr summed up for him: "We are all agreed that your theory is crazy. The question which divides us is whether it is crazy enough to have a chance of being correct. My own feeling is that it is not crazy enough." To that Freeman added: "When the great innova-tion appears, it will almost certainly be in a muddled, incomplete and confusing form. To the discoverer himself it will be only half-understood; to everybody else it will be a mystery. For any speculation which does not at first glance look crazy, there is no hope."

Speeding

Freeman toyed with two designs for the starship. One he called conservative, the other optimistic.

The conservative version was a "heat-sink" spaceship. Its bottom would be made of a good heat conductor, like copper. A hemispheric copper pusher plate would absorb the energy of the ship's hydrogen bombs and then re-radiate it. To absorb a megaton of energy, five million tons of exposed surface would be necessary, so the ship would be enormous. Acceleration would be gentle, so the ship would not need to be especially sturdy. It would be a spidery structure twenty kilometers in diameter. Unloaded, it would weigh ten million tons, half of which would be the copper hemisphere. Its fuel would be thirty billion pounds of deuterium, loaded into thirty million bombs. With its bombload racked away, the ship would weigh forty million tons. The bombs would explode ten kilometers beneath the hemisphere, detonated at intervals of one thousand seconds, to allow the copper to dissipate the energy.

These specifications, wrote Freeman, "represent the absolute lower limit of what could be done with our present resources and technology if we were forced by some astronomical catastrophe to send a Noah's ark out of the wreckage of the solar system. With about one Gross National Product we could send a payload of a few million tons (for example, a small town like Princeton with about twenty thousand people) on a trip at about 1,000 km/sec or 1 parsec per 1,000 years."

A parsec is roughly three light-years, or three quarters of the way to the nearest star. A heat-sink ship leaving Earth at the time Saint

Augustine was bringing Christianity to the Anglo-Saxons would have reached Alpha Centauri at about the time Freeman brought these calculations to the attention of the public.

"As a voyage of colonization a trip as slow as this does not make much sense on a human time scale. A nonhuman species, longer-lived or accustomed to thinking in terms of millennia rather than years, might find the conditions acceptable."

Freeman did not find the conditions acceptable. Voyages of *human* colonization were what interested him. The heat-sink design was only to prove feasibility in principle. Freeman doubted that a heat-sink ship would ever happen.

If bomb-propelled ships were ever built, he believed, they would be of the optimistic design, compact and rugged vehicles something like Orion, but scaled up in size. They would be momentum-limited, not energy-limited. Instead of absorbing the bomb's heat energy, the pusher plate would shuffle it off in a puff of vaporized ablating material. The optimistic ship would be more expensive (three thousand dollars per pound of payload, compared to three hundred dollars for the heat-sink ship), but it would be lighter and faster. Unloaded, it would weigh only a hundred thousand tons. It would carry just three hundred thousand bombs. The deuterium for the bombs would cost only ten percent of one Gross National Product. Where the heat-sink ship would accelerate slowly over a hundred years, the ablation ship would accelerate quickly over ten days. Its maximum velocity would be 10,000 km/sec.

This velocity was, Freeman noted, "just about what one would reach by 'surf riding' on the expanding shell of debris from a supernova remnant like Cassiopea A."

Freeman wanted to tap the velocities that God employs in the larger brushstrokes of His Creation. He craved the sensation of a celestial surf ride.

It was in 1958 that he proposed his starship. Behind his mild and professorial exterior, then, lurked a lust for speed that would have dismayed the most reckless of the duck-tailed, leather-jacketed dragsters of that period. Freeman's zero-to-sixty time was an appallingly small fraction of a second. His vehicle would not have squealed away in the smell of hot rubber; it would have vanished in a thermonuclear flash and a whiff of vaporized metal, traveling at more than three percent of the velocity of light, covering ground at the staggering rate of one parsec per century.

At that speed, he wrote, "these missions could reach many nearby stars in the course of a few centuries." He predicted that, barring catastrophe, the first interstellar voyages would begin in two hundred years.

"Was he serious?" I asked Ted Taylor, years later.

"I don't think so," Taylor answered. "In his characteristic way he wanted to push something to the limit. H-bombs per unit of energy are a lot cheaper than A-bombs. They're also a lot hotter, a lot more energetic. He asked himself what principle you'd have to use to be able to use H-bombs."

"The starship was like an existence theorem in math," says Freeman himself. "It was to prove if you could do it. I never really believed in it. My heart was in a ship you could put together in a few years to tour around the solar system. But I have always been interested in other intelligent beings. From that point of view, the starship interested me."

--- 30 ---

Black Hole

In 1971 Freeman indulged his interest in other intelligent beings. He accepted an invitation to the First International Conference on Communication with Extraterrestrial Intelligence, held in Byurakan, Soviet Armenia. The conference roster included nearly everyone who had contributed to the quasi-science of exobiology. Most of the contributions had been theoretical, necessarily, for exobiology remains a science without subject matter. Freeman was invited not for his work on Orion, but because of a short report to

Science written ten years before. In it he had pointed out that interstellar radio signals were only one possible manifestation of extraterrestrial intelligence. Another was infrared radiation.

Technological civilization expands very fast, Freeman had reasoned. After three thousand years of growth in a solar system like our own, it would be a logical development for a high civilization to have disassembled one of its larger planets in order to build an energy-capturing shell around its sun. If this has happened, he wrote, we are wasting our time searching near visible stars. We should look instead for dark, room-temperature objects about the size of Earth's orbit which radiate as intensely as the star hidden within, but radiate in the far-infrared.

Freeman's report took up only a single page of *Science*, but it has caused a lot of discussion. Cool stars similar to the sort he postulated were unknown when he wrote, but more than a thousand have been discovered since, and some of these are sending out strong radio signals. The signals are likely natural in origin, and Freeman himself leans to that view, but other scientists wondered. Were these "Dyson civilizations"?

Freeman disowned his civilizations, arguing that the infrared stars were appearing in places where astronomers know that new stars are forming. It was to be expected, early in a star's evolution, as its natal cloud of dust contracted and began to heat up, that it would pass through a room-temperature stage. But Freeman's doubts did not discourage everyone. When five hydroxyl sources were discovered lying in a nearly perfect circle in the zone of space called W 3, astronomers suggested, half serious, that this was a federation of Dyson civilizations.

Now, at the conference in Armenia, Freeman's mood seems to have been quietly testy. A gathering of theoreticians is not his cup of tea. Such a gathering produces more abstract argument than he likes.

One morning began with a discussion on the probability of the existence of extraterrestrial civilizations. Because there is no way to estimate this probability in the absence of evidence, the talk turned philosophical. The scientists debated the meaning of probability. Almost everyone but Freeman was having a good time. Wanting to change the drift of the proceedings, Freeman designed a tactic during lunch. "I have six points which I shall go through quite briefly," he said when they reconvened. "The first is: to hell with philosophy. I came here to learn about observations and instruments and I hope we shall soon begin to discuss these concrete questions."

Freeman's hope was not to be. His presentation was followed by a talk by N. S. Kardashev, of the Institute for Cosmic Research, Soviet Academy of Sciences. Kardashev was interested in the collapse of supermassive objects, and the possibility that extraterrestrial civilizations were taking advantage of this phenomenon. He gave a little background. If an outside observer were to watch a spaceship approach a contracting mass larger than 1.5 solar masses, he said, the observer would observe a peculiar thing. "As the spacecraft draws closer to the gravitational radius, all processes observed would be extended indefinitely in time; whereas for someone aboard the rocket, the processes will take place in the usual time scale. This is a well-known effect. Let us examine what happens once the gravitational radius is reached. To begin with, the external observer will not observe this at all. The occupants of the spacecraft will reach the center in a period of time, $t = rg/C = 10^{-5} (M/M.)$ seconds. After that, everyone will probably assume them to be lost, but some new models suggest they may remain very much alive." The contraction of the mass and the spacecraft, explained Kardashev, would not proceed to infinite density. Somewhere close inside the gravitational radius—or "Schwarzschild sphere"—they would stop, and then would expand.

"They return," said the Russian. "But the main question is, Where do they return to? For the external observer, they will never emerge. In an infinite period of time they will still not have emerged. From this, we draw the conclusion that our space is much more complicated than it seems. Sakharov assumes that there is an infinite multitude of spaces separated from one another by infinitely large times. This provides us with a time machine which enables us to cover infinitely large time intervals in small proper times. This is rather abstract."

"Yes, very abstract," said Dr. Morrison of MIT. "It is a great trip for electrons but I would hate to send a spaceship on it."

"Do not be afraid," said Kardashev. "The flight conditions may be normal. The density, radiation, and gravity gradient may be safe for life, if the electrical charge and the mass are sufficiently large."

Kardashev reminded the gathering that supermassive objects through which we might enter the past are called white holes. Our avenues to the future are black holes. During the brief time expansion of the white hole, he speculated, a traveler might see all the past of the universe, and in the black hole, all the future. Kardashev concluded by suggesting that investigators concentrate their searches around white holes and black holes.

In the question period, Dr. Morrison asked about the tidal stresses on passengers entering one of Kardashev's holes.

"The tidal stress," answered the Russian, "depends upon the dimensions of the body relative to the gravitational radius. Such estimates have been made and everything seems to be quite satisfactory."

But Dr. Gold of Cornell was uneasy just the same. "I thought if the radius was only two kilometers or so, the stresses would be very large and a human being would certainly be drawn into a long, thin thread."

"Of course," answered Kardashev, "but for a very short time, you must remember."

"I don't wish to be a long thread even for a very brief moment," said Gold.

Drs. Gold and Morrison, it seems, shared Freeman Dyson's impatience with abstraction. So did the Russian Shklovsky, a scientist whom Freeman much admires. It was Shklovsky who delivered Freeman's favorite line at Byurakan.

"Like other scientific meetings, this one had its lighter moments," Freeman has written. "At one point, an astronomer digressed into a rambling and improbable theory of mental creativity. He told us that our powers wax and wane with the eleven-year period of the sunspots, and he illustrated his theory by enumerating all the great discoveries of Newton and Einstein that were made at times of maximum sunspot activity. The Russian astronomer Iosif Shklovsky leaned over to his neighbor and whispered loudly, 'This theory was invented during a deep sunspot minimum.' "

Sunspot-minimal thinking is common on Earth, even among minds of the caliber convened at Byurakan, and Freeman despairs of it.

We will now enter a black hole in this narrative, for a glimpse, maybe, at the motivation behind the starship, behind Freeman's desire to find another intelligent race.

At two o'clock one morning, in a time that belongs later in the story, on a dark and narrow road, Freeman and I conversed wearily, our eyes fixed on the curves ahead. I had been driving all night through the darkness of the British Columbia rain forest. I was talking mostly to stay awake at the wheel. I asked Freeman whether, as a boy, he had speculated about his gift. Had he asked himself ever, or much, why he had this special power? Why he was so bright? The physicist's face was blank with fatigue when he turned to me, and his answer was uncharacteristic of him.

"That's not how the question phrases itself. The question is Why is everyone else so stupid?"

—— 31 ——

Total Madness

"Someone asked me the other day, if he gave me one billion dollars would I build Orion?" mused Freeman. "The answer is quite obviously no. That surprised me."

Freeman went away for a short while, following cerebrally some ramification of Orion, of the billion dollars, or of his surprise. Then he popped back into the conversation. No matter how long Freeman is gone, he never loses the thread.

"Orion was a dirty and very primitive way of going into space. At that time, bombs were going off all around. Our little contribution to fallout would have been only a small fraction of the total—one percent."

During the Orion project, he said, only Linus Pauling and a few other scientists were much concerned about the hundred megatons of fission products that atomic testing was releasing into the atmosphere. Since then, the attitudes of the scientific community, and Freeman's own attitude, had changed. He no longer considered it acceptable to detonate nuclear bombs in the atmosphere.

After the death of Orion, Freeman ceased to think much about space travel. It was not until the 1970s, and the public's warm reception of Dr. Gerard O'Neill's ideas on space colonization, that his interest returned.

"Gerry O'Neill is very much the space-cadet type," said Freeman. "He and I have been good friends for many years. Gerry had been thinking hard about space colonization for a long time. He got to the point of really trying to figure out how to colonize space, simply using conventional stuff. He went public. I'd taken for granted that the public had lost interest, that Apollo had bored everyone to death. Nobody was interested in the thing, and I'd given up on seeing it in my own lifetime. O'Neill revived me. He was on television all the time. He even got some money from NASA. There was substantial interest, not just from space cadets, but from normal people too."

Gerard K. O'Neill is a neighbor of Freeman's, a professor of physics at Princeton. He wants to build free-floating colonies in space. The design he prefers is a coupled pair of parallel cylinders, each closed by a hemispherical end-cap. The cylinders would rotate about their long axes to provide residents with an Earth-normal gravity. In his Model 1, each cylinder has a diameter of six hundred feet, is three thousand feet long and has a rotation time of twenty seconds. The interior walls are divided longitudinally into six regions, three "valleys" of farmland alternating with three zones of windows. The axis of the cylinder is pointed toward the sun, and light planar mirrors positioned outside the windows reflect sunshine in. The mirror angle is varied to allow for dawn, for the stately passage of the sun across the sky, and for sunset. Weather, season, temperature, and length of day are regulated by mirror angle. At the outside end of each cylinder is a big paraboloidal mirror that never looks on the night. It collects solar energy around the clock to run a steam-electric plant. The mass of Model 1 is about half a million tons—that of a large supertanker—and its two cylinders would house ten thousand people.

The colony would have to be far enough from Earth and moon to avoid frequent eclipses and the consequent shutdowns of solar energy. The best spot, O'Neill thinks, is near the point on the moon's orbit designated L5. Most of the colony's raw materials would be transported to L5 from the moon. The lunar surface, O'Neill points out, is rich in titanium and oxygen, as well as aluminum and silicon.

From the Earth, in vessels like NASA's space shuttle, ten thousand tons of material would be ferried to L5. Half of this would be liquid hydrogen, which, when combined with the oxygen in the moon's surface, would produce forty-five thousand tons of water. The rest would be food and equipment. At L5, construction crews would process the aluminum into the castings, wires, and cables of the colony's twin cocoons.

Eventually larger colonies, with twenty-mile interiors, could be built, O'Neill thinks. Bicycles and electric cars would be adequate transport in a world of such dimensions. There would be no internal-combustion engines, no dirty energy, no air pollution. Food would be fresh, never growing more than twenty miles from market. Skiing, sailing, and mountain climbing would be possible. There would even be clouds in O'Neill's sky. The professor, who is a glider pilot, made some calculations and found that his colony would have enough atmospheric instability to provide him with lift. At high altitudes the old dream, man-powered flight, would become a breeze. Skindivers could dive without having to equalize the pressure in their ears. Terrestrial species endangered by pesticides would find a refuge. There would be no pesticides in the colonies. There would be no pests.

O'Neill with his colonies, like Freeman before him with Orion, is averse to wasting time. He would like to see progress in his own lifetime. He believes the first colony can be assembled as early as the 1980s, and would cost no more than the Apollo project.

"The strange thing is," said Freeman, "I find O'Neill's colonies completely unappealing. I would say they're a fine place for a weekend, but . . . Anyway, they turned me off completely. We had arguments over it. I bet Gerry he wouldn't get anyone to sign on.

"The kind of style I would much prefer is where a bunch of nuts build themselves an old tin can in the backyard and go themselves. More in the style of George. I'm not interested unless it's cheap. I set as benchmarks the level of costs for the *Mayflower*. It's quite easy to figure out what that level was.

"With the *Mayflower* there were two kinds of people. There were the planters, the ones who actually went, and the adventurers, who supplied the money. For a planter, his one share in the enterprise cost seven years of work. The adventurer invested fifty pounds. The total cost was about five thousand pounds, which today is the equivalent of about twenty million dollars. Somebody who is not a millionaire, but is just a little bit crazy, might put five years of salary into it. You raise a hundred thousand dollars a head that way. So you get two hundred people, both planters and adventurers. That's about the right size for a colony.

"O'Neill's colonies are much too big. They're too sanitized, bureaucratized. That's the first thing I noticed about them. O'Neill says the cost of a colony is twenty billion dollars—to start. For that you get a big colony, of course. But that's the number everyone believes. It's the accepted dogma that everything you do in space costs billions of dollars. I say we should do it for twenty million dollars. You have to do it for twenty million before I'm interested. Nobody in NASA would take this seriously for a moment. For them this is total madness."

South Again

The sun was bright, the swell was gentle. The serpent head of the baidarka furrowed open ocean. We were heading south. To our right was a blue horizon—the Gulf of Alaska. Somewhere beyond the edge lay the Alaska Peninsula, the Aleutians, and Kamchatka. To our left, the pale granite underpinnings of the American continent rose streaming from the sea and then fell back.

Torch Bay receded behind us. We took a last look back at the cirque and the waterfall before they passed behind the point. As Torch Bay closed to us, the next bay unfolded.

Our paddles dipped and pulled. Power flowed into George. His decision was made, his canoe was underway, and his doubts had departed. He was full of a sense of himself.

We slid over patches of offshore kelp. The recumbent stalks made a rubbery sound as the hull scraped over. The stalks were a dark, smoky olive-green that glistened in the salt water and the afternoon light. Some were as thick as hawsers. From the bulbs at the ends sprouted leaf-tassels of a translucent spring-green. The tassels were incandescent and flame-shaped when you looked toward the sun at them. The kelp stole the baidarka's momentum, but gave it back when the prow broke free. It is not that way in other boats. Kelp instantly fouls the prop of an outboard and it locks up a rowboat nearly as fast. In the dory that summer we had battered away at the kelp, trying to get the oars between stalks. At the end of a stroke, each oar, festooned, weighed sixty pounds. In the baidarka it was easy to drive the paddle blade between the stalks and easy to get purchase among them. Baidarkas are kelp boats. In them Aleuts once pursued sea otter into the seaweed. For sea otter, the kelp canopy is like a lawn, and they like to doze or fool around there. Baidarkas were the ants at that picnic. Now, in the twentieth century, George's baidarka passed us easily from the canopy of one sea forest to the canopy of the next.

The prow was full of gear, and a yellow nylon hatch-cover sealed the forward hole. George sat in the middle hole, and I sat in the stern. That arrangement would fix his back in front of me for the rest of the voyage. Seldom has a biographer observed his subject so closely.

When we slipped the elastic of our paddling skirts around our chests, the baidarka became airtight. If I rose in my seat, George's skirt would collapse and wrinkle. If I sat down, his skirt would balloon. Seldom have biographer and subject been so intimately connected.

We passed a small island, a smooth granite dome with a little grass on top. It was rounded and awash, like a fallen asteroid. "Does that kind of island turn you on?" asked the son of Freeman Dyson. "No trees. It's the kind of place I'd like to come and camp for a few days."

We passed a minke whale, endless back and small fin going in opposite directions.

We reached Cape Spencer and streamed with the tide through the jumble of islands at the tip of the cape. The islands were big blocks of granite. On top were spruces, very dark, each stamped with individual character by the sea wind. The channels through the islands were pastures of kelp, and all the tassels pointed in our direction. As the tide propelled us through, George glassed the Cape Spencer light. According to his intelligence, the lighthouse was to be automated sometime this month. He buttoned his binoculars back in their case and took up his paddle again. "I think it may already be abandoned," he said. "Places like that are full of good things." He considered going ashore to scavenge, but decided the baidarka was already too heavily loaded.

Turning Cape Spencer, we spotted a salmon troller several miles away. We heard it almost as soon as we saw it. "It's amazing how far away you can hear boats," George said. We smelled it too; traces of diesel fumes came and went on the wind. "I like diesel," said George. "I get high off it. It makes me think I'm *moving.*" He liked the sound of diesel engines too, he added, and he liked the sound of buoys. "I like wilderness. But I like seeing boats, too . . . the different kinds of people."

The day had clouded over, but a good wind was driving us toward Inian Pass on the other side of Cross Sound. Inian Pass was the entrance to Icy Strait, and that was where we wanted to go. George said something about our good luck, but mentioned it somberly, without any visible pleasure, taking care lest he change it. Cross Sound was an open body of water, and he worried about it. If the weather changed in the middle, we had no harbor to run to.

As we crossed, evening came on. The excitement of departure was gone now. We were no longer fresh. We had settled into our paddling rhythm. It was somewhere in the middle of the sound that the trip really began.

The sky had turned gray, which would be its normal color on the voyage. The sea was gray and choppy. The near islands and the ridges of the mainland were of a grayness nearly black, and the far islands and ridges were gray in diminishing half and quarter tones. The mists that obscured some islands, and the lens clouds that capped some ridges, were of a grayness nearly white. All the grays were fluid. The clouds flowed over the landforms, the landforms flowed into the sea, the sea flowed with its tide. The baidarka, slender and blue, bisected a broad gray world. Its deck held the only color in creation, its accouterments the only detail. Its shape was the only one fixed. That would be the story of our voyage: the baidarka as constant as a compass needle as the shoreline unfolded smoothly and continually ahead, and the sea passed beneath in a hundred changing moods and textures, and the sky flowed away above, forming and re-forming. I found my eye returning fondly to the canoe. I took comfort in the blond wood of the masts, the translucent blue of the fiberglass, the holes in George's Peruvian sweater, the nap on his wool cap, the green of his eyes when he turned around. The baidarka was an island of human warmth in the midst of the elements.

The canoe changed size, I noticed. Sometimes, when I was studying the grain of its masts or the weave of its captain's sweater, the baidarka was the whole world. It seemed surprisingly wide, for a kayak, and perfectly safe. Other times, when I looked west at the horizon and felt its reach, remembering the hundred thousand storms the gulf had spawned, or when the chop caught my attention by suddenly slapping the hull, the baidarka shrank. It seemed, then, to bisect the sea as thinly as one of those widthless lines in geometry. The canoe was not much broader than my shoulders, and unloaded it weighed less than I.

George looked back at me. "When we get to civilization, we'll have trouble making decisions," he said. "There are no decisions now. We know what we have to do. We have a goal—south. Every day we can get up and know exactly what to do—get on south."

Out in the sound, flocks of phalaropes swam away from us with their head-bobbing motion. Pairs of murrelets looked wildly at us, then did their surface dives. They raised up a little, then shattered the water with their foreheads, as sudden as karate masters but without the yell. Bonaparte gulls flew over, and tufted puffins. I saw a horned puffin, my first of the summer.

Chichagof Island, on what had been the far side of the sound, was drawing close, and we could make out individual trees on shore. By the time George found a cove with a suitable beach, the island was darkling. Using driftwood logs as rollers, we slid the heavily loaded baidarka up the pebble slope. George pitched his one-man tent from the bowline and crawled inside. The tent was coffin-sized, tailored to his dimensions. A football player would not have fit. For a time George lay on his belly looking out. He and the serpent head of his baidarka studied each other down their common bowline. George dropped his eyes first. He turned his head on the side and went to sleep.

The next day dawned gray, except for a small patch of blue in the direction we were going. We took that for a good omen. George said he liked to watch the blue while paddling; it gave him heart. By noon our prow was pointing at the snowy peaks near Chilkoot Pass. The patch of blue stood like a beacon over the mountains, which were distant and white in the sun. "It's clear weather over the Yukon," George said. I found I could watch snowy mountains for a long time without boredom. The mountains in front cast pale-blue shadows on those behind. I wondered what it would be like over there. That was Canada. The mountains were in another country.

We saw a barge so distant that the tug pulling it was invisible. George glassed it, as he would glass all barges and log booms on the trip. "What I really like to do," he confided, "is tie up to log booms without them knowing it. For me that's just like catching a good wind."

This was the mode of cryptozoic travel practiced by Huck Finn on the Mississippi. George had introduced it to the Pacific Coast.

Near the entrance to Hoonah Bay, we passed a small, forested island. We found ourselves studying it closely. It had a lot of small-island appeal. It would have taken two minutes to walk across. "They don't show any islands smaller than that on the chart," George said. "On the chart it's just a dot. In Seattle an island like that would cost fifty thousand dollars." In Seattle, I figured, it would cost a lot more than that. Yet here in Alaska we were so wealthy in islands that we didn't even bother to land.

When we had passed the island, George tried an experiment. He climbed out of his manhole, lay on his back on deck, feet toward me, and tried to take a nap. It was his first attempt at this, and it took some tricky balancing, but finally he wiggled secure. "This is *great*," he said, addressing the sky. "I'm going to do this more often." From where I sat, George made a gunsight. His bare feet were the rear sight, framing the front sight of his nose. In my manhole I felt like von Richthofen. I scrunched low and aimed. George's septum pointed deviously toward the blue patch of sky.

While George slept, we came upon a seal sleeping on the surface. Her pale pelt was beautifully mottled with dark spots. Her nose was in the air, just like George's. As we passed, I spoke to her in the conversational tones I'd heard George use in addressing seals. I didn't want to startle her or awaken George. I told her she should be glad I wasn't an Aleut. She didn't hear me at first. Then she started, looked at me for a moment with her big, dark-adapted eyes, and dove unhurriedly.

In the afternoon we went ashore for fifteen minutes to rest and stretch. I poked around in the forest. The vegetation was already very different from that of the outer coast of Glacier Bay. Here the land had been free of ice longer, and the forest was older. The trees were wide-boled, and there were huge cedars now among the spruces. The trees grew big right down to the high-tide line. The beach was bright in the sunlight, but a step away, through holes in the wall of trees, the shadows looked black. When you stepped inside the forest, the light was muted and cathedrallike. The trees were widely spaced and as old as druids. The canopy stole all the light, leaving none for other plants, so the understory was open. There was no devil's club or thickets of young trees, as in the new spruce forest at Torch Bay. If I'd had time, I could have struck out unimpeded in any direction over the moss carpet, but I heard George calling me from the beach. I rejoined him there, and we slid the canoe into the water.

We paddled until it was almost dark. Entering Spasski Bay, we began looking for a camp. George passed up a couple of gently sloping sand beaches. He prefers steep beaches, because on those it is not necessary to haul the canoe such a horizontal distance to be safe from the tide. Turning a point in the bay, we came upon a motorboat. The outboard was tipped out of the water, the cowling was off, and a man was bent over it. We had no tools to lend him. We went by quietly—at twilight a baidarka's passage is ghostly—and I don't think the man saw us. He was the first stranger we had seen in months. Turning another point, we saw a cabin, our first in a long time. Below the cabin was a pier, and on the pier another man stood watching us come in. Twenty yards out we stopped paddling. The canoe glided in, and George reached to fend off the piling, then caught it with his hand. The man above was dark-skinned and looked part Indian. He asked where we were heading. When George answered Vancouver, the man looked first incredulous, then disgusted.

"You don't have good sense," he said. He looked down at the baidarka and shook his head. "Where are you coming from?"

"Torch Bay," said George. The name rang no bells with the man. "Beyond Cape Spencer," George amplified.

The man started to move off, as if our lack of good sense might be catching. Then he stopped and looked down again at the biggest kayak in the world.

"So, what do you call this thing?"

"A canoe. A big canoe."

"A big canoe, huh?" He looked a little friendlier. "Well, I hope you make it to Vancouver. I think you're absolutely crazy."

The next day the patch of blue sky appeared again. It led us southeast to Point Augusta, where we went off the old chart. George got out the new chart and fixed it on the deck in front of him. Paddling, he looked from the landforms to the map, then back again. Sometimes his paddle paused in the air as he bent to study closely some feature of the two-dimensional country. After missing a beat or two, his stroke resumed. His head came up and he watched the three-dimensional country. "I like the British Columbia charts better," he said. "They're smaller. These charts in Alaska cover too much ground. In British Columbia you can go across a chart in a day, and you think you're really moving."

Rounding Point Augusta, we entered Chatham Strait. For several miles we ran down the strait's west shore, then a wind came up. We raised sail and crossed to the east. The old shore fell behind, and soon we could not see the trees for the forest. In the middle of the strait we were in limbo. Both shores were vague.

Then, on the new shore, individual trees began to take shape. The wind was fickle, and we resumed paddling.

A light rain began to fall. We ignored it at first, then we made ourselves some raingear. The Aleuts had sewn their paddling parka, the *kamleika*, from sea-mammal intestine. We used Hefty plastic garbage bags. The idea had come to George in Torch Bay, and he had borrowed a packet of bags from the camp commissary. We cut holes for neck and arms and slipped the bags on. They worked well. Our wool shirtsleeves got wet, but wet wool is warm. Paddling in a garbage bag was better than paddling in the stuffiness of a cagoule or a rain parka. The only disadvantage was the crackling of the bags as your shoulders rolled with the double paddling. It wasn't much of a noise, but I was accustomed now to the silence of the baidarka, and I was happy when the rain stopped and I could take the plastic off.

Down the strait we could see the white, perfect triangle of a summit on Baranof Island. The peak appeared to rise straight from the strait. The foothills below the mountain, and all the rest of Baranof Island, were cut off from us by the curve of the Earth. Chatham was a big strait. It stretched on far past that mountain; then there was another strait, and then another. The sky over the peak was blue, and we continued to chase it.

The next morning we caught up with the blue sky and good weather. The wind was light and intermittent, and while it blew we took turns napping, one of us disappearing inside his manhole to lie down as best he could, the other steering. At noon the last breeze died, and we began a steady paddling.

We worked hard, and by early afternoon our water bottles were empty. When we came abreast of a good-sized river—we saw its avenue through the trees on Admiralty Island—George turned in to refill. A flock of surf scoters had gathered off the river mouth, and as the baidarka neared, the ducks thundered off. Their feet pounded the surface, their wings beat it frantically, they wobbled from side to side, in an interminable comic takeoff that never climaxed. Their panic continued long after the need for it had ended. They lathered the water white way out into the strait. The panic subsided, then started again when one duck suddenly remembered us anew. In retreat the thirty scoters made a roar like heavy surf.

One hundred fifty yards out, George tasted the ocean. It was nearly fresh; the river ran stronger than it looked. We entered the mouth and the water shallowed under us. The stones of the pavement below were rounded and naked. They were river stones, very different from the algae-bearded, sea-changed stones that floored the strait. Inside the river mouth, another flock of scoters thundered off, making way for us. We turned a corner, and the strait disappeared behind us. Suddenly we were on an inland river. The banks were close on either side, and the spruces grew tall around us. George signaled for me to stop paddling. We glided toward shore, and the only sound was a scrape of the rudder reins against the deck as George made a slight course change. At the last moment he reached out and grabbed a clump of grass to stop us. I grabbed another clump. Holding on against the current, which was gently trying to flush us out, we looked around. Upstream, where the slough narrowed and became a river proper, was a small rapids. Above the fast water a young eagle was harassing a scoter it had trapped in the shallows there. The eagle dove at the duck each time it tried to surface and escape to the slough. It takes a pair of eagles to catch a scoter this way, and this one got away. The water was still slightly brackish, but George began filling his bottle with it.

"It's good for you," he said of the brackishness. "Chichester drank a pint of seawater a day."

"Chichester's dead."

"He is?" George looked thoughtful for a moment, then came up with the explanation. "He also drank a pint of gin."

Our bottles full, we let the current take us out. As we passed the entrance, a seal surfaced. "Hello!" George shouted. "How many salmon are running up this stream?" The seal looked at us, but didn't answer. It was privileged information.

We continued down the strait. After turning several points, we caught up with a migration of jellyfish, or crashed a convention of them; it was hard to tell which. The medusae pulsed everywhere around us, disks of pale-orange protoplasm expanding and contracting in the dark, cold water. Turbulence from George's paddle would swirl back, and the jellyfish image would stretch and shatter. George obliterated dozens in that harmless way, and I watched them all go, not bored, not fascinated—simpleminded, the way you get sometimes in the wilderness or on the water.

Whales were blowing out in the middle of the strait. They were too distant for us to see, but the sound travels so intact over these waters, and the far lungs were so mighty, that the whales seemed to be right beside us. It was a human sound but immeasurably larger. Throughout the afternoon we listened to the heroic exhalations. We looked in vain for the source; then finally, five miles away, we saw a spout. The whales were humpbacks.

At six in the evening, the sun had five hours' elevation left, yet it was already difficult to look westward. The sky seemed to have been storing light throughout the long day, and the west was saturated. There was a thin, bright stratum of haze over the strait. The strait's oily undulations were full of light, and so were the far mountains. We heard the blowing of some sea mammal coming toward us out of the brightness, but it hurt to look for it. For a time we had the disembodied sound for company, then, hands shading our eyes, we saw them—a pair of Steller sea lions hunting leisurely this way and that, and finally straight at us. They were as big as small whales. They moved in perfect synchrony, curving together out of the lambent surface. Their flanks were long and glistening, compendiums of the swell itself. George spoke to them, but they were not interested. Their big leonine heads and whiskers nosed back under.

From the sea, the blowing of the lions and whales came and went, but from land the warnings and chatterings of birds were continuous. Ravens and gulls cried at us and berated one another. Each time we rounded a point we heard the laughter of a new pair of eagles. Eagles enjoy the view from promontories, and each point had been staked out by two of them. All day long the bird sound unfolded unceasingly to our left, and the sea-mammal respiration came fitfully from our right.

The sun was low above the western mountains when we spotted the village of Angoon. We worked our way toward town against the tide, and it was slow going. For a long time the buildings got no larger, then we began to catch up on them. A mile from the town pier we passed a drifting skiff with the outboard tipped out of the water. In it a young Tlingit couple were fishing and watching the sunset. The man wore long hair and a headband. We said hello, and he waved curtly. As we passed, he said, "You'll never get anyplace in that."

At the time I was annoyed. He looked like a revolutionary Indian, in his long hair and headband, but he didn't have the revolutionary idea. He didn't know a revolutionary boat when he saw one. Later, remembering something in his tone, I wondered if he hadn't been speaking with irony, from his racial experience.

We turned in for the pier. Through the pier's pilings, we saw an Indian woman walk down to the pebble beach at the pier's foot. She dumped a cardboard box of garbage below high-tide line and set it on fire. She was watching it burn as we came up, and she didn't see us. The pier was tall and rickety and labeled with a tiny sign, ANGOON. Three children on top stopped playing when they saw us. They began commenting as we drew close. The pier had a ladder, and George steered for it. He seized the low rung to stop the baidarka's momentum. At this, one of the small boys above immediately began jerking in his fishline. We watched the lure bob and spin upward and vanish over the edge of the platform. Three dark heads appeared against the sky, looking down on us. "Hi!" George called. The heads ducked back. We tied up. Stiffly, after twelve hours of paddling, we climbed twenty-five feet to the top. The children were in retreat. "Hello," George tried again, but without luck. We followed them shoreward, stretching our legs. The children joined an older girl at the foot of the pier. When we reached them, George tried a third time, "Hello." The older girl nodded without looking at us.

Angoon was our first town in a long time. We were tired but excited. This was civilization, sort of. Most of the houses on the waterfront were on pilings. The planks were warped and weathered, and the buildings leaned this way and that. On the hilltop was a boxlike building with a few tiny windows in random spots. It looked like an old gymnasium or a cannery, if there is such a thing as a hilltop cannery.

The odors were not those of Western civilization. Angoon had the sweet smell of decay I knew from Asia and South America. The dogs were big, sullen Indian dogs. There were no little dogs, no lap dogs. The Indian dogs looked peculiar about the eyes. They looked crazy, I thought, or maybe just different. We passed a wooden church with a spire that once had been white. We passed a dark, beady-eyed old man sitting on a porch, staring straight ahead. His face in repose was fierce. He looked very much like the Geronimo of that famous photo of the chief in exile in Florida. He nodded at us as we walked by. Kids passed on bikes, but did not look at us. For most of the town, we seemed not to exist. Angoon wasn't unfriendly, exactly, it was just a township of another universe. We passed through insubstantially, like rumors. In ten minutes we had come to the end of main street. We about-faced and headed back.

On our second pass through town we met a middle-aged woman who gave us our first Angoon smile. We passed Geronimo again, and once more he nodded fiercely. I thought I glimpsed a white man, bespectacled, through the window of one of the houses. A missionary? Then we were back at the beginning of the road. For something to do, we read the bulletin board. We learned that someone was selling some fiberglass pipe. Gas was fifty-four cents a gallon. People getting G.A. checks should report monthly this year, not at the end of the season, as before. When there was nothing left to read, we headed down to the pier.

We were both a little worried about the baidarka.

"Can you imagine what it would be like in Angoon without the canoe?" George asked. I had been thinking the same thing. The canoe was fine, of course, tied up where we left it.

It was quarter to midnight as we pulled away from Angoon. Twilight was fading, and dusk was gathering in the town. The moon was rising full, the weather was still clear, and we decided to paddle all night. We were almost out of earshot of the pier when two girls on bikes stopped there and shouted after us.

"Hey, what are you guys' names?"

"I'm George and he's Ken."

"Where are you going?"

"South. From Yakutat to the south. To Prince Rupert."

No one could think of anything to add. In the isolation of Torch Bay, George and I had lost all our small talk. We had waved good-bye and had resumed paddling, when one of the girls thought of something. "Hey, what are those sticks?"

"They're masts. For sails," George shouted.

That really exhausted our subject matter. We waved good-bye again.

There was a shortcut back to Chatham Strait through a channel south of town, and darkness overtook us as we paddled through it. The channel was narrow, and in the dark the sawtooth skyline of the spruce forest loomed above us. The moon was hidden by the trees. We turned a corner in the night and came upon two seiners anchored near shore, side by side for company. Lights were on in one wheelhouse. As we slipped by, close under the twin sterns, we heard a man's voice but couldn't make out the words. The seiners never knew we were there.

The channel opened up again. The spruce shore no longer loomed above us, and the moon reappeared above the trees. The strait was still calm. The surface was all glassy undulation. A line of reflected moons danced there, merging and pulling apart. As we left the confines of the channel, the sounds of the strait returned. They traveled even better at night. Somewhere to our left an eagle laughed its crazy falsetto laugh. Gulls complained from invisible rocks near shore. A whale was blowing somewhere ahead, and a moment later we heard seals, their noise smaller, more rapid, varied, and human than the whales'. Sometimes the seals snorted or coughed. The night waters seemed crowded, until you remembered that you were hearing everything within a compass of several miles. There was plenty of room around each sound, when you corrected for how well sound traveled here.

The moon set behind a cloud, and the strait darkened. The phosphorescence of our paddles was suddenly brighter. Each stroke sent backward a luminous pale-green ball that vortexed apart and faded.

We settled into our paddling rhythm. We had been up for twenty hours now. Our motion was mechanical. We were a little stupid from fatigue, and part of the beauty of the night was lost on us. We took turns napping but we were too tired to sleep well.

George was dozing below when I realized that a humpback was drawing close. The explosions of its lungs came increasingly louder. I had been plotting its course without thinking about it, and suddenly I knew it would intersect our own. I wondered dully what would happen if the whale was rising when our paths crossed, but I was past worrying. Then the whale blew right beside us, and the spout erupted in the moonlight. I heard the inspiration that followed the blowing. The second sound was siphonal, like air and water going down a pipe. The mist hung in the moonlight, then settled out, and I heard the whale blow again, more distantly.

I was dissatisfied. I didn't know why. The sound should mean more to me, I thought. Whales. *Whales.* The great whales. I knew there was a message, but the sound was too big, or I was too tired. It was like riding a wave with a period so great you couldn't feel the roll of it. I wanted to think clearly, but I had been paddling too long for that.

At four in the morning, four hours after the daylight had departed to the southwest, it returned in the northeast. The sky in that direction turned green. West of us the snowy peaks on Baranof

Island clarified, then turned pink. The day was on us. We paddled until eight that morning, then found a beach and headed in.

We didn't know how weary we were until that afternoon, when, trying to rise, we fell back. For the rest of the day we lay about on the beach, like driftwood cast up by the strait.

—— 33 ——

My Opinion

Resting in the wan sunlight, I thought about the Dysons, father and son.

Sometimes it seemed to me that both were caught up in a kind of ghost dance. Both were hoping, like the plains Indians of the 1890s, for resurrections of ways of life that are past recall. George hadn't realized that the day of the Indian was over; Freeman hadn't seen that the white man's day was in its twilight. George was wishful in thinking he could bring canoes back to his coast—if he really thought that—and Freeman had failed to hear the poppings and bucklings of the technological edifice upon which his hopes for the comets depended. But George's was the ghost dance I felt comfortable with.

Freeman's argument that interplanetary space is necessary as frontier was wrong, I thought. We have as many spatial frontiers on Earth as we ever did. Freeman liked to invoke Columbus ("Everything I say may well be as wrong and irrelevant as Columbus's reasons for sailing west. The important thing is that he did sail west and we do go into space.") but I could invoke Columbus too. Before that discoverer came, the Indians and the Norse had certainly come, and maybe the Irish, Egyptians, Phoenicians, and various lost tribes of Israel. It was still a new land that Columbus found.

Joe Ibach, the Glacier Bay prospector, had once rambled all through the Torch Bay country we had left behind. He ran a trapline between Graves Harbor to the south and Icy Point to the north. In a valley near Torch Bay, we had found the fragments of Ibach's skis—big wide things, more like snowshoes than the equipment of downhill skiers. We had set these relics down carefully, exactly where we found them. They were evidence that one Joseph Ibach had known this country, but in no way did they diminish its wildness for us. Ibach had died alone in his cabin in 1960, and the secrets of the country had died with him. They were waiting for us to rediscover.

Long stretches of the coastline from where we lay south to Vancouver Island were deserted now, after the busy days of dugout canoes, when small villages had stood everywhere. The country was all waiting to be known again. Most discovery is rediscovery. The best discoveries are personal, anyway, and not the kind commissioned by queens and scientific academies. The idea that Earth's landscapes have been used up in some way was, for me, peculiar.

Freeman, looking three thousand years into the future, saw Jupiter disassembled to make an energy-capturing sphere around the sun: "It seems a reasonable expectation that, barring accidents, Malthusian pressures will ultimately drive an intelligent species to adopt some such efficient exploitation of its available resources. One should expect that, within a few thousand years of its entering the stage of industrial development, any intelligent species should be found occupying an artificial biosphere which completely surrounds its parent star."

What a strange thing to expect of an intelligent species! The expectation proceeded from a theory of evolution and history very different from my own. To extrapolate, from a century or two of industrial development, three thousand more years of it was not good science. Freeman had a linear view of history, convenient for a man of his tastes, but out of date. He seemed to think that high technology was some sort of end point, that science itself had some sort of mandate. The only things enjoying anything like a mandate from evolution, as I understood it, were coelacanths, scorpions, and sharks. The only things with a mandate from history were peasants and taxes and whores. For Freeman to expect artificial biospheres around intelligent stars was no more reasonable than for the old Egyptian astronomers to have expected giant pyramids out there.

Even if one were to assume that our evolution from now on would be electronic, I thought, one would not be led to expect, from present trends, anything so ingenious as energy-capturing solar shells. One would expect a titanic amplification of rock and roll. A new, lowbrow music of the spheres. Our radio astronomers should not be listening for "$E = MC^2$" in code, or anything so elegant. They should be listening for a funk beat.

In conversation once, Freeman conceded me a number of horrible mistakes that technology had made. "But, don't you see," he urged, "we have to fix them, and we have to keep trying."

Why? I wanted to ask. I had my own theory, but could not express it to Freeman politely. Technology forges on, not from any need of the species, but from the need of certain of its more brilliant members for interesting games to play.

"Earthbound," for Freeman and those of his persuasion, is a common, sad pejorative. For me the word has a snug and comfortable sound.

Freeman has faith in the hospitality of space, and I have faith, almost equally groundless, in its inhospitality.

In speaking of Mars after the Viking landings on that planet, Ted Taylor, who dreamed with Freeman of sitting at Orion's controls on a Martian voyage, told me something that, from my faith, I choose to regard as a warning. "It seemed in prospect," Taylor said, "a much more exciting world than it turned out to be."

Even if Freeman proves right, and man's destiny is in the stars, I think we will remember the youth of our race as the best time. Through the windows of our spacecraft, Jupiter will be an inspiring *sight*, before Freeman disassembles it, but what lies out there for the other senses? I have a theory that Columbus, Erickson, and Magellan, in their old age, remembered the sand of new beaches between their toes, the winds of new continents on their faces, the strange smells, the strange calls in the forest, as much as they remembered the sights. Our sensibilities evolved on Earth, and will be most rewarded there.

But that is only my opinion.

—— 34 ——

Tyee

Three days after leaving Angoon, we rounded Point Gardner. We were out of Chatham Strait at last. We had begun to feel like prisoners of the strait, and it was good to see its wide mouth close behind us. The weather over Frederick Sound was good, but we felt too weak to cross. Our fatigue after our all-night paddle had allowed various illnesses to catch up with us. A broken blister on George's hand had infected, as had a blister and a devil's-club cut on mine, and we both had fevers. We decided to recuperate at a place called Tyee, where the chart showed an abandoned cannery.

From a mile out, George glassed the cannery pier, looking for a place to tie up. Drawing closer, we saw that the landward end of the pier had collapsed. The pier would do us no good, but we headed for it anyway. George made a small adjustment of the rudder rein, and we slipped between the pilings. Looking up at the underside of the platform, we saw sky through missing planks in it. We emerged from the coolness, George made another small adjustment of the rudder, and we ran up on the beach.

We moored to some bushes below a row of small cabins. The cannery workers had lived here, apparently. We poked around. The cabins were full of broken glass and shingles from roofs that had collapsed. We walked down a ruined boardwalk to the mess hall, a two-story frame building on pilings. Inside was one remaining table and a cast-iron stove as big as a Japanese car. The kitchen had two deep sinks and was separated from the eating room by a partition with a little window where you passed in the trays for washing. I passed in an imaginary tray. I remembered KP and the Army. I had a good idea about the kind of jokes that had been told in here, and about the frustrations. Tyee was as poignant, in its way, as Pompeii; or so I thought that day.

We walked over to the cannery buildings, where big iron engines and flywheels and pulleys rusted in place. I found these artifacts especially interesting, after Torch Bay and its absence of human things. This had been civilization, more or less. We walked outside again. The cannery, the mess hall, the row of cabins, the boardwalks, were all disappearing under thimbleberry bushes and tall flowering grasses—a fragrant demise. I like places like Tyee, but Tyee made George uneasy.

Two of the cabins had been renovated by Indian hunters from Kake, a village to the south. We knew their identity and origin from the graffiti on the walls. The hunters had put plastic over the windows and had stuffed rags into the chinks. They had turned a third cabin into a slaughterhouse, and the floor was covered a foot deep with deer bones. We picked the nicer of the renovated cabins. In it we found some Aunt Jemima pancake mix and a little rice. George cooked up the rice on the old stove. In the back room were metal cots with cardboard spread over as mattresses, and I unrolled my sleeping bag on one of them. George wouldn't use any of the several cots. He unrolled his bag on the floor with the head outside the door. He would have preferred sleeping entirely outside, but there was no place to pitch a tent. All the land was covered by thimbleberries or by ruins.

George told me, now, how sick he had been the day after our paddle past Angoon. First he had been unable to get warm in his bag, then, for the next two nights, he had sweated. "I was so sick I lay in my bag and couldn't talk. I had all those thoughts about dying in the wilderness."

I admitted, then, that the same thoughts had crossed my mind. The lymph node above my infected hand had swollen. I had begun to feel those imaginary twinges from the appendix that come the minute you go under the weather when out of the reach of doctors. George, on hearing "appendix," brightened. "I know how to take it out," he said. "That's why I kept this deer antler. You make a small hole and hook it out. That's how the Indians did it." I thanked but no-thanked him.

In the 11:30 twilight the mosquitos came in. After ignoring them for a while, I got out my tent.

The previous night, in rolling up the tent on the beach, I had trapped dozens of amphipods in the folds. Unrolling it now, I allowed them to escape. They snapped and crackled away, exploring their new surroundings. The sound diminished into the corners of the room, like a dropped handful of bird shot spreading outward. I pitched my tent on the floor, crawled in, killed the mosquitos that had entered with me, and went to sleep.

The next morning George returned from a brief exploration, anxious to leave. He had not slept well, he said. He had been kept awake by someone hammering in the forest. Investigating this morning, he had seen the print of an enormous gum boot on the beach. "Sasquatches," he told me. "Maybe they've taken to wearing gum boots to fool us." He didn't smile as he said this, and I wasn't sure he was joking. I asked if he was sure the hammering was supernatural, and not made by a woodpecker or some other animal. "No," he said. "It was a spirit. These places hold them."

We ate a quick breakfast before leaving. As I chewed, I read the cabin walls like the back of a cereal box. Most of the graffiti were in felt pen. One read, *Nov–Dec 1972. Saw 82. Killed 17. Missed 11.* Another read, *Andrew Wright missed his first deer, Tyee 1973, but intends to get his first one tomorrow.*

Studying the lettering of this second entry, I decided that Andrew Wright had not written it himself. His father had, I was almost certain. His father had written it in part to make Andrew feel better about missing the deer, in part to impress on him the importance of succeeding tomorrow.

A third graffito concluded the story. It was made out in imitation of an official proclamation, with a black felt-pen border around it.

It said, *Andrew Wright got his first deer, Nov 21, 1973*.

George was fretting over the time we had lost in Tyee, so I finished eating quickly. As we got up to leave, George added his own message to the wall.

> *Didn't hunt,*
> *Didn't kill,*
> *Came here*
> *And sat still*
>   *—Dyson, 1974*

—— 35 ——

Ravens

As the canoe traveled south, it transported George deeper into his old way of perceiving the world. He had heard the spirits hammering in the forest at Tyee, and had seen the giant impression of the sasquatch gum boot on the beach. Soon he was talking not just to seals and sea lions, but to ling cod. ("Come on fish, bite. There are two hungry people up here. We're not going to sell you. We're not going to put you in cans.") I could talk to fish too, but I could never make it sound like conversation. Some places spooked George, for no reason that I could grasp; other places seemed to charm him. His way of seeing things was somewhat different from mine. It was dramatically different from his father's.

"The picture of the world that we have reached is the following," Freeman Dyson had written. "Some ten or twenty qualitatively different quantum fields exist. Each fills the whole of space and has its own particular properties. There is nothing else except these fields; the whole of the material universe is built of them. Between various pairs of fields there are various kinds of interaction. Each field manifests itself as a type of elementary particle. The particles of a given type are always completely identical and indistinguishable. The number of particles of a given type is not fixed, for particles are constantly being created or annihilated or transmuted into one another. The properties of the interactions determine the rules of creation and transmutation of particles.

"Even to a hardened theoretical physicist it remains perpetually astonishing that our solid world of trees and stones can be built of quantum fields and nothing else. The quantum field seems far too fluid and insubstantial to be the basic stuff of the universe. Yet we have learned gradually to accept the fact that the laws of quantum dynamics impose their own peculiar rigidity upon the fields they govern, a rigidity which is alien to our intuitive conceptions but which nonetheless effectively holds the earth in place."

The atoms of Democritus, and Newton's particles of light, and Freeman's quantum fields, were pebbles on the Alaskan shores where we beached the canoe each night.

The days became indistinguishable. We pressed on south, and the straits and channels gave way to other straits and channels. In the end these became indistinguishable too. Our hands, blistered by the paddling, were painful and felt larger than life. They were patterned with salt from the seawater that ran continually down the paddle shafts. The same pattern formed every day. Going ashore only to sleep, we pushed off in the mornings upon waking. The beaches became indistinguishable. We departed them too quickly for any to feel like home. Above our morning beaches, the canoe seemed to levitate. The log rollers on which we hauled out the night before blended, in the early light, with the gray of the beach stones, and the blue canoe appeared to float eight or ten inches off the ground. It seemed a magic vessel, anxious to be on its way.

Not a day passed without whales. The sound of their blowing was always around us, like the respiration of gods. We were trespassing, but with indulgence, I felt. We were like small boys who have sneaked into Neptune's room and hear him breathing in his sleep.

There were always ravens. There was the concussion of raven wingbeats as they crossed the strait, flying over us. They always seemed to have some black business on the other side, and they made beelines over. *Whumpf, whumpf, whumpf.* There was the odd assortment of raven cries, intelligent and varied, like language. Ravens hopped over the beach stones, worrying things with their big, all-purpose beaks. Ravens cawed in the treetops, warning the forest of our approach. Ravens cocked their heads to watch us with beady, black, cynical eyes. One day forty ravens came raucously over in a flock, descended on one tree, then left it immediately for another. The passage of forty ravens was as ominous and unsettling as that of several million locusts.

In most of the mythologies of the North, Raven was both the trickster and the creator. That the Indians and Eskimos would make him trickster was easy to understand. Ravens have a lot of tricks. That the aborigines would make him creator makes sense too, after a while. There is the blackness of ravens, like the black of original night. There is the way they pop up everywhere, like the power behind things. It was a good combination, trickster and creator; it made it hard to take anything too seriously. That was a virtue the native view shared with Freeman's view of the universe. Making a stern and jealous god of Raven is nearly as difficult as forming one from quantum fields.

According to the Tlingits, whose waterways we were now navigating, it was Raven who brought light into the world. In the beginning, light was the possession of a rich man who kept it to himself. Raven determined to steal it, and he hit on a plan. He made himself small and arranged to be swallowed by the rich man's daughter. A bitter pill, it turned out. The girl became pregnant and in nine months gave birth. Her child was precocious. His black eyes were so bright they made people uneasy. The bright eyes traveled rapidly over the bundles that hung high on the walls of the rich man's lodge. When the child was old enough to move about, he crawled to a spot beneath one of the bundles, cried bitterly, and pointed up. "Give my grandchild what he is crying for," said the rich man. "Give him that one hanging on the end. That is the bag of stars." The child played with the bag, rolling it around on the floor of the lodge; then accidentally he opened it. The stars flew up through the smokehole. They scattered across the sky, arranging themselves as they are today.

The child began crying for a second bag. The grandfather resisted, until it seemed the child would cry himself to death. "Untie that next bag and give it to him," he said at last. Playing with the bag, the child found an opportunity to open it accidentally. The moon flew up through the smokehole and took its place in the sky.

Only the sun remained, and the child began begging for the bag containing it. By now the grandfather had noticed how the child's eyes moved around peculiarly and continually changed colors. He suspected that this was not an ordinary infant. With a sense of resignation he untied the last bundle and brought it down. As soon as the bundle was in the baby's arms, the baby uttered the raven cry, *Gaaa!* and flew with the sun up through the smokehole.

This was not the version Freeman taught at Princeton. But in Tlingit country, in George's baidarka, watching ravens every day, you could see how it might have been that way.

"*Gaaa!*" cried the ravens, or "*Tok!*" and sometimes George answered. Like most people who live close to the land, he is a good mimic of animals. His *tok!* is perfect. *Tok!*ing, he could pass for Raven himself.

—— 36 ——

Starbuck

Approaching Kuiu Island, we saw the patchwork pattern of clear-cutting in the forest. "I don't like logging," George said, "but it sure makes you feel at home." In British Columbia there is a lot of clear-cutting, and that patchwork was familiar to him. I hated seeing it. A short time later, still miles from shore, we smelled sawdust and gasoline. Our noses, fine-tuned after several un-polluted months in the wilderness, could detect one or two parts per billion. "It's good to smell logging smells again," George called back to me.

George's passion for the south was all-consuming. I did not share it. The baidarka's captain wanted to drive south every day; the crew wanted to linger. I had no aluminum awaiting me in Vancouver, no plans for a big canoe, and I saw no reason to rush. I wanted to explore the forest behind our beaches, or occasionally climb one of the peaks above us. George always had a reason we should not. There was always a tide we had to catch, or a bit of good weather we ought to take advantage of. To George the idea of missing a tide was heresy. I came to regard his drive to the south as monomania. I was no match for it. I played Starbuck to his Ahab, muttering a lot, but unable to deflect him.

Relations steadily soured between us. I was irritated by George's singlemindedness. He was irritated by my taking notes. He had made it clear he didn't think much of my profession. People in the North, he warned me several times, were suspicious of writers. Too many writers had come up and written exploitatively of the real people. Far too many bad books were written as a general thing. What the world did not need was another bad book. The story of the canoe had to be told right. Without ever saying so, he let me know he didn't trust me to do that, and was sorry he had ever agreed to it. Whenever my notebook was open, George's mouth stayed shut. Formerly, getting his story had been like pulling teeth; with his mouth closed even that was impossible. At our campfires he was often withdrawn and distant, as he had been years before, according to his mother, when confined on that Maine island with the compulsive marshmallow eater.

On only two occasions did George regard me with something like approval.

Once was when I retrieved a sea-lion shoulder blade that he himself had found, then discarded. Needing something to keep my duffelbag out of the dampness at the stern, I used the shoulder blade for a plank. It seemed a small thing, but George gave me a glance of surprised respect. "That's a good thing to have," he said later. "It's good to find a use for it."

The second occasion came at dinner one night. Our fishing luck had been bad, and I was hungry for protein. Remembering that I had seen the foxes of Torch Bay eat the amphipods that live under beach rocks, I collected several dozen in a jar. At first George watched me in amusement, then his look turned reflective. In his face I saw dawning a new regard for me. My attempt to imitate the foxes impressed him.

"They should taste like shrimp," he predicted. A moment later he amended that. "They'll be all shell." No matter how the amphipods turned out, one of George's statements would be right. In natural matters, George likes always to be right. I tossed the amphipods into boiling water, and they quickly turned a promising seafood red. I cooled them off, selected a fat one, and bit crisply through its chitinous shell. It tasted horrible. I couldn't remember tasting a worse bug in all my childhood. I offered one to George, who tried it and spit it out. "See, all shell," he said.

I felt guilty about taking all the little lives, so I forced myself to eat three or four. If they didn't kill the foxes, they wouldn't kill me. I scattered the remaining tiny carcasses on the beach stones. Something else would finish them.

My experiment, or its failure, brightened the evening for George. He cooked the rest of the meal in good humor. He made a pot of rice, then emptied a packet of green-pea soup on top of it. The packet was part of the stash of surplus food he had lifted from Torch Bay.

"Geez, this is poisonous-looking stuff," he said. "I'll have to take their word for it that this is food." He ruminated, stirring the soup. "It's amazing the stuff they pass off as food. It's barely enough to let you survive. Just enough to let you sit in front of a TV set."

He ruminated some more.

"I've seen so many messed-up people. And they think it's *them!*

They think it's *their* fault they can't do anything. It's the white bread they eat."

The soup was poisonous-looking, all right, but it tasted fine. George ate all of his portion, I noticed.

We pushed south. The shape of today's islands and fiords was, by the day after tomorrow, dim in my memory. The forested ridges were green or gray, depending on whether the sun was shining. When the sun broke through strongly, the colors were intense, but they clustered at the cool, blue-green end of the spectrum. There was an exception, a thin band of tropical color at waterline, where orange and purple starfish clung to the rock. We ran close to that vein of warm color, for the current was usually strongest beside the strait wall. The kelp was our current indicator. When the tide was running strong, Vs of water rippled on the downhill side of the kelp tassels. When the Vs rippled against us, we seldom tried to fight it, but pulled out or moored to the kelp and napped until the tide turned. When the Vs rippled south, George always wanted to run with them.

He didn't like to waste time fishing. When we came to a likely looking patch of kelp, or found a promising underwater rock on the chart, we would pause, but never for long. While I held a bulb of kelp to stop our drift, George would unwind his handline from its board, and the silver lure would flutter slowly out of sight. George would yank a couple of times. If there were no bites in the first three minutes, he would re-coil the line and reach for his paddle.

He mentioned one day, at the end of a fishless week, that limpits were edible. That was good news to me. I was always a little hungry now, and I was eager to try them. Passing through one shallow channel at low tide, we saw big limpits on the bottom, and George consented to stop. We rolled up our pants, stepped barefoot into knee-deep water, and began collecting. The system was to sneak a knife blade under the edge of the coolie-hat shell before the limpit sensed you and tightened into the rock. Wading, our shins and feet were pale in the icy water. They quickly went numb. We collected until our fingers too went numb and ceased working efficiently. It became difficult to surprise the limpits. Prying an alerted limpit from the rock was hard work, and we barked our fingers. I wanted to collect inefficiently for a little longer, but George was anxious to be on his way. There was a tide to catch. We sat back gingerly at the edges of our manholes, steadied the skitterish baidarka, then swung our legs in. We took up our paddles and resumed paddling south.

I might have shared George's passion for the south, I thought, if I had believed more strongly in the big canoe, the grail toward which he was paddling. But I was not sure about the big canoe. As I understood its purpose, from George's sparse hints, the super-baidarka was to rescue him from solitude. Sitting in one of its central manholes, he would surround himself with friends or family. I had encountered a similar wish before, in other solitary people. Someday they all would have a place in the country, a refuge where, around themselves as nuclei, they would gather a sympathetic group of people, and human relations would run smoothly. I had daydreamed that myself. So had Freeman. "A truly isolated, small, and creative society will never again be possible on this planet," he had written, at the beginning of his work on Orion. Freeman's place in the country was simply farther out.

But we were kidding ourselves, I thought. It would not be the way we imagined. We tended to forget how things go with people. The dream came when the runty social animal in our natures whined louder than usual, and the dominant solitary animal was forced to listen. Once we established our communal places in the country, or built our big canoes, or set up our labs in the asteroids, the solitary animal would roar again.

I suspected, too, that the big canoe was too grandiose a notion, like Freeman's plan for a space ark the size of Chicago and destined for Alpha Centauri. I suspected that the bigness was evolution in the wrong direction.

Emerging from Rocky Pass, we headed across Sumner Strait. The chart showed a village, Point Baker, on the strait's far side. We looked for the village with our binoculars and saw a number of salmon trollers clustered where it was supposed to be. We headed for the trollers. We were almost across when the tide began to rip, and we paddled hard against it. A huge flock of phalaropes was feeding in the rip, along with humpback whales. Ahead the humpbacks blew, raising spouts like those sent up by heavy artillery. One whale showed his hump, then his flukes as he sounded.

At the entrance to the cove at Point Baker stood a small island. Several children were playing on the island, and they stopped to watch us come in. One of the boys was black. He was the first black human I had seen for a long time, a solemn little boy of about six. He looked out of place, under the gray Northern sky. It didn't look healthy for him. I was easily impressed, after my weeks of wilderness, and his presence here seemed a wonderful mystery.

Point Baker seemed a metropolis. There were *dozens* of people. One motherly lady from Oregon invited us aboard her cabin cruiser. She looked at our hands and gave us salve for them. She gave us beers. It was great to be mothered, I thought. It was great to drink beer. We saw an Afghan dog, and it seemed an animal from a fable.

After fifteen minutes in town, I glanced at George. I saw that he was on edge. With a sinking feeling I asked what was wrong. He muttered that he was ready to go. I couldn't believe it; we had been looking forward to visiting Point Baker for days. "But we just got here!" I protested.

For George fifteen minutes was enough. It occurred to me then that for George the journey was the destination. Reluctantly I finished my beer. We paddled out of the harbor, passing again under the solemn gaze of the little black boy. I wondered what his story was. Now I could never know. Point Baker fell behind, and the serpent head of the baidarka once again swung south.

In Ketchikan I jumped ship. Duffelbag in hand, I waved to George as he paddled out of Ketchikan's small yacht harbor. The baidarka's thirty-one feet seemed very long with only one man in the middle of them.

For several days George continued south alone, he would tell me later. Near Prince Rupert, in Canada, he hitched a ride with an old Indian in a salmon boat. The Indian told him good stories all through that night. When they reached George's home waters, he thanked his benefactor and resumed paddling. He had decided to spend some time on Hanson Island, one of the middle rooms in his nine-hundred-mile house, and he headed there. Entering the cove where his friend Paul Spong lives, he was greeted by a pod of killer whales. He counted twenty, maybe more. The killers blew and jumped all around him, a twenty-one-whale salute. They let him know he was home.

Junk

"You've got to reduce the cost by three factors of ten," Freeman Dyson once said, in discussing the economics of space colonization. "One factor comes just by having fewer people. The second factor of ten, which is fairly easy also, is having people willing to risk their necks. The way NASA works, they can't afford a single mistake. Everything is very safe, and the expense is enormous. The safety systems are triply redundant. That's fine, if you can't afford to fail.

"For the third factor of ten, you need better technology. You can't get there using existing rockets. That's the factor of ten that Orion would have given us. That's why I'm a space cadet.

"But there are other ways.

"The way the *Mayflower* people did it was just to wait a hundred years after Columbus. Columbus was a proper government expedition. Spain and Portugal conducted the equivalent of Apollo, and a hundred years after that, you could buy a *Mayflower* secondhand. You'll be able to buy up all kinds of junk from NASA and Apollo, too. You'll find a lot of old ships that a bunch of nuts would be able to parasitize. It may even be easier in space than on Earth. In space, garbage doesn't disappear, it just lies around. It's a question of collecting it and putting it together."

George and I drove down a bumpy levee road near Vancouver, looking for a junkyard. Nearly a year had passed since our return from Alaska. On our left was flat, wet Northwestern farmland, much of it returning to brush. On our right was the logjammed river. George had not visited this particular junkyard for some time, and he was no longer certain where it was. He decided we had passed it, and he asked me to turn around. We drove back, this time with the logjams on our left. We passed scattered levee-road businesses. The pavement undulated, as pavement will do on a floodplain. George was looking for an aluminum rod and a piece of aluminum plate for a rudder.

We found the junkyard and parked outside. At the gate was a sign requesting visitors to check in at the office. George ignored it. He strode past and into the yard. Looking around him, he muttered that he didn't like the look of the place. It was much neater than the last time. That was a bad sign, he said. He began poking around in bins of scrap aluminum. He wore patched pants, a riddled sweater, and a $1.50 pair of Communist Chinese tennis shoes. Stray hair straggled out from under his wool watch cap. He looked like one of those derelicts you see poking around in city garbage cans, only sadder, because he was so young. He found an aluminum rod that looked good and he set it neatly beside the bin. We moved on.

Two men were conversing beside a mountainous scrap heap in the middle of the yard. One was wearing a business suit, the other a hard hat. The hard hat ignored us for a while, then broke off his conversation and walked fiercely our way. He was a white man but it was hard to tell, for his face and his blacksmith's forearms were sooty from his labors. His eyeballs glared white in his dark face. He was the Infernal Junkman, it seemed to me, but George stood his ground. The junkman asked what we wanted. George began describing the rod and plate he needed, when the junkman interrupted to say he didn't have it.

"Can we look around?" asked George.

"I told you we didn't have it. What's the point?"

With that, the junkman turned and walked back to his important conversation with the man in the business suit.

George made his way without haste toward the gate. "That's what always happens," he said. As soon as you found a nice junkyard, where they let you pick around and take anything you wanted for fifty cents a pound—the price they got for scrap—then inevitably they decided to go big time. They didn't want to sell little stuff any more. The neatness *had* been a bad sign, as George had suspected. A connoisseur of junkyards, he had seen it all before. The same guy had been very polite to him the last time.

George paused to pick up the aluminum rod he had stashed beside the bin. He held it beside his leg as we passed the office, not hiding it exactly, but not making it conspicuous, either. His face was impassive. He tossed the rod in my car, and we drove away. "I'll just buy that plate," he said. "I don't mind. But I felt obligated to try the scrapyard first."

—— 38 ——

A Specimen
of Intelligent Life

The path began, narrow as a game trail, at the foot of George's tree, ran uphill through the bright, tall green of salmonberry bushes, passed a small clearing and a vegetable garden, and ended at the door of his workshed. The workshed had seen a lot of weather. It stood gray and ramshackle between the spring-green of the cleared land in front and the dark evergreen of the forest behind. It was not quite twelve feet wide, but it was fifty feet long. It once had been somewhat shorter—too short to accommodate what George had in mind—so he had knocked out one end and lengthened the building. The addition was a simple framework of two-by-fours on which he had stapled clear plastic. Visible through the plastic was the battered easychair in which George did much of his thinking. The chair faced the rear of the shed, for the target of his thoughts lay within. Next to the chair was the stove that had warmed him through the past winter's work. The stovepipe ran up through the plastic ceiling, and smoke curled white against the dark forest behind.

Inside, the shed was spartan. The walls were decorated only at intervals of twenty feet or so. In the bright end of the shed were nautical charts, one of the Atlantic, one of Southeast Alaska, one of British Columbia. In the shed's shadowy middle was a black-and-white photograph of Navajo shepherds on horseback in Monument Valley. Farther on, paper templates for the work in progress hung from a nail, and across the way was a blurry black-and-white photograph of *D'Sonoqua* under sail. There was a color photograph of George's three-man baidarka, pulled high on a stone beach. There was a blueprint for a twelve-man kayak sixty-two feet long. Beside one of the twelve manholes a human figure was sketched for scale, and in its hand was one of the enormous paddles that would propel such a canoe. There was a second blueprint, this one more carefully done, of a less ambitious six-man canoe.

Beside the stove was a desk cluttered with drawings and notes. The drawings were businesslike. There were a few scribblings to test the nib, but otherwise no doodling. George had committed pen to paper only to draw kayaks in cross section, or to detail kayak parts. The notes were mostly shopping lists, and in the way of shopping lists, they spoke volumes.

Pepper	Oats
notebooks	oil
long johns	sunflower seeds
wheat	
alfalfa seeds	Insulate floor under table.

There were books. One, the *Alcoa Structural Handbook*, lay open on the desk. The others filled a shelf at the far end of the shed. *Antarctic Pilot, 1961. British Columbia Pilot, 1963. American Practical Navigator, 1962.* Wylie's *The Essentials of Modern Navigation* (1941), of which George was the third owner, to judge by the names inside the cover. *Fortunes in Formulas for Home, Farm, and Workshop, Containing Up-to-Date Selected Scientific Formulas, Trade Secrets, Processes, and Money Saving Ideas,* published by Hiscox and Sloan in 1907.

There was *The Restless Universe,* by Max Born. On the fly was a handwritten note from Dr. Chen Ning Yang, winner of the Nobel Prize for Physics. "George," wrote Dr. Yang, "I was greatly thrilled to hear from you last week that you are interested in particle physics. I recall the excitement and the sense of anticipation I had thirty years ago upon reading this book by Born. Hoping that you will enjoying this book as much as I did. I picked it up at the bookstore for you. Best wishes—Frank Yang." George had *not* enjoyed this book by Born, which Dr. Yang had sent when George was a boy in Princeton. "Those unified-field scientists are all so crazy," George says. "I have my own unified-field theory. The trouble is, you have to go through so much bullshit to learn to talk to those guys in a way they can understand. That's why I wanted that book."

There were other books, *Moby Dick, Alice in Wonderland, The Bark Canoes and Skin Boats of North America.*

And in the middle of the shed, running nearly its entire length and occupying it so widely that there remained only a slim aisle to walk around, was an enormous canoe.

It was the biggest kayak in history, a realization of the six-man model blueprinted on the wall. It was forty-eight feet long, yet not quite five feet wide. It lay upside down on a row of benches, waiting to receive a second coat of blue paint. The first coat, catching the sunlight at the bright end of the shed, glistened as if still wet. In the dimness of the shed's middle, highlights shone on a smooth dark hull.

The canoe was composed almost entirely of the three most common elements in the Earth's crust, oxygen, silicon, and aluminum. It was an abbreviated version of the planet itself. It was both more and less than it seemed. It contained just two hundred pounds of aluminum, three hundred pounds of glass and resin, two hundred of plywood and string, and one hundred sixty of spruce planking, yet these were spun into a cocoon of great strength. The six manholes were arranged with single holes fore and aft, and two pairs of holes side by side in the middle. The prow curved up into a dragon head. The aluminum tube of the keelson was filled with a few symbolic handfuls of British Columbian earth. Beneath the yew step that would receive the forward mast, cemented in place with clear epoxy, was an old gold coin minted in France. It showed Saint George slaying the dragon.

"It's totally new," George told me. "It's a new kind of consciousness. If the spaceships come, and they want a specimen of intelligent life, this is what they'll take."

The aliens would be especially interested, he predicted, once the canoe had its bubbles in place. He explained that he was going to make Plexiglass domes to cover the manholes when storms came up. At sea, passengers would look out dryly at the weather, and the domes would double as hatch-covers when George was in port. With the domes in place, the canoe would look like a huge water insect, or like a spaceship.

"It's so strong, it's ridiculous," he said. "It's much stronger than I ever thought it would be in the beginning. But each time I started something, I'd see ways to make it stronger." The canoe contained no ferrous metals and not a single nail. It was lashed by twelve thousand feet of string, any four strands of which could lift the entire boat. "The only thing in it with negative buoyancy is the fiberglass, and the spruce boards alone are enough to float that. That doesn't mean anything—everybody claims their boat is unsinkable. But it *is* strong. It's stronger in each of its parts than necessary. It's as strong as possible according to the present knowledge on this planet."

George had decided to name the canoe *Mount Fairweather,* after the white peak that had guided him to Glacier Bay, and had guarded him there, the mountain that many believe to be the most beautiful on Earth.

The canoe had begun in late summer of 1974, shortly after George had returned to Hanson Island from Torch Bay. He found a perfect Sitka spruce, windfallen, on the island, and with the help of a friend, and an Alaska Mill, he chainsawed it into planking for the floor of the canoe. This first chore was the hardest physical work he would do. The big spruce was a difficult tree to jack around, and the chainsawing was rough on his arms. It took three days and two gallons of gas. George cut into the tree without calculation, but the planks came out exactly the right length. "It was luck, or intuition, or something," he says. The boards were thirty-seven feet long. He could have cut them out in shorter lengths, but it was fun chainsawing the whole tree. "And it shows where the boards came from. Anybody who looks at that boat will know it was made near a forest. You don't get thirty-seven-foot boards anywhere else." He tapered the planks with a hand saw and sent them down to Vancouver on a friend's boat. He left them to dry through that winter and part of the spring.

In October 1974 George extended the shed. He spent a month drawing his templates, then began building in earnest. He formed the keelson first and joined the ribs to that. His aluminum was the kind used in packframes and airplanes, alloy 6061 T6, with copper, magnesium, and silicon in it. It came in twelve-foot sections that he had to splice together. He machined his own internal sleeves for the splicing, on a simple lathe that he built for the job, and he epoxy-bonded them in place. He bent the tubes into the proper curves by hand, and this took a lot of time. Next time he builds a canoe, he plans to spend a few days to make a hydraulic bending jig.

When all the tubes were bent, George haywired the frame together. In the haywire stage, he could move the various elements about easily and get them right. The wiring was fun, because the canoe took shape so quickly. Big sections of it grew every day. As he saw his idea materialize, George's confidence grew. Kids came around to check his progress—the tough, ragged kids of Belcarra Park, pale-skinned from the British Columbia winter—and George cut them small lengths from his big rolls of wire. They played happily with the wire while George labored. By Christmas the haywiring was finished and the canoe's skeleton was complete.

Flying squirrels were raiding the tree house. To get away from them and closer to his work, George moved to the workshed, sleeping in a small loft above the center of the canoe. He kept a box of clothes there, and a mattress.

For a month he lashed the canoe. Lashing, he believes, is the only way to put a canoe together. "You're not messing with the structure," he says. "Lashing strengthens, instead of providing stress points and weakness." In the lashing, as in everything, the boat was ridiculously, redundantly strong. "You could cut half of the lashings in the boat—three-quarters of them—and it would still be entirely seaworthy."

Twelve thousand feet of lashing would have been an intimidating task for one man, and for the first time in his canoebuilding, George asked for help. His neighbors responded by holding sewing bees for him. One Sunday he counted nineteen people in the shed. For the most part his assistants were the young, long-haired, wool-shirted, denim-overalled people who live marginally, like himself, in the forest around Belcarra Park. They pulled the lashing tight manually and clamped it, pulled it and clamped. "This place was like some kind of huge operating room," George says. "The sewing parties were really good parties. They got *too* good, and I had to stop them. Forty people came, and nothing got done. What was done was no good and had to be ripped out."

George lashed on alone, aided now and then by Henry, the crazy poet. Henry once spent three full days working on the hull lashings, punching in at eight in the morning and punching out at five in the afternoon. He did good, careful work and recited his poetry to anyone who happened by.

> *Frome the watters of terrestial tears*
> *Of the raindrops of the blood of soul,*
> *Frome the woumbs of the godesses of the gods*
> *Of heavean of godmother earth of godmother nature,*
> *Thee and me Aeliscahre Aumaeli,*
> *Mother, Father, one breath in all the Aeliohim*
> *Of every sun and every moon and every plannet*
> *And asteroid too,*
> *Of all the elements, Aumaeli Aumaeli. . . .*

The lashing was pleasant exercise for the hands, and not really tiring. The hard work was in George's trips to the forest to cut the firewood to heat the shed to keep his hands warm. On rising, George would cut wood for an hour to get his blood circulating. His stove was made from a forty-five-gallon drum, and he burned whole logs in it. By the time he had finished with a log, the cutting and burning, it had warmed twice.

The stove roared, the hands worked, the winter passed, the canoe quickened.

When the lashings were tied, George first washed them with acetone, then coated them with epoxy. "The boat's strength depends on the epoxies, so it has to be done right," he told me. "During epoxying, everything has to be surgically clean. No smoking, no dust, no fingers. The important thing is not to put anything into the boat that isn't having all its strength used."

In the hospital smell of acetone, George sealed the open ends of tubes, puttying them in with epoxy mixed with fillers. In places where he needed a lot of epoxy, he admixed microspheres for lightness. The idea of microspheres—microscopic glass balloons—both pleased and repelled George. They were an instance of the ambivalence he feels toward technology. Microspheres were certainly nice for making canoes, but as he worked with them he wondered how broadly the idea was being applied. Once I heard him say, as he mixed up a batch, that he thought microspheres, or their equivalent, were probably being mixed into processed foods.

George lashed the thirty-seven-foot floorboards in place with one-inch intervals between, decking the entire shallow U of the hull's cross-section. This decking would protect the fiberglass from anything sharp in George's cargo. It would warm the interior, both in color scheme and as a buffer between the paddlers and the cold fiberglass. It would keep passengers and cargo dry, in the unlikely event the canoe bottom got damp. The interval between boards would admit a sponge, if necessary. George covered the boards with six coats of epoxy, giving them a permanent shine.

He anchored the yew steps for his three masts with thirty

aluminum screws. The yew had been cut on the northern British Columbia coast. George had not cut it personally, "but Michael Berry did, which is as good as myself." Michael Berry, a neighbor of George's in Belcarra Park, is competent at many things, and is probably George's best friend.

George covered the finished frame with unbleached cotton, sewing the sheets together. The sewing went more quickly than he had expected, and in two days the job was done. He left to attend to other business, and the canoe rested, white as a seabird, for several days. While George was gone, Stewart Marshall, an artist friend, dropped by the shed. "He saw all that stretched canvas," says George, "and he couldn't resist." Marshall painted the decks and sides with designs in the Northwest Indian manner. When George returned and saw the paintings, he was angry at first, then he began to like them. He noticed that Stewart had left spaces in the design. They needed filling in. They cried out for George's own signature. (It is my opinion that Stewart left the space for other reasons, just as Michelangelo left a little space between God's outstretched hand and Adam's, but George was sure of the artist's intent, and he was, after all, owner of the canoe.) He mixed his paints and added a crab and a flounder, in a simple, cheerful manner. "I can draw, when it's something I know something about," he says, and this is true. Having added a bit of himself to Marshall's mural, George felt much better.

He wet the cotton and laid on the first layer of fiberglass. It went on wrinkled, but straightened itself in the course of the night. George was impressed. The canoe seemed to be assembling itself.

"Things like that were happening. All through the construction of the boat, things happened that made it seem predestined. Like the gold coin. The way the gold coin came along is mystifying to me."

On the day of George's birth, his mother had set aside for him a gold coin showing Saint George slaying the dragon. She had kept it all those years, then had sent it to Belcarra just in time for him to place it beneath the mast step.

"There was another thing that happened . . . it was almost too much to tell about. One night in my tree house I had a dream, very vivid. In the dream I had an aluminum flute. It was during the days I was working with aluminum, bending tubes. I've never played a flute, or any other musical instrument. In my dream I was playing it to whales.

"That next morning a guy came around who I hadn't seen for at least a year. He was a flutemaker. Once I had helped him drill a flute. I almost did a somersault, because that's all I had been thinking about that morning—the flute in the dream and how to get it made. So I gave him an aluminum tube. He'd never made a flute with aluminum before, but a week later he sent me this flute. He said it was the best flute he'd ever made. I picked it up *and I could play it.*

"That flute really helped keep the project on track," said the grandson and namesake of Sir George Dyson. "When you're putting all your energy into a canoe, it's good to have something else. I made a connection between my canoe and music. I equate flutes with whales. Because Paul Spong is always playing flutes to whales. It seems that anybody who has anything to do with whales plays flutes. When I have a flute, I think of whales.

"If nothing else works I can make a living making flutes. I can copy this one. I want to copy the dimensions of the flute on one of the tubes inside my canoe, in case I lose this one."

Often during the building of the canoe, George let himself go fallow. He sat in the easy chair by the stove, playing his flute, or sipping salmonberry tea, or just thinking. He looked through narrowed eyes at the length of canoe running at him from the dim end of the shed. From the dim end of his unconscious, ideas would come at him.

One time he was experimenting in his imagination with hydrofoil outriggers that would permit *Mount Fairweather* to sail upwind. It occurred to him suddenly that the hydrofoils might be made so you could join them together to make a dinghy. His spirit jumped at the economy and versatility of the notion. Another time, as he studied the prow's dragon head, which rested, like a great hound's, at the foot of his easychair, it occurred to him that he might install red running lights as eyes. Then he would drill into one of the aluminum tubes inside the dragon's head and connect it to the butane tank that he was going to install for cooking. The dragon's nostrils would shoot a flame twelve feet long. "Out at sea, at night, people wouldn't know *what* made that," he told me later.

Sometimes after a day's work, George slept in the canoe. He found the curve of the spruce floorboards perfect for sleeping. He did not have to lie curled up, as he did in his treehouse, but could stretch out six times over. Occasionally George worked inside the canoe late into the night. His shop lamps shone through the fiberglass, illuminating the deck paintings like stained glass. It was, he says, unbelievably beautiful. He wondered how the paintings would look at sea, illuminated by the moonglow of phosphorescence.

———— 39 ————

Streets of Longing

Mount Fairweather was to be launched on June 21, 1975, the summer solstice. A month later, if all went well, George was to be reunited with his father. Both men had decided they were long overdue for that. The accomplishment of the big canoe, I was convinced, had a lot to do with George's readiness. The reunion was to take place on Hanson Island. The big canoe was the vessel that would convey George there, both physically and psychically.

George hurried to finish her in time. He accepted my offer to help, which surprised me, for I knew the small regard he held for my mechanical ability. His surrender, more or less cheerful, to the idea of interdependence was new to me and seemed to mark a fresh chapter in his life.

I drilled holes for lashings in the rudder plates. The drill was dull. It had lived a long life. George's philosophy is not to buy tools, but to build his canoes with whatever chances to come his way. The drill just happened along, like his welding glasses and his grinder. He bought only a file, some sandpaper, and a few other small items. I leaned my weight on the drill to compensate for its dullness, using a stump as a workbench. The day was warm and I worked without my shirt. The aluminum was bright under my knee and steadying hand, and the sun scintillated from the circular buff marks. Delicate whorls of aluminum flew from the drill and littered the ground. The whorls of metal were mixed evenly with whorls of wood, for after completing each hole, the drill bit into the stump.

George emerged from the shed, dressed for painting. He was frightening. He wore an old, once-white shirt buttoned to his throat, and pink rubber gloves, and the old-fashioned welder's goggles with blinders on the sides. There was a scarf on his head and his beard was wild. He looked like an insane moonshiner or a mad backwoods scientist. He asked me to break off my drilling and help him apply the second coat to the canoe.

We applied the paint with rollers. When we finished, Stewart Marshall's abstractions still showed through clearly, as if through a blue watercolor wash. George was happy about that, but confided that the paintings eventually would have to go. He planned to sail to Hawaii someday, and blue would be impossible for such a trip. He would have to paint it over with opaque white, to keep it cool. He regretted the necessity, but function came first. The nemesis of fiberglass is the sun, and the ultraviolet had to be kept out of the fibers. A consolation was that Stewart's art would continue to show inside. At tropical noon, the interior of the canoe would become a cathedral, the light streaming through Stewart's stained glass.

When it came time to sand the second coat, George changed his costume somewhat, shifting the scarf to his face, bandit-style, and covering his head with a paint-flecked wool cap. His big nose protruded above the scarf. He now looked like a mad Arab scientist. He always did the sanding alone, not wanting to inflict on anyone else the particles of fiberglass and paint that filled the shed.

When the sanding was done, he stripped off all his clothes, became the essential George again, and disappeared into the sauna.

Later George sat in his easychair, set a plywood board on his lap, took out a circular slide rule, and did some figuring.

"You look like your father's son," I said.

He smiled. "This is the only calculation I've made for this boat," he mused, and he explained that he was figuring the ellipse for the Plexiglass bubbles. He had designed the manholes, and the bases of the bubbles, as ellipses, so that the bubbles would fit inside when it came time to stow them. He made a measurement with a fragment of an old tape measure, then made a notation on the plywood. "I did this boat without a real tape measure," he said, and he smiled slowly at his own eccentricity. "It was a real hassle, too."

I asked him if he ever detected in himself the mathematical heritage that had come from both parents. "Yes," he said. "The perfection of the canoe is a manifestation of it. The desire for perfection in this canoe."

His calculations complete, George sketched the ellipse on the template of the plywood.

Freeman was on George's mind.

"Do you remember that photo I sent you?" he asked me.

I remembered. In April he had sent a photograph of the canoe in its haywire stage. Skinless, the canoe had looked like one of those reassembled skeletons of aquatic dinosaurs, or of whales. "Yep," I answered.

"I sent a print of that to my father. But that's the only one I sent. I don't know—is it a good one? Does it give a good idea of what's happening with this boat?"

As he put the finishing touches on *Mount Fairweather*, George thought a lot about children. There was a new batch of babies in Belcarra that season, and posterity was on his mind. It was important to have children when you were young and flexible, he told me. He himself was twenty-two and he was beginning to get uneasy. The big canoe, he believed, would be a safe place for children. They could crawl around on the smooth spruce floor under the covered deck. There were none of the dangers that you had in open boats.

I imagined how it would be for George's children. Stewart's Northwestern abstractions and George's crab and flounder would be the painted animals on the long crib of the canoe. The little Dysons would learn to paddle before they walked. They would grow strong on salmon and brown rice and berries. The grand-children of Freeman and Verena would learn the mathematics of the tides. The great-grandchildren of Sir George Dyson would play on aluminum flutes to humpback whales. It all sounded fine to me, though I thought George should get a woman first.

On June 19, two days before the launch, I visited the shed and found it empty. George was off babysitting, again. The Belcarra people recognized his rapport with children, and he was in heavy demand. With the launch only two days away, and the canoe still unfinished, I wondered at his priorities. I lit the burner under the coffeepot, and while it heated I poked around.

Stopping at his bookshelf, I opened a volume called *Communication with Extraterrestrial Intelligence*. It was an account of the conference his father had attended in Armenia. The fly was inscribed, *To George from Freeman, Christmas '73*. Turning the pages, I came to a discussion in which Marvin Minsky, an expert in computer intelligence from MIT, observed, "It is probably easier to communicate with a Jovian scientist than with an American human teen-ager." Freeman must have agreed with that, I thought.

I moved to George's cluttered desk and glanced at the papers on it. Among his sketches of canoe ideas and his shopping lists were typewritten notes to himself. Most were fragmentary. George had preserved them, just as he preserves in conversation bits of aborted sentences and pieces of ideas. In discourse he prefers the elliptical to the well-thought-out.

One fragment went: "I have a great and well-founded fear of these cold northern waters, and a respect for the fatal consequences to be met in a very few minutes, [a respect] that grows with the occasional taste of icy spray or bootful of green ocean water. This fear has rarely come to me in my canoe but shows up often at times . . ."

And that was all. The fragment ended.

Shuffling through, I found one paragraph that was complete: "I am once again among those streets of longing—for the fresh sea air, the open hills and forests, and the nourishment and shelter that the richness of the wilderness provides for me. I am, however, among friends: but what are friends in a city of five hundred thousand? Where is the room to feel the one true soul among all these others?"

—— 40 ——

Launch

The third planet, making its old rounds, approached the point on the ecliptic at which its northern pole tilted most sharply toward the sun. Its dark side rotated toward the star, and daylight fell on the inlets and archipelagos of British Columbia's long, fractured coast. At first light on the solstice, the land was lost under the white of rainclouds, but as the longest day lengthened, the whiteness burned off. The launch day turned bright and propitious, and the people gathered. By early afternoon there were fifty celebrants in the yard. The new arrivals greeted George, entered the shed to admire the canoe, then went out to take the sunshine.

The hair was long, both on men and women. Most of the men were bearded. There were plaid shirts in quiet colors and embroidered smocks. There was much wool and unbuttoned raingear. Some people came in bare feet and some came booted. There were several babies in crocheted carriers, slung Indian style against their mothers' breasts. Children old enough to walk did so very freely, and several dogs explored with them. Somehow it was never noisy. Even the dogs were well mannered, showing polite interest in one another. George's people made a gentle tribe. There was wine and beer, and several joints circulated, but no one partook heavily. The people had the canoe today, and the summer solstice, and a rainless afternoon in British Columbia. None of these required artificial aids to appreciation.

A girl in overalls approached George with a rose and tried to stick the stem in his wool cap. He grinned broadly through this operation, which ended unsuccessfully. The rose would not stay, so the girl just handed it to him.

Henry the poet arrived, in a Greenpeace T-shirt and an old tweed jacket. He wore a leather headband and his gray hair fell to his shoulders. In his hard ex-longshoreman's hand he carried the manuscript of a poem he had begun the night before in honor of the canoe. The top page was in green ink, and there was a whole sheaf of pages under it. Henry is prolific. "I was working on this at daylight," he said. "Did you feel my presence?"

"Well," said George, smiling. "It was raining."

The playful irony did not bother Henry. "The raindrops are the angels' tears," he said.

A young woman arrived, and Henry embraced her. He held her for half a minute, rocking gently from side to side, his eyes closed beatifically. This was to be his style with all the females at the party. His craziness had some advantages. "George will slay the old dragon again," he predicted, as he signed the makeshift guest book. "The Rome-Rockefeller-Disraeli crowd is the dragon now."

I wondered if he meant "Israeli." Either way, it seemed an odd coalition.

The canoe was upside down on its rack. At a given moment the bottom halves of four or five people showed under it, heads and shoulders inside the hatches, like kids at holes in a circus tent. I found an unoccupied manhole and poked my head inside. The canoe's spruce floor, with its six coats of epoxy, made a polished blond ceiling. The interior was full of blue light. Between the six manholes there were three conversations going. The nearest pair of manholes were discussing the strength of the fiberglass.

"You could hit it with a hammer, and nothing would happen."

"Well. Not very hard."

"George says you can."

"Well. You could drop a hammer on it, I'll bet."

A man in a ponytail joined us, sticking his head inside. He held George's aluminum flute. He put it to his lips and began to play, and the notes resonated beautifully inside the blue chamber of the canoe. "Oh wow!" said a young man. "Oh no!" said a young woman.

I ducked out of the canoe. I saw George gesture with his cup at his friend Michael Berry. "Do you notice anything funny about drinking ginseng tea out of a Styrofoam cup?" George asked. "East meets West."

George's sister Katrina arrived with their mother, who had flown in from Alberta, where she was now teaching. Katrina entered with animation, passing a huge bouquet across the canoe to George. Dr. Huber-Dyson entered more quietly. She seemed preoccupied. She and George did not touch, but they smiled at each other.

When Henry the poet learned Dr. Huber-Dyson's identity, *he* hugged her. She is an attractive woman with a lot of Old World elegance. "Bless you," he said with much feeling, holding tight. "Bless you. Bless your indwelling soul." Dr. Huber-Dyson looked uncomfortable. She stood an inch or two taller than Henry, and was a bit stiff in his frayed-tweed embrace.

A man named Dave stood at the stern, stroking the hull. He was, I learned, a fiberglass instructor at a Vancouver night school, and he had assisted George in the fiberglassing. I asked what he thought of the canoe. "It's fantastic," he said. "As a one-of-a-kind, there's nothing like it." I asked if the canoe was strong. "*Strong?*" he said. "When you figure that the tensile strength of the aluminum is from forty to sixty thousand pounds per square inch, and the strength of the glass fiber is around twenty-two thousand pounds per square inch . . . yes, it's strong. It's not only tough, but the fiberglass flexes. The boat is flexible when it hits something."

"Like a sharp, pointed rock?" I asked. Dave wasn't sure about that. "It would take a fall of twenty-five feet," he guessed.

Near us a man was enumerating the strengths of the canoe. ". . . and the lashings are nylon, which allows some play. You could drop this boat off a thousand-foot building, and nothing would happen to it."

"Nothing," agreed Dave.

"That's something I'd like to see," said the enumerator. It would have been a spectacular demonstration, all right.

At the foremost of the six manholes, someone was explaining the canoe, and George's plans for it, to a middle-aged woman. "It's beautiful," she agreed. "But how will he find five people who want to go in the same direction?"

Outside in the sun, Henry was reciting poetry to anyone who passed within range.

> *Aeli Schaum, Aeli Schare, Aeli Aeli,*
> *Aeli of all the Aelioihim of every tribe in Heaven,*
> *On earth and sea and air all breathe,*
> *Aeli make thy presence known to all from first to last*
> *Who has played a part in the building*
> *Of George's kai yahk kahnew. . . .*

I asked Henry if I could read his poem, and he gave me the manuscript as a present. He was tired of carrying it around, he said. It was all in his head, anyway.

The poem was twenty pages long. Some pages were in green ink, some in blue, some in red. Henry printed everything in capital letters, with no punctuation. His lines did not scan, but ended whenever he ran out of room. The poem itself ended similarly, simply stopping in the middle of a sentence. Henry produces poetry the way a factory loom produces fabric—by the yard, and it can be cut off almost any place.

Very little of the verse was actually about George's canoe. Most of it was angry and political: "I wish that all of the greedy gluttonous paricitical death dealing warmongers of corporate pimps at the whores convention of the tax and proffit babilonion seduction of the money credit system that would let all perish for there gold and graven immiages on there dollar bills that is not even worth as much as a quacking duck or a crowing hen for both of these feed a starving man . . ." and so on.

I found only one reference to the canoe, a line in which Henry alluded to his work on the lashings: "Aeli did bless every knot that I did tie while I did breathe the breath of spirit . . . the very breath of love divine returns to all this day and forever more that looks upon George's kah yahk . . ."

I asked Henry what language his "Aeli" and "Oumaeli" came from. No special language, he answered. Those words went back before Babylon, way back to Atlantis, and to Lemuria, the lost continent of the Pacific. Atlantis and Lemuria went down together in sin, much as the North American continent was going down now.

"It's just like automatic writing," Henry said of his poetry. "You've heard of automatic writing? It comes into my head and I write it."

I looked for George and found him in the shed with Michael Berry, discussing his next move. Before he went anywhere, he said, it would first be necessary to cut his sails or make paddles, then find some crew. As if on cue, a small boy entered *carrying a paddle*. The good-ominous quality of that was lost on nobody. George and Michael Berry exchanged glances.

"Hey!" said George to the boy. "Let's go! Where do you want to go?"

The boy had no immediate ideas. Instead he studied the canoe. "This is a neat color," he said.

"You like it?" asked George. "Tell me." He was eager for the boy's opinion, as he never was for an adult's.

George began disassembling the prow end of the shed. He pulled back the plastic wall, then hammered out the two-by-four crosspieces. He stationed people around the canoe, fifteen to a side. Using a system of slings he had devised for turning the canoe during construction, he and the crowd turned the hull right-side up. Then, at his signal, with a great cheer, the canoe lifted. As it came off its braces, there was a loud popping from the stern. The canoe was adjusting to the change in stresses. The people winced at the noise and hesitated, and seeing that, George grinned broadly. "Don't worry, it's strong," he said. He had not doubted for an instant the strength of his creation.

With whoops and children's high-pitched yells the crowd set off. They marched like Christian soldiers under the battering-ram of the great kayak. The procession was too big for everyone to fit under the hull, so many flanked it, some shooting pictures. It was exactly the kind of human enterprise that drives dogs hoarse with ecstasy, and a band of them ran furious figure-eights around and through the bearers' legs. Two more cautious dogs kept their distance, barking with a high sense of injustice, as if at some great animal revived from the Triassic just as a trick on them. Ravens flapped off their branches and sailed away through the trees, cawing. Their wings showed very black, even in the deepest shadows of the forest.

George directed things unobtrusively. There was a rose in his cap—someone had figured a way to make it stick there. A matching rose bloomed in the forward mast hole. George's mother shot some photographs—she no longer seemed preoccupied—and then she waded in and put her shoulder under the canoe. Henry led the way, chanting in a pre-Babylonian tongue and waving a feather fan given him by Ben Rose, the head shaman at a big convention of one hundred and fifty tribes at Bragg's Creek, Saskatchewan, where Henry had been made an honorary shaman. From time to time he glanced back to see if anyone noticed the figure he cut.

After a hundred yards on the gravel road, the canoe turned left down a dirt path leading to the water. Salmonberry bushes impinged on either side, and the canoe passed with much rasping of twigs and snapping of branches. Its movement was liquid. The bobbing motions of our forty disparate strides worked to cancel each other out, and the canoe glided smoothly, as if already on the water. The dragon head, riding high above the head of the tallest bearer, moved imperially through the dappled sunlight of the forest.

The people in front, who had to swing the prow each time the path turned, called back for less speed. Their requests were polite until they came to the bridge; then they got fierce. "Slow up! We're on the bridge!"

As the canoe left the bridge, the bearers began drumming on the sides. They made a savage din. The canoe broke thunderously out of the forest and onto the park lawn, where the Kingsway Frozen Food Company was in the middle of a picnic. A softball game was in progress, and the players turned and watched us. Henry, our holy point-man, had begun to slacken his step, but now he straightened, waved his fan more smartly, and chanted louder. I saw him sneak a glance at the picnickers, checking his effect on them.

We set the canoe down in the grass above the water, and Henry began a benediction. It started well:

"God bless everyone who has tetched this canoe. I drink a cup of love to this canoe. Blessed the miners of the bauxite that made the aluminum for this canoe; blessed the petrochemical workers that produced the fiberglass resins for this canoe; blessed the textile workers that made the cloth for this canoe; blessed the . . ."

After a while, though, the benediction began to become Henry's unending chant, and everyone had heard that before. We listened stolidly. Energy began diffusing from the event. Then a dog named Squirt jumped up on the canoe, and the interruption provided a sort of beachhead. Several other dogs followed Squirt's lead—they seemed to like the scratching sound their nails made on the buffed wax of the deck—and one of the men brought out a bottle of champagne. The cork popped very high, and the crowd cheered. The man handed the bottle to Henry, who accepted it—a little resentfully, for he understood its purpose. He stepped out of the limelight.

"Don't laugh at an old fool," I heard him say. "An old fool may be wiser than you."

Emotion still ran high in the dogs, and with no moving canoe to chase, a fight broke out. Henry watched it with interest.

We carried the canoe down to the water. The prow ploughed into Indian Arm, and a second champagne cork popped. People climbed aboard, carrying an odd assortment of paddles and oars.

Mount Fairweather was about to take off on its maiden voyage when someone noticed that George was not aboard. I was astounded that he would pass up this first trip. I decided that the sacrifice was a kind of gift to the people. But the people prevailed upon him to go, and he joined the first group. Barefoot and grinning, he straddled the narrow stern and paddled off. The boat was as overloaded as a Ganges ferry. Passengers were sitting two and three to a manhole and were clinging to the decks, yet the canoe rode high on the water. It did look smaller now, however. *Mount Fairweather* did not fill the ocean the way it had filled the shed.

Later, standing on the deck of the Belcarra Park snackbar, George watched as a third canoeload of passengers set out.

"It's a canoe," he said meditatively. "It's a system everybody can handle, you know?"

He studied his canoe.

"The lines are all right. You don't know until it's in the water. It'll look better when it's not riding so high. With a thousand pounds of fresh water, a thousand pounds of groceries . . ."

"Take it easy," said Henry, who was leaning on the rail beside him. "Go slow, George."

I rested my own elbows on the rail, next Henry's, and I watched the dragon head breasting the waves and the slim body following behind.

"On Loch Ness it would create a sensation," I said.

George nodded. "It's almost a biological organism."

When the last passenger had disembarked, we pulled the canoe up on the beach, and the party adjourned to the lawn above. It had been a long day, full of people. For a little solitude, I walked back down the path toward the shed. The path was very quiet. The day in the forest was, as usual, darkling an hour before the day outside. The path was littered with twigs and the green, maple-shaped leaves of salmonberry. The canoe's rough passage had brought a false autumn to the path. I reached the shed, and it now seemed very big and empty inside. The door stood open, and Styrofoam cups lay around. I headed back to the park lawn and the party.

The celebration was winding down. I poured a cup of wine and walked down for a twilight look at *Mount Fairweather*. A red-haired boy of about nine was sitting on a drift log above the canoe, alone with it. He had posted himself like a guard.

"Did George ask you to watch it?" I asked.

"I wanted to watch it," he replied.

I sat on the other end of his log, and together we watched the great canoe.

VI

La Jolla

After the launch, I drove down to La Jolla, California, where Freeman Dyson was attending a symposium. Freeman had completed the western leg of his journey toward his son. At the conclusion of the symposium he would travel the northern leg. Driving south, I felt like an emissary between them.

The wet skies and coniferous forests of George's country fell behind, and after three days driving I entered the desert of Freeman's country. The Southern California coast near La Jolla was new to me, a strange terrain of tawny, sunbaked hills, each crowned feudally by an aerospace lab. One of these labs was General Atomic, where Freeman had worked on Orion. After the Ice Age look of George's glacial inlets, Freeman's twenty-third-century hills were unsettling. I thought I liked George's country better, but I approved of being warm and dry.

Freeman and his colleagues at La Jolla were working on a classified problem for the Navy. The proceedings were secret, so I had to talk with him after work. We met at his hotel. I was shocked, again, by his resemblance to his son. He was a smaller, neater, slightly paler version. He asked for news of George, and I gave it. I delivered a message—that Freeman was to bring one of George's sisters to the reunion, if at all possible. Then we walked at Freeman's brisk pace to the Jolly King restaurant next door.

"I'm not a gourmet," he said. "I live on hamburgers. I hope you don't mind."

I didn't mind, personally, but I winced when I imagined

George's reaction. He would not be pleased by his father's diet. This evening Freeman ordered, as usual, the Jolly King "combo" hamburger and a Coke. *Brain food*, I thought.

As we waited for our quarter-pound patties of slaughtered steer, shot through with steroids and chemicals, undoubtedly, and enriched with microspheres, Freeman sat very erect and still, like a man listening for a small noise. This was not likely what he was doing, for the Jolly King was full of clatter and conversation, and we were talking ourselves. The attentive look was a sham, I decided. Freeman was practiced at setting his body in a neat, alert posture at the table—a good safe place—and wandering off. He would return occasionally to animate his hands or eyes. He spoke with vestiges of his British accent, diluted by thirty years of exposure to American English and by some other influence I could not identify. German? Freeman speaks that language and he had just returned from a year at the Max Planck Institut für Physik und Astrophysik in Munich. He spoke slowly, pausing often to follow a thought or search for a word. In the red vinyl booth of the Jolly King, the physicist was wildly out of context. He looked as peculiar there, in his way, as George would have looked in his L. L. Bean hat and gum boots. Freeman, who is not quite of this Earth, was not of the Jolly King at all.

I asked about his role at the symposium. He had an idea, he answered, for unscrambling the sounds of the sea in search of submarines. "The sea is a . . . difficult, distorting medium," he said. "I want to find out what you can learn about submarines from their sound. If you can unscramble . . . Well, about all you can do now is put hydrophones in and listen."

Freeman was preoccupied at the symposium by thoughts of submarines and military strategy, and here in the Jolly King he began thinking them aloud.

"The really bad decisions, I think, were made in 1930, long, long ago, when it was decided to go in for bombers in a big way. It's been going on ever since. An offensive strategy. If we'd had a defensive strategy, we would also have had a navy which would have been not so much interested in fighting wars all over the world.

"World War II, I think, has never been understood. For ten years after World War II, everybody thought it was great. It was a grand crusade against the powers of evil, and so on. Now there's a sort of feeling that it was actually a pretty disgusting business. But nobody really understands why it went bad."

"Why did it go bad?" I asked.

"*Because of this bombing!*" said the former RAF mathematician. "It wasn't even an effective weapon. Without it we would have ended up with a clean victory and not a dirty one. It would have left the world with a tradition of fighting in a somewhat more clean fashion. I don't think we would have used a nuclear bomb."

"And you hate submarines, too."

"Yes. U-boats—subs. They have a thoroughly bad history. I mean, ever since they've been invented, they've been used for bad purposes. They never did any good to anybody. They cost the Germans World War I, in a way."

"By bringing the Americans in?"

"Yes. It was the same stupid business. It was technically so good. They had these submarines that could sink ships right and left, so they just sank all sorts of ships."

There was, said Freeman, a dangerous Dr. Strangelove aspect to submarines. Missile subs were isolated, unnatural environments, with crews subject to all sorts of claustrophobic pressures, and the captain was king. A sort of collective insanity was possible.

"It's a typical example of a weapon that's tactically good but strategically terrible. I think submarines will always be like that. It's the same with this stupid missile submarine. You see, it *looks* lovely. The U.S. has forty-seven missile boats, the Soviet Union has fifty-three, or whatever it is. We have these hundred submarines cruising the oceans, and it's all very fine. They have this beautiful deterrent. The Russians will never shoot, for if they do, they know their country will get wiped out. But suppose you wait a little longer, and you have five or six different countries with these submarines, and then somebody starts firing them at you. How do you know who the hell it was? Anybody can start that. The deterrent doesn't work."

I asked Freeman if he could explain, simply, his new idea for detecting subs in a noisy sea. He laughed and shook his head. "No. It's mathematics. It's my trade." It was also, I found out later, a military secret.

"My real interest in this sort of thing," he confessed, "is in its application to astronomy." He explained that the big problem with earthbound optical telescopes was turbulence in the atmosphere. He had an idea for a new sort of telescope. Its mirror would be rubbery, so it could be wiggled about. Television would record the image and feed it into a computer, which in a hundredth of a second would alter the mirror's shape, correcting for the atmospheric distortion.

A woman in the next booth was listening. Catching snatches of our conversation about subs and computers, she had tuned in her own unscrambling apparatus. I saw her glance curiously at Freeman.

"My task now is to get the astronomers interested," he said. "Then in five years or so it might come about. There is no interest yet in the United States. But the Russians are very interested. As a matter of fact, I got an invitation from the Russians just the other day. They have a new observatory in the Caucasus. I'll be leaving in November."

The woman looked sharply at Freeman. We were in John Birch country, I remembered. The woman saw a strange, large-nosed scientist with an odd accent conferring with a young bearded man in wire-rimmed spectacles. We must suddenly have looked very much out of context indeed.

"So you're going over to the other side," I said to Freeman. We laughed. The woman looked at us in alarm.

The next afternoon we sat in the same booth. We ate the same "combo" hamburgers. Freeman had brought along the paperback he was reading during breaks in the symposium, and I asked for a look at it. It was an interlinear version of *Slaughterhouse-Five*.

We ate our hamburgers, drank our Cokes, and spoke of a number of things. I answered Freeman's questions about my travels in the Brooks Range of northern Alaska. He asked if I had ever seen igloos. I had not. Eskimos don't build igloos in Alaska anymore. I told him a little about the canoe trip down from Glacier Bay with George, and he told me about Orion.

Toward the end of his Orion period, I learned, the people at General Atomic had offered Freeman a job—a vice-presidency, with stock options. Apparently a brain like Freeman's meant a whole franchise; it was like signing O. J. Simpson or Abdul-Jabbar. "If I had taken it, I would have had three swimming pools by now, living like a real Californian," said Freeman. "That was my chance." I studied his face for traces of irony, or for real regret, but I couldn't read anything there.

He told me that the Orion men had not been totally inattentive to detail in the interior design of their ship. They had given some thought to space suits, but these they would have worn only during the trip. When they got to their destination, they would have built themselves a habitation in which suits were not necessary. "We thought a good deal about what we would do when we got there. We had a definite picture of the icecap on Mars as being a good place to start. Partly for the reason that you could dig into it and make big caves."

"That's why you asked me about igloos?"

"Yes." He smiled. "It's remarkable how easy it is to build igloos. My children build igloos in Princeton sometimes. And it actually works. It welds itself together so beautifully. Only in Princeton it doesn't last very long."

I asked if the Orion people ever laughed at themselves.

"Yes. It was impossible to take the whole thing seriously, all of the time."

Freeman admitted that Orion's shock absorbers might have presented problems. "The shock absorbers were the guts of the ship. And shock absorbers are not usually built in that size." He laughed at the understatement. "They would likely have been a big snag for the engineers." He admitted, too, that lubricating the pusher plate between explosions might have been a problem. "I don't know if it would have worked in real life. A half second was too short a time to spray it well. I preferred just letting the pusher plate ablate—but not too much, of course."

His thoughts strayed away for a moment, then returned.

"Again, it's the question of the *Mayflower*. When the time came, when the ship was all ready to go, we would suddenly think of all the things we had forgotten. I'm sure we would have had just the same kind of scramble at the last minute that the pilgrims had. Those people were frantically arguing about how they were going to buy their provisions, and so on, only a few days before they were supposed to sail. I'm sure it would have been like that with us too."

We spoke then of Orion's lift-off. The awesomeness of that spectacle came home to us, and we laughed. It was the same kind of crazy laughter that comes when you roll a boulder off a cliff, or light a cherrybomb under a can. (*Kaboom!* Haw, haw.) If it was comedy, it was comedy that made no sense. I suggested to Freeman that our laughter was some sort of pre-rational Big-Bang atavism, and he seemed to agree. He nodded, anyway.

"It would have been quite a ride," he said, and laughed again. "It was during that time that I took the kids to Disneyland. We went on all the rides, but I couldn't find one that felt like Orion."

Freeman's laugh was identical to George's. Laughing, both Dysons drop their chins to their chests and look out under their eyebrows at you, shyly, like small boys testing jokes. The laugh is silent but the shoulders shake. Could George have *learned* the trait? I didn't think so. The laugh seemed to come straight from the genes.

In the adjoining booth a man and his wife were drinking their coffee. The man was large and fit, with a healthy head of gray hair, and he sat in the same seat occupied yesterday by the woman who thought Freeman was going over to the Russians. The man heard Freeman mention teaching.

"You're a professor?" he asked, across the low partition. His accent was Midwestern.

"Yes," said Freeman, who turned toward the man with a small, blank smile.

"A professor of what?"

"I'm a professor of physics."

"Physics," the man repeated, raising an eyebrow. "Where do you teach?"

"Princeton."

"*Princeton*," the man repeated. (*"Camelot,"* his inflection said.) "That's where Einstein was, wasn't it?"

"Yes."

"Tell me, is physics a pretty tough course?"

"It . . . it depends. For people who have the talent, it's not difficult. For some people it's totally impossible."

"For you it's not difficult."

"No."

"Let's see, what's the law of physics? 'For every motion there's an equal and opposite motion'?"

"Very good."

"And, 'An object in motion tends to stay in motion'?"

"Yes. More or less."

The man from the Midwest looked pleased that these verities had gone unchanged, or that he had remembered them right.

"Tell me," he said. "I've heard that when Einstein was in Princeton, he would have two colleagues with him whenever he went down the street. He would work only in a large, empty room with a blackboard and nothing else. Is that true?"

"I don't know. It could well be true. I didn't know Einstein."

That satisfied Freeman's questioner, who nodded as if the Einstein story had been verified. He and his wife finished their coffee, rose, and wished us good-bye.

When they were gone, Freeman said, "I wish I had gone over to see Einstein. I was much too shy." He told me about Helen Dukas, an old family friend in Princeton. She had been Einstein's secretary and later George's babysitter and honorary grandmother. She still visited the Dysons regularly for Sunday tea. "A very bright woman," he said. "She was Einstein's personal secretary and general factotum for thirty-five years. She is very competent—commensurate with the task, which was considerable. Helen tells me that I should have gone over to see him—Einstein would have enjoyed it."

Our coffee came. I asked a question I had been saving for a good moment. Would Freeman mind my being present on Hanson Island for his reunion with George? He thought about it briefly. "That will be fine," he said. "It might even be better to have someone else there. There won't be much happening, though—there isn't enough time. This will be just to break the ice."

I asked Freeman if he approached the reunion with any trepidation. He did not, he answered quickly. Our checks came.

"Tell me," I said, as we rose. "I understand that during Orion, you insisted on working alone in a large room, with nothing in it but a huge blackboard. Is that so?"

For an instant Freeman looked at me as if I had gone mad. Then he remembered our neighbor, and laughed the Dyson laugh.

I was oddly pleased that he had not computed my joke instantaneously. I had stumped him for a moment. It was not a fair competition, I suppose, but it allowed me to think that in certain mental processes I was not quantum leaps behind him.

That night we ate at the Jolly King again. There was a Chicano family in the next booth, this time. They spoke together in Spanish and asked Freeman no questions about Einstein. Neither were they worried about his imminent defection to an observatory in the Caucasus.

Again our talk rambled. Freeman spoke about the NASA style and Apollo. He didn't think the taxpayers had got much for their Apollo money. Then he told me about the TRIGA reactor that he and Ted Taylor had helped design. The reactor's remarkable safety was the result of something called the "hot-neutron effect," which he explained to me. TRIGA had been a great commercial success, and fifty-seven of the reactors had been sold. The idea for Freeman's own contribution to TRIGA had come, he said, when he was walking down La Jolla Boulevard, just outside a Mexican restaurant.

While he spoke of TRIGA, Freeman's mind had been busy with Apollo, apparently, for suddenly he skipped back to it.

"I'm as old as Slayton. Maybe there's time left. For that one thing, I forgive them the idiocy."

In the next booth, a boy of about six, the youngest member of the Chicano family, sat across the partition from Freeman. Something about the physicist interested him, and he turned his dark, Indian eyes in Freeman's direction. He did not look directly at Freeman. It was more Freeman's voice, I decided. I had the crazy, fleeting notion that this boy was an incipient physicist and he was absorbing some kind of knowledge from Freeman's tone. There was some lesson, unconscious maybe, coded in the amplitude of Freeman's soundwaves, or in the periodicity of his sentences.

Freeman felt the boy's eyes and turned. The two exchanged shy smiles.

Freeman and I talked for a while, then Freeman did a strange thing. The boy had been resting his brown hand on the partition between booths. Freeman's hand came up of its own accord and laid itself alongside. Man and boy gravely studied their two hands, side by side, then Freeman abruptly withdrew his.

The boy's father glanced at Freeman, puzzled. Freeman himself looked surprised. We were all confused, I think, except for the boy. The boy seemed to have noticed nothing out of the ordinary.

The next day Freeman and I walked down the La Jolla beach. A section of sand, far north on the bay's curve of cliffs, is set aside for nude swimming and sunbathing. I had brought no swim trunks, so we walked there. Freeman had made the hike several times before,

225

in training for the reunion with George. He believed he would need to be fit, and he was conscientious about getting exercise every day.

We passed under the tall wooden pier that serves Scripps Institute of Oceanography, and we waded several shallow streams in the sand. These streams, said Freeman, were overflow from holding tanks at Scripps. It was a watershed he knew something about.

North of Scripps the cliffs began. They were desert cliffs and they crumbled into the blue desert of the Pacific. On top, against the blue desert of the sky, stood mansions, some designed by Caligula, others by Arthur C. Clarke. They sent me into mild future shock—future discomfort, anyway. Freeman set a fast pace, and soon we were past the zone of mansions and the clifftops were wild again.

There were round pebbles of magnetite up there, Freeman informed me. Back in the Orion days, he and George had explored the clifftops. George, who was then five, had asked why the pebbles were round. Freeman pled ignorance. George advanced a theory. "I think the pebbles are round because of magnetism, the way the Earth is round because of gravity." Freeman had been impressed.

"Unfortunately, it doesn't happen to be quite true," he said now, seventeen years later. But it had demonstrated a scientific sort of thoughtfulness that he had seldom marked in his son.

Freeman told me that La Jolla residents gather on the same clifftops to watch the migration of gray whales, and that he and George had joined them. Once Freeman had taken George on a boat tour out to see the whales up close. I contemplated this as we walked. I liked the idea of George seeing his first whales from these Frank Herbert cliffs. He had stood like a captive prince under the space-age mansions, watching the ancient migration. When he grew old enough, he followed it north to his destiny.

Freeman took a long, quick stride. George would be pleased by that, I thought.

The walking reminded Freeman of his first arrival in Princeton, and he told me about it. On getting off the train, he had walked two miles in from the station. "As I walked along, I thought how strange it was. Here I was, twenty-four years old, going to teach physics to Robert Oppenheimer." The lesson, said Freeman, was quantum electrodynamics and his Greyhound-bus discovery. "Oppenheimer was extremely difficult. I went in to give this first presentation, and I couldn't get out ten words before he would interrupt to say something."

"Was it criticism?"

"No, I wouldn't say that. *Invective.*" Freeman laughed. "He liked to talk more than listen. In time Oppenheimer understood what I was talking about. I suppose he forgot that he'd ever been opposed to it."

As we walked, Freeman searched the sky along the cliffs for hang-gliders. He saw none, and was disappointed. He told me that on his previous walks he had seen at least one or two of the manned kites. He supposed that the wind must be wrong today. The hang-gliders were wonderful, he said, and I really should come back to see them.

A small hawk was riding the cliffside thermal. The sun was above it, and its wingtips were incandescent. The hawk appeared to give Freeman no consolation. He did not follow its flight.

On the La Jolla beach, clothed people and naked people made distinct populations. They were separated by more than a mile of unoccupied sand, and by a peninsula of boulders that had spilled from one of the decaying cliffs. We crossed the no-man's-land, and when we came among people again, they wore no clothes. I felt alien in my cut-off jeans.

Freeman nodded toward a naked girl, brown all over, about four years old. "I find it very pleasant, the children," he said. We walked deeper into the naked country, and Freeman pursued his thought. "I find it very civilized. I don't know—there seems to be a kind of innocence. But it may be entirely my imagination."

Two very healthy young women passed, walking in the opposite direction. I turned my head to watch them. Freeman looked to see what had caught my attention. He cast about, but couldn't find it. His eyes shifted ahead again.

We came to the center of the colony, the most densely populated part, and Freeman stopped. He spread out his hotel towel. He liked to swim in a busy part of the beach, he explained, because he worried about riptides. A lot of swimmers were an indication of safe water. We undressed, and I discreetly looked Freeman over. The physicist was thin, but not scrawny. His shoulders were not broad, but his chest was deep. He had a greyhound build. He still looked like the high-school runner he once had been. His skin was pale, for his work had kept him indoors this summer.

Freeman swam straight out to sea, way beyond everyone else. I watched him a little nervously. He diminished against the long gentle swells, his head getting smaller and smaller. Having said he liked to swim near people, he was stroking out into an empty ocean. It occurred to me that in this ambiguous instinct of his, in this ambivalence toward crowds, he was very like his son. I was relieved to see him at last turn back.

When Freeman emerged, he toweled off fast. "I don't have enough fat on me," he explained. "The chill gets to me very quickly." He was shivering, and his kneecap was jumping spasmodically. It surprised me, for the Southern California water was almost warm. This will not score points with George, I thought. Compared with the Gulf of Alaska, where George and I had swum daily to build up our survival time, in the event we overturned, this water was tropical.

When Freeman was dry, I studied him, circumspectly. He should have looked funny, I thought. There was the big Dyson nose, and Freeman's salty hair was sticking out in all directions. He was thin and still shivering a little. The naked astrophysicist. But some essential seriousness in Freeman prevented him from being funny at all. There were those Dyson eyes, gazing seaward, then gazing at the throng, and seeing—what? Quantum fields? Quantum fields that cavorted here as bathers and as breaking waves? Or was his attention fixed on some sort of Universal Innocence?

We headed homeward. Coming to the end of the naked country, we put on our pants. Freeman pulled on one of those gray, sleeveless sweater-vests worn only by physicists and higher mathematicians.

The day's walking had made his bare feet tender. He seldom went shoeless, clearly. We came to some rocks, relatively smooth and harmless, and he paused to put on his shoes. George would not like that, I decided. I realized I was keeping a tally. Minus one point for Freeman.

Shod now, he could no longer wade and had to jump the streams that flowed from Scripps. I watched his broad-jump form critically, and I was amazed. He had astounding spring. He cleared the stream by a big margin, and glanced back to see if I had noticed. In his youth he had run the steeplechase, I remembered. I watched with admiration as he jumped again. George would like *that*. Plus one point for Freeman.

The sun was setting red through the tall pilings of the Scripps pier, but it was not the sunset that Freeman remarked on, as we passed. It was the edgewave. The edgewave, he told me, had been discovered here at Scripps. A mathematician had figured it out. The edgewave comes and goes with a period of about a minute, no matter what incoming waves do. It is important to the formation of beaches. It was odd, said Freeman, that it required discovery at all, since it is so readily observable. He was amused that it had taken a mathematician to put his finger on it. Scripps was very proud of its edgewave, he said, smiling.

The sun set smoky-red, the ocean turned pastel, the physicist regarded the wave.

We tried a shortcut back to my car, climbing a steep vacant lot between beachside houses. At the top of the hill, shutting us off from the street, was a high Cyclone fence. Freeman slowed as we came to the fence, and I asked, solicitously, if he thought it was too high. "Oh no," he said. "It's just that ... I don't suppose a policeman would happen to come by right now?"

"I doubt it," I said.

I was amused. What did a policeman care? The worst he would

do was tell us to go back. In this situation, George Dyson would not have paused for an instant. Minus one point for Freeman.

Freeman looked furtively up and down the street, then leapt up, agile as a boy, chinned himself on the fence, and vaulted effortlessly over.

"I don't like fences," he confided, when I had joined him on the other side.

------ 42 ------

Reunion

Freeman walked with his daughter Emily down the path to George's tree. The two were pausing in Belcarra Park on their way north to the Hanson Island rendezvous. Freeman wanted to have a look at the tree house. George had traveled this path less than a month before, in departing himself for the rendezvous, and as Freeman followed it now he sniffed about, in a dignified and figurative way, for clues. He was hot on the trail of his son.

Freeman climbed to the top of the ladder at the base of the Douglas fir, tipped back his head and sighted upward. The bottom of the tree house was barely visible through the spokes of branches and clusters of needles. Freeman lost himself in thought. Finally he looked down at Emily and me and he grinned indescribably. "This is quite extraordinary," he said.

He ventured no higher in the tree. He descended, and we walked back down the path to join Gwen and Allen Martin for herb tea. The Martins lease the land on which George's tree house and workshed stand. Freeman wanted to meet them for the same reason he wanted to see the tree—to learn from George's friends, as from his circumstances, the manner of man his boy had become.

The Martins had spread a blanket on the grass of the clearing in front of their house, and had set Fainne, their new baby, loose on it. The sun was warm. We watched the baby and the sunlight on the waters of Indian Arm, and we stirred honey into our tea. From the beginning, conversation languished. Nobody seemed to mind. Freeman was absorbing George's country and finding it beautiful. He was delighted by the Martins. There is a kindness among the forest people of Belcarra that reaches its peak in that couple. "I was quite overwhelmed by them," he would tell me the next day. The Martins, for their part, would comment on Freeman's gentleness. They were delighted by his resemblance to his son, by the shoulder-shaking Dyson laugh and how little it had changed between generations.

Fainne, the baby, crawled purposefully and repeatedly toward the blanket's edge and the grass beyond. Each time she was about to make her escape, someone would set her back in the center. This treatment finally made her cry, and Freeman volunteered to hold her. Perhaps he saw, in her drive for the breeze-stirred grass beyond the blanket, a metaphor for his own discontent in the confines of this solar system; perhaps he just liked babies. For the duration of the tea he held her, declining all offers to relieve him of that burden. "I find there is a tranquillity in holding a baby," he said.

The next day Freeman, Emily, and I stood at the rail of the ferry to Vancouver Island. The sea wind was southerly, blowing down from George to us.

A propos of nothing, Freeman spoke.

"A baby is one of the magic things in the universe. Like that baby yesterday. She was absorbing things, storing them. How could she do it? All the things a baby has to know . . ."

Then babies grow up, I thought. Long-haired and untidy, they smoke marijuana and build kayaks in their rooms. Remembering Freeman and yesterday's baby, I wondered again how it was that he and his own child could grow so far apart.

Emily and her father stood close together. Often on the crossing he put his arm around her, affectionately and for the shared warmth, and she seemed to like it. Emily was fourteen, a year older than George had been when, surly and unreachable, he had built his first kayak in his room. She was a fragrant, tidy girl. She scarcely remembered her brother. "I remember I got his room," she said. "The dirt was *that* thick." She wrinkled her nose and held thumb and forefinger several inches apart.

It surprised me to learn that George had been dirty, for I had always known him to keep a neat canoe and a clean, if ragged, person. Freeman was surprised, and a little disturbed, that Emily did not remember more about her brother.

We went inside, ordered coffee in the ferry cafeteria, and talked. Freeman told us that when he himself was fourteen he had started a religion. Unhappy with the Christian notion that the heathen are doomed for reasons out of their control, he had begun a sect of his own. "I was convinced suddenly that all people are the same. We are all one soul in different disguises. I called it Cosmic Unity, I think. We . . ."

Here Freeman paused, carried off by his thoughts. Emily muttered something.

"What?" I asked her.

"Emily hates it when I stop in the middle of a sentence," explained Freeman. He reached out to lay a hand on her cheek. She accepted that—no hard feelings either way. He concluded his story. "I seem to remember that I even had a convert. Cosmic Unity lasted about a year, I think."

I asked Emily if she had ever started a religion. No, she said, that would be crazy.

At Nanaimo we left the ferry in my car, drove northward a hundred and fifty miles through the forest on the lee side of Vancouver Island, and at Kelsey Bay took another ferry. We steamed north, deep in George's country now. The steep fiord walls of Johnstone Strait were patterned with forest. Patches of virgin trees alternated with patches in various stages of regrowth. The mountains above were dark and boreal. The sky was gray. The air was colder.

In the evening we turned into Beaver Cove, where we were to meet George for the trip to Hanson Island. On entering the cove, we scanned the inner shore and its labyrinth of log ponds for his canoe, but could not see it. As the ferry neared its slip, the passengers began descending to their cars, and at last we had to join them. By the time we reached my car, many motors were idling. The ferry's engines reversed and the water churned in the slip. "The big moment," Freeman said, as the pilings groaned against the ferry's weight.

I saw George first. He was walking down to the slip, wearing a knit cap and a stiff waterproof coat. I had seen him more recently than his family had, and I was familiar with his costume and his gait. "There he is," I said.

"You see him? Where is he?" Freeman asked. Then he saw his son, and watched him for a moment. "Yes, that's the man."

Freeman leaned out the window and waved, but it was dark in the maw of the ferry and we were just one of many cars.

"Every time you wave, he looks away," said Emily. "It's too dark in here."

Freeman continued to wave, fruitlessly.

We sat and studied George in the rumble of idling engines. The big moment dragged on. First the lane to the left of us moved out, then the ferryman waved to the lane on our right. We were among the last cars to leave the ferry. When we finally pulled up beside him, George recognized us. Grinning like fools, he and his father shook hands.

—— 43 ——

Dukhobor

George had not picked us up in his canoe, for the wind wasn't right. He came instead with a friend, Will Malloff, in Malloff's new speedboat. At the moment Malloff was the sole inhabitant of

Swanson Island, across Blackfish Sound from Hanson Island. His wife Georgiana was temporarily off-island. When she is home, Swanson Island has its full complement of two inhabitants.

Malloff is a big, bluff, pipe-smoking man in his forties. He is the inventor of, among other things, the Alaska Mill, which is in wide use in North America by people returning to the land. George had used one of Malloff's mills to chainsaw the floorboards for *Mount Fairweather*. Malloff is also a logger, and he runs a one-man, one-tractor operation on Swanson Island. Today he wore a plaid wool jacket and heavy size-thirteen boots. He was aware of Freeman's credentials as a scientist, but did not seem particularly impressed. He made no attempt to conceal his testy amusement at scientists and their world. He called the physicist "Dr. Freeman." He liked George, clearly. He would wait and see about George's father.

George passed our dunnage to Malloff, who stowed it in the speedboat. When it came to Freeman's leather suitcase, Malloff wrinkled his brow in amusement and looked at George. *What's this?* his eyes asked. A leather suitcase was out of place and comic here, apparently. George just shrugged. He swung my old Army dunnage bag over, and this Malloff accepted without comment of the eyes.

The five of us and our luggage jammed the cabin. Malloff was worried about the weight, so he and George changed the prop on his new Mercury outboard, substituting a blade that would pull the load better. "I don't know how they know what they're doing," said Freeman, the theoretician, as he watched this mysterious operation.

We pulled away from the bleak little logging town of Beaver Cove, passing acres of log ponds. Then we left the cove itself and entered the chop of Johnstone Strait. The sky was overcast. The wind was brisk but not particularly cold.

Halfway home to Swanson Island, the Mercury broke down.

At first Malloff thought that the engine had simply overheated. He gave it a few minutes to cool before yanking on the starter cord.

Nothing happened. The big man cursed under his breath. He yanked and yanked, and the small cabin filled with his male smell. It was a frontier aroma. Malloff's brow darkened savagely and histrionically—he does not have a frontier stoic's face—and he yanked and cursed again, this time above his breath. His black mood filled the cabin like his smell. I admired the engine's stubbornness in refusing to start in the face of it. Malloff gave an extra hard yank, and nearly hit George in the nose. George pulled his head back and smiled just perceptibly. *Canoes can't break down like this,* his smile said.

Malloff pulled off the cowling and monkeyed with the engine. He leaned out over the back and asked George to pull the starter cord. George did so. "There's fluid coming out of the spark plugs," Malloff informed us. He tasted. It was salt. "Headgasket," he said. "It's blown a headgasket." He was in a bleak mood to begin with—his wife was gone, and he had just spent the morning fixing another outboard—and now this. Freeman felt badly that our weight had overburdened the Mercury, and he apologized twice.

We were drifting, fortunately, into Double Bay, one of the few occupied coves in that country. A young man named Ron Moe, a friend of Malloff's, was on the water working on his boat, and he rowed over in a dinghy. On learning about the headgasket, he prepared immediately to tow us home to Swanson Island. He shouted to his wife Julie, who stood on shore, and asked her to get sleeping bags. It was so late in the evening now that they would have to spend the night at Malloff's.

"My bathwater is just getting hot!" she shouted back. A hot bath was a luxury, clearly, for she stood for a time on shore, debating with herself. Should she take a boat ride and human company, or the bath and a night alone on her island? It was a close thing. Will and Ron urged her gently to forget the bath, and after a minute they prevailed. Her decision made, she did not second-guess it, and joined us in good spirits. Freeman was much impressed, he would tell me later, by the frontier helpfulness.

The Moes' inboard diesel, turning over slowly and reliably,

towed us home. Now and again Ron laid his hand on the plywood that covered the engine, testing the temperature, making sure it did not overheat. A marine diesel in its simplicity is an engine that even George Dyson approves of. We plugged away eastward into the dusk, and the three British Columbian men exchanged information. Ron told George and Will about a new kind of cod-jigger with a spring on it, so you didn't snag. They talked about Mercury outboards—how well those run when they are running, how difficult to repair when they're not. They talked about tide rips. They talked about the weather. Freeman followed this coastal conversation closely, turning from one speaker to another. He was cold. He hunched in his thin nylon jacket against the sea wind, but his face was rapt. Mostly he watched his son.

George looked good. He was brown-skinned and relaxed. He did not look often at his father or sister, but his eyes embraced them in the avoidance, and he smiled almost continually.

As we entered Freshwater Bay on Swanson Island, we saw the canoe. *Mount Fairweather* was moored to the raft off Will Malloff's beach. George had added three masts since I last saw her. The masts were made of blond wood and had a pretty rake to them. The Plexiglass domes were finished and all six were in place. They had worked perfectly. The bubbles were a smoky blue, and in the twilight it was hard to see inside them. They gave the canoe a veiled intelligence. Ron Moe laughed with pleasure on seeing the canoe again. "God, what a beautiful thing," he said. Freeman murmured his assent.

George did not hear his father, apparently, for as we tied up a minute later he asked Freeman what he thought. Freeman repeated, louder, that the canoe was beautiful. He confessed that he thought he would like it better without the domes—just the classic Aleut lines. The astrophysicist, oddly or not, did not like the spaceship look. George nodded, glad to have the opinion.

Emily seemed to like the domes well enough. As we came alongside, she leaned and ran her hand over the smooth curve of one.

Stepping ashore, we were inundated by dogs, big Rhodesian ridgebacks, which Malloff breeds. The ridgebacks were lion-colored. They were heavily muscled, like lions. In Rhodesia they are used to hunt lions, and Malloff got his first pair, he claims, to protect his livestock from Swanson Island's mountain lions. The ridgebacks slammed into us at a friendly eighth of the speed at which they slam into prey on the veldt. When they had subsided, we walked inland. We passed a litter of giant bones the dogs had gnawed and abandoned. It looked like the site of a Pleistocene kill by dire wolves.

Malloff had come to Swanson Island four years before with fifty dollars and a chainsaw. In those four years he had built an entire settlement. Above the beach, in a slash in the forest cleared early in his logging, was a small, scattered town of sheds and buildings. Rust-colored and ramshackle, they stood at various angles to one another. Some were high against the green edge of the forest, some low near the gray stone of the beach. Some tilted crazily. Malloff had found the pieces of his town abandoned in various places and had assembled it here by barge. He had not yet straightened everything out, or found a use for all the structures. Two of the buildings were workshops for Will and Georgiana. One shack, raised on pilings, served as a greenhouse. The space beneath the greenhouse had been meshed in, and was hissing with geese. Nearby was a large coop hysterical with chickens, and near the coop was a kennel squirming and yapping with ridgeback puppies, and behind the kennel was a huge vegetable garden, covered by net against the birds. In the garden several escaped hens scratched among rows of lettuce. There was a duck pen too, netted over against bald eagles. There was an aviary for pheasants. The aviary was a pyramid twenty feet tall, made of huge timbers draped with mesh. Piles of tools lay all around. There was an open-air blacksmith's shop. Will's tiny caterpillar tractor was butted up against a tree, as if tethered there.

Georgiana Malloff is an artist, and the shack nearest the main house was her studio. Inside, her only furniture was a small wood stove, which warmed her when she worked in winter. Her paintings lined the studio walls, white-matted against the weathered wood. They were pastel and understated. Outside, her sculpture, big and bold, lay or stood everywhere in the clearing her husband had made in the wilderness. There was a massive stone rose. There was a great wood mask with flowers for eyes. There was a Panlike figure in blond wood, part Picasso and part Tsimshian. Totem poles of rounded abstract forms sprouted like mushrooms from the grass of the clearing. The poles leaned above the beach, greeting visitors. They huddled unfinished beside the studio, draped by canvas. They stood in exile at the very edge of the slash, their lines mingling with the first rank of trees. Sometimes, George told us, you came upon her poles far from here, standing alone in clearings in the forest, like artifacts of a forgotten civilization.

The Malloff settlement testified to the energy that two isolated people, undistracted by trivialities, can unleash. Here, I could not help thinking, was the kind of small colony that Freeman Dyson advocates. It was a smaller group than his small group, but the principle was the same.

Freeman had fallen silent and thoughtful. He and Emily followed, listening, as George showed us around.

Will shouted a dinner invitation, and we broke off and headed for the main house. The main house was a rebuilt shed. Will had made it as tight as a ship, for warmth. The only extravagance, from the standpoint of heat loss, was a big picture window that looked down on the water. Will asked us to remove our boots, and we padded inside in our socks. Everything in Malloff's lair was big. There was a row of size-thirteen gum boots, cork boots, and moccasins, to which we added our own puny footgear. There was a coffeepot as big as a barrel. There was a frying pan as big as a manhole cover, in which Will is accustomed to frying a dozen eggs and six or seven potatoes simultaneously. There was a big bowl of oversized, gnarly pipes.

Will dumped or wrestled Rhodesian ridgebacks off the chairs, and invited us to sit. George fired up the stove, and the house heated quickly. It was, Ron Moe informed us, a neighborhood joke how hot Will kept his house. Will smiled and grunted.

George made a giant salad from the garden. He boiled potatoes, and brewed mint tea. In Georgiana's absence, he had been the cook on Swanson Island. Will brought out salmon in jars, one jar plain, one jar alder-smoked. We ate seriously, without much talk. Will urged us on, saying he had canned too much salmon and wanted to get rid of the stuff.

After dinner the coastal talk resumed. We learned that Ron and Julie Moe had been lighthouse keepers. There is, they told us, a small fraternity of families who support themselves by tending lights on British Columbia's lonely coasts. With automation that fraternity is diminishing, and the Moes had left it. In partnership with another couple, they started a homestead near Cape Scott on the northwest coast of Vancouver Island. Their house was so remote that walking in took five days. It was not so remote, however, that they could escape the long arm of bureaucracy. The government had incorporated the region in a park, and the Moes had been forced to sell out. They had moved here and were trying to accustom themselves to the relative crush of people on this leeward side of Vancouver Island. They now had neighbors breathing down their necks not more than a couple of miles away.

When Julie mentioned that their former partners at Cape Scott had moved to the Queen Charlotte Islands with a new baby, Freeman was interested. He asked Julie what she thought about rearing children in the wilderness.

"I've thought a lot about it," she said. "I don't know. It's pretty scary." Freeman nodded. He seemed to find this a sensible answer.

Will Malloff told us stories of Saskatchewan.

His grandfather in Saskatchewan, he claimed, sometimes ploughed with twenty-three horses abreast. The old man was so strong that he could handle that many. On Saturdays he would drive his team to town with a tankful of grain, sell it, and buy flour and groceries. That done, he would tie the team outside the bar and commence to drink and fight all day and most of the night.

Early the next morning, before light, his friends would pour him into his tank and set the horses loose to find their way home.

Will's grandfather was a Dukhobor.

The Dukhobors, a sect founded in Russia in 1785, are, according to Will, a "hard-working, loving, not-killing-anybody people." The Dukhobors steer stubbornly by their own reading of Scripture and they deny the authority of temporal government. Czarist Russia was not the best place imaginable for Dukhobor pacifism and Dukhobor stubbornness, and the Dukhobors suffered. Will told us of persecutions in Russia, and of a forced resettlement in a region annexed from Turkey by the Czar. "The Turks were pretty tough, and they didn't take kindly to colonists the Russians sent in. Living among the Turks was supposed to make the Dukhobors bear arms." It didn't work out that way. The Dukhobors proved such gentle and industrious neighbors that the Turks couldn't find anything to hold against them. The Dukhobors survived to emigrate by the thousands to Canada in the 1890s, most moving to the plains of Saskatchewan.

The name Dukhobor derives from the Russian for "spirit wrestler." If Will Malloff, stocky of frame and tenacious of mien, was typical of his people, then it was a good name, I thought. Malloff had left the Dukhobors when he was young, but the Dukhobor had not left Malloff. Building your own colony on your own island is a very Dukhoborish thing to do. Here on Swanson Island, Malloff was about as isolated from temporal authority as an Earthling can be.

Freeman was interested in this story of emigration to distant places. He drew Will out with questions, and the Dukhobor warmed to the tale. He described for us the simplicity of the life in the Saskatchewan colony, and the hard work, and the good sense.

"But you left," said Freeman, when Malloff finished.

"Oh yeah. I had to get the hell out."

Everything changed, Will explained. Young people were coming into the community with no idea of what it was all about. The leaders became corrupt. They were no longer interested in hard work. There was nothing to do but go.

Ron Moe volunteered that he was not so sure. It seemed to him that the newcomers eventually might have got the idea and merged with the community. He had seen that happen in British Columbia with young people who moved here to start communes. At first the young people had been exclusive. Wanting really to start from scratch, they had avoided the sourdoughs and other indigenes. But in time they came around.

Ron, the lighthouse keeper, the homesteader who once had settled as far from people as he could, was an optimist about human nature.

Malloff shook his head. He reminded Ron of the Finnish colony nearby on Malcolm Island. The Finns had built a town they named Sointula, "Freedom Town." The colony had a hopeful name and a promising start, but soon it suffered a schism. The split occurred between the intellectuals and the farmers. "The intellectuals wanted to contribute their intellectualism," said Will, "and they wanted the farmers to contribute their farming. The farmers didn't like that. The community has been there seventy-five years, and the split is getting worse."

I would make my bets with Will, I decided. It seemed to me that the rapprochements of human history were back-eddies, that the main flow was in the other direction. The tendency in matter was toward entropy, in biology toward speciation, and in human affairs toward factionalism. At all levels of organization, things like to fuss and fight. I said something along these lines, and Freeman agreed. When it comes time, he said, people just have to leave.

"I'm interested in how much use you make of machinery here," Freeman said to Will. "That surprised me."

"Yes, I like machinery," Will answered, and he waited for Freeman to follow up. Freeman did not. Whatever the physicist was driving at, he let it alone for now. After a bit more conversation, Freeman excused himself and he and Emily went to bed.

When they had gone, George told Will about his father's idea for a computer-corrected telescope. Malloff, the inventor, was fascinated. When he learned from me that Freeman was going to Mother Russia to sell the telescope idea—and that Freeman spoke some Russian, besides—Malloff the Dukhobor got excited.

The next morning at the breakfast table, Will greeted Freeman in Russian, and the two men exchanged Russian pleasantries. Will asked about the telescope. Freeman filled him in. The conversation turned to the possibility of the existence of extraterrestrial life and to the problem of communicating with it, a subject that interested both men. Will asked if Freeman had read Shklovsky. Freeman had. He *knew* Shklovsky, in fact. Hearing that, Malloff got excited again. The slender physicist was winning the big Dukhobor over. For a while the two men discussed the Russian astronomer and his unconventional ideas on alien intelligence.

"Does he have trouble getting funds?" Will asked.

"I don't think so. He's a legitimate astronomer, with a fine reputation. You don't get into that academy without that. He's made a number of important discoveries. I think he's the most imaginative man they've got."

By the end of breakfast, the talk on extraterrestrial life had exhausted itself. Will seldom had conversation like this on Swanson Island, and he didn't want it to stop. "Tell me, Dr. Freeman, what are some of your other hobbies?"

Freeman hesitated.

"Well. I've been interested, for a long time, not just in communication but . . . but in learning how to get men like yourself into space."

Will raised his eyebrows in surprise. Freeman went on to explain, briefly, his ideas for space colonies, and the table fell silent. *What have we here?* said the eyes of the two backwoodsmen, and the backwoodswoman. In a few minutes, though, Freeman's ideas began to be familiar and not so crazy. Will Malloff, if I interpreted correctly the angle of his brows, was ready to be interested in the idea in the abstract, but had no intention of going into space himself. Ron Moe listened, not saying much. Finally, as we stood from the table, Ron spoke.

"I'll go," he said, "if you promise me there'll be salmon out there. And cutthroat trout."

Will's first chore that day was to repair the Mercury outboard. He had decided to make a new headgasket himself, cutting it from a spare sheet of copper, and he headed to his workshop for a tool. Freeman tagged along.

The workshop was a barnlike, three-room building with a heavy door carved in bas-relief by Georgiana. Inside, stacked like a painter's canvases, were more huge doors. Georgiana once must have gone through a carved-door period. Beyond the stacked doors were tables jumbled with Will's tools and inventions. The master of Swanson Island paused to show Freeman a lathe he was rebuilding, then showed him a power sander he had invented for rounding the corners of the furniture he makes. Next he picked up a power handsaw he was in the process of inventing. "This is just a prototype, of course," he said. "I had to make some adjustments in the length of the stroke. The stroke was too short. I had to lengthen it, and I ran into some problems with balance."

Here Malloff abruptly stopped, as if he had caught himself, once again, in an explanation too abstruse to interest others. I had seen Freeman catch himself similarly in his explanations of matters astrophysical. I knew that in this instance Will was mistaken; Freeman *was* interested in the problem of balance in a piece of machinery. Orion. The TRIGA reactor. Freeman handled the saw, impressed. He returned it carefully to Will, who tossed it carelessly back on the pile.

Ron Moe joined us, and we walked down to get the ailing Mercury. On the beach we passed the dory that Will had built when he first came to his coast. The dory had carried him and his chainsaw here to Freshwater Bay. It was the seed of all that followed, the first artifact of the Malloff colony. It rested, faithful as Crusoe's first dugout, on the gray stones. Ron Moe pointed in passing to the floor planks. They were pocked and roughened by hobnail boots. "Will's the only man I know who'd build a dory by hand and then wear those boots in it," he said.

The Dukhobor smiled and did not deny it. He waded out in his gum boots to the speedboat. He bent over the Mercury outboard. Reaching back for the vise-grip pliers in his pocket, he had a thought. Hefting the pliers, he looked at Ron.

"I won't let him send me into space unless I can take my vise-grips."

"I can't send you," corrected Freeman. "You have to want to go yourself."

—— 44 ——

Hanson Island

"This is a very comfortable canoe," said Freeman. "It's so solid—like a rock."

The physicist began experimenting with his paddle, first with a burst of short, fast strokes, then a longer, slower series. He abandoned the experiment in midstroke, his paddle upraised, and began watching the water drip from the blade. On hitting the ocean, the drops made silver beads that danced on the surface. They dervished and disappeared.

"I wonder why the water forms those beads," he mused.

George smiled, without interrupting his steady paddling. "I've wondered about that for years. I've always been meaning to ask you. Could it be electrical?"

"Maybe. But I would guess oil."

We were bound for Hanson Island, having said good-bye to Will Malloff that morning. George sat in the stern paddling hole, watching his father and sister, who occupied two of the central holes. I sat in the forward hole. The canoe was so long that snatches of the conversation were lost to me.

I did hear Freeman point out that the prow had swung away from our destination.

"Most efficient vector," George answered.

"Oh. Of course," said Freeman.

On Hanson Island George had prepared a camp for his family. He had found a spot at the edge of the forest, among last trees looking down on a rocky promontory. A previous tenant had built a tent platform, and on this George erected, for Freeman, a tall Explorer tent he has owned since childhood. Nearby he pitched a second tent for Emily. For himself he pitched his two-man tent some distance up the hill. I found space for my bag under the roof of his small storage lean-to.

On the next point, separated from George's point by a hundred yards of crescent beach, was Dr. Paul Spong's house. Dr. Spong comes to Hanson Island in the summer to study the killer whales that hunt the salmon-rich waters around the island, and for the past several years George has joined Spong there. The hundred yards of beach allowed the Dyson family privacy, when they needed privacy, yet was not far to walk for company when they wanted that. During their five days on Hanson Island, they usually ate breakfast on their own point, and supper at Spong's.

Spong's table was often crowded. There was Dr. Spong, his wife Linda, and their six-year-old son Yashi. Stewart Marshall, the artist who had painted the designs on *Mount Fairweather*, had built a simple house nearby and usually ate with the Spong family. Jim Bates, George's old captain on *D'Sonoqua*, visited once, as did George's friends Michael and Maureen Berry, and several others in his circle. George's people are migratory, wintering around Belcarra Park and summering around Hanson, Swanson, and Malcolm islands.

Breakfasts at George's point were less populous—just George, Freeman, Emily, and sometimes me.

"We're getting tableware," said Freeman, delighted, as I arrived for breakfast one morning. George was carving a spatula and some spoons from pieces of wood. He finished these quickly, set down his knife, and took up his hand axe to make plates.

"That's a nice axe," said Freeman. "Did you make it?"

"Yes. Well, I found the blade. It was discarded in an Indian village. I made the handle. I epoxied in the head. It's a good axe, because it's small and you can carry it around." He tapped four times with the axe, splitting off four cedar shakes for plates. "You don't expect a hand axe to last long, because it does so much work. But this one has. It's the epoxy."

Epoxy, he explained, was the only way to put an axe, or a canoe, or anything else together. He believed that the Polynesians may have had an epoxy. In Captain Cook's writings he had found reference to a special native mixture of tree saps. "It set up real good," George said. "It was better than anything the Royal Navy had."

George sent Emily down to the shore to forage, and in a while she returned with a bunch of limpets. George put them in the coals of the fire, and Freeman shook his head ruefully. "I'll try anything once," he said.

After the mollusks had cooked for a minute, George made tongs of a pair of sticks, lifted the shells from the fire, and deposited them sizzling on the cedar plates. As Freeman took his plate from George, I noticed a peculiar thing. The son's hands were older than the father's. George's hands were brown, nicked, and weathered. Freeman's were not.

Freeman looked down at his plate. When cooked, the antennae of limpets shrink to little Satanic ears. The naked shellfish become pink, embryonic devils. "The thing to do is shut your eyes and eat it," Freeman suggested to himself. He followed his advice, then opened his eyes in surprise. "It's far better than it looks," he said. Emily chewed her limpets without comment and slowly, a tiny bite at a time.

"You didn't know what I've been doing," said George one morning. "Except for one letter every six months or so. Is it pretty much what you expected?"

"No," answered Freeman. "I'm surprised to find you with so many people. I had imagined you as some kind of a hermit."

"I don't know how that rumor got started."

"Well. I suppose it was the tree house, for one thing. Living one hundred feet up in a tree. I had imagined that it was somewhere in the middle of the wilderness."

"No."

"And I think it's good. I'm glad you're not a hermit. I don't think it's good for one, in the long run. Being a hermit."

We ate the breakfast George had fixed for us—oatmeal mush with sunflower seeds, raisins, and honey—and we looked down at the waters of the channel. The tide was beginning to rip out in Blackney Passage. George asked Freeman about the Dyson family fortunes. Had Freeman encountered many Dysons in his recent trip to Europe? Freeman had not. He reported that there were not many Dysons left. In the past fifty years, the Dysons had produced few children, and the name was dying out. Not that Freeman really cared. The genes survived, said the father of five daughters, and that, he supposed, was the important thing.

George told Freeman about flying squirrels. He had returned to Belcarra this last winter to find his house full of pine cones. There were pine cones under the bed and pine cones under the table. "Flying squirrels are almost . . . intelligent," he said. "They had unscrewed the lids on my jars—things like that. They . . ."

He was interrupted by Yashi Spong's high-pitched, carrying cry. The boy stood at the far end of the beach, on the Spongs' point. He shouted that killer whales were here, and he gestured seaward. We saw the fins of the pod rising in formation, well offshore. We set down our tea.

Killer whales are something to see. In those illustrations showing various whales and their relative sizes, killer whales don't look so big. Next to sperm whales or any of the big plankton-eaters they are not, but next to any other living creature they are huge. And there is the way they carry themselves. Nothing in the sea worries them. Their dorsal fins flag their fearlessness, rising nearly vertically, like the tails of dominant wolves. Nothing in the ocean cuts the water more beautifully. You can't really see killer whales in the big tanks at various Marinelands and Sea Worlds. You have to see them free, blowing on a cold strait. Freeman and Emily took turns with George's binoculars, watching the tall fins and listening. The whales blew like loggers using dynamite in a distant range of mountains. Emily noticed something through the glasses.

"That one has a fin that curves the wrong way."

"Yeah," said George. "That's the bull. It might even be old Forward Fin."

The whales proceeded down the coast. We saw flukes for an instant, and then the whales were gone around the point. Blackney Passage was empty again, except for the roilings of the tide rip.

"Well," said Freeman afterward, in the silence, "are you planning to people the Earth with Dysons?" He spoke as if the question naturally followed the whales.

"Not so many," George said, smiling. "One or two maybe." He paused, then continued. "It's amazing how easy it is to take care of them. I've watched certain people I know. It's good when the parents are involved in something larger. That makes a big difference in the cooperativeness of kids."

"Yes," said Freeman.

"Do they still hunt humpbacks?" I asked, on another morning. We had been discussing various whales.

"Yes," said George. "It's funny. On the endangered list for the world, humpback whales are about third. Blue whales, fin whales, humpbacks. But in Alaska, they're still pretty common."

"How is the minke whale doing?" asked Freeman.

"All right," George answered. He told us a little about minke whales, then added, "There was a sei whale that lived right around here. He stayed here all the time."

"What's a sei whale?" asked Emily.

"It's like a big minke whale. He's even shyer than a minke. He just stays all by himself and never says anything to anybody.

Somebody shot him. Paul found him with about four hundred rounds of high-powered rifle bullets in him."

One morning over mint tea, George told Freeman about the *I Ching*. Millennia of Chinese experience, said George, had gone into the writing of that book. He explained how you threw coins to determine, through the medium of chance, the hexagrams that marked the stories that guided you. It was important to read the *I Ching* without skepticism, he said. The hexagrams were no good to you unless you accepted them on faith.

I glanced at Freeman, the rationalist, for his reaction to this warning against skepticism, but I could not read it.

"What kind of advice does it give you?" Freeman asked.

"It depends on what kind you need, what kind of questions you ask."

"What kind of questions do you ask?"

"That depends."

"What do you think about this idea of a radio?" asked George another day. "Some people think I'm crazy to want to put one in this canoe."

"No, no," said Freeman. "I think it would be very good. Both for you and for me. I think a radio in the canoe is a good idea. That's what I like about you—you're not a purist."

When breakfasts were done, the Dysons usually strolled over to the the Spongs' to visit. Halfway there, high on the beach cobbles, was an old bathtub. Outdoor tubs are one of the customs of the country. "It's a great experience," George told his father. He explained that you waited until high tide, when the water came close to the tub, then you dipped it full, lit a fire beneath, and cooked yourself like a missionary. "Yes. Wonderful," said Freeman.

The Spong house is a high-ceilinged, free-form affair built of driftwood around a big boulder. It is part Kwakiutl lodge, part Arab tent; rough-hewn in its timbers, yet airy and full of Persian rugs and pillows. It is not the shiptight sort of house that a Dukhobor would want to winter in, and Will Malloff likes to joke about Dr. Spong as carpenter. Spong does not winter there. He makes no claims for himself as carpenter. His main business is whales. For several summers whales have been plentiful, and he has not got around to finishing his roof, half of which is still covered only with plastic. The plastic is great on sunny days, but on rainy days the Spongs run about positioning bowls under the leaks. The single big room is busy always with static from Spong's hydrophones. The hydrophone wires run out into the cove, where they eavesdrop on passing whales. The sound is powerfully amplified to pick up the faintest cetacean grumble or aside. Motor vessels tend to come into range suddenly, and the noise is horrendous. Someone leaps up and runs to turn down the thunder of the screws.

When the hydrophones pick up whale noise, Dr. Spong is often the first to hear it. In the middle of conversation he changes expression. An odd, introverted look. *"Orca,"* he says.

Faintly, pealingly, a note materializes in the static. It begins as regally as an elephant's trumpeting, then suddenly shifts incredibly higher. Spong and his people go to the window, or walk out onto the point to whistle at the whales or play flutes to them. Dr. Spong's interest in killer whales has swung, as often seems to happen with students of whales, from the scientific to the mystic and personal. Spong's main wish now is simply to be with whales, and the music he plays to passing pods is part of that. He never refers to killer whales by that common name, which he feels is a bum rap. He calls them by their Latin name, *Orca.*

Spong is close-mouthed about *Orca.* Freeman and I questioned him about the whales, but neither of us learned much. Spong seemed reluctant to discuss his research. I began to suspect that he had made the whales some unspoken, perhaps telepathic, pledge of confidentiality in return for what they would let him learn. He was as loyal to *Orca* as a shaman to a totem animal. Sometimes his manner suggested that he knew far more about killer whales than he could possibly communicate, and he was annoying. Sometimes he seemed to mystify his work unnecessarily. It may have been, of course, that the mystery was real, inherent to his huge subjects.

The people who had gathered around Spong were not the sort that wear white lab coats.

Stewart Marshall, the artist, seldom even wore shoes. His hair and beard grew long and wild, and his skin was deeply tanned. He wore loose and holey sweaters against his bare brown skin, and his pants were daubed in many colors where he had wiped his artistic fingers. His girlfriend was a nineteen-year-old Danish girl named Nina. She too went barefoot, and she wore a bangle on one brown ankle. Her blond hair formed ringlets in the damp sea air, and the ringlets framed a face that was the Victorian ideal—out of style now, but pretty. She had been in Canada for just six months and spoke little English. Freeman liked to listen to her. "It's strange," he told me once. "The words are all those of the American dropout, but the accent is so Old World." Nina kept to herself and was given to sudden, small laughs at private thoughts. To my ear, her laughter rang melancholy, and hinted at some recent trouble or confusion, but she may simply have lacked a Danish-speaking person to share her thoughts with. I saw her gay on two occasions. One was on the beach when we cooked some hotdogs Freeman had brought. She laughed with pleasure at the idea of cooking, in this land of vegetarians and fish eaters, hotdogs on the beach. The other time was in George's canoe. "This boat!" she cried, "I love this boat!" and she gave herself completely to the paddling. Michael Berry, George's best friend, was bearded and quiet. He lived in the cabin of his boat with his wife Maureen and their infant son. Painted in black letters on the cabin's outside were all the trades he was jack of: OXY-WELDING, MECHANICAL, SCUBA-DIVING.

Paul Spong was the only beardless male on Hanson Island, besides Freeman. Dr. Spong has become a naturalist-politician, a lawyer for whales, and his smooth chin may be a concession to appearances. He travels a lot to cities, and had just returned to the island from a campaign in Europe. His hairline recedes from the front, and he wears his hair moderately long. His accent, like

Freeman's off-British, is difficult to place. It is Kiwi overlain by Canuck. Spong is a native of New Zealand who has spent many years in Canada. Linda Spong was dark-haired, good-looking, solid and sensible. Freeman admired her. "Of all the ladies up here, she seems the most sane," he told me.

One of the visitors to the island was the young woman called Muffin. She was an old friend of George's and had attended the launching of the big canoe. She was large-eyed, pigtailed, and more noticeably pregnant than she had been at the launch. She was a vegetarian. It was in a discussion of her beliefs about food that I first noticed a coolness come between Freeman and George.

Freeman's stepdaughter (George's half-sister) Katrina was ill, and both men were worried about her. One evening George told his father that Muffin had cured a similar illness through diet, and he argued the benefits of vegetarianism and fasting. If Katrina followed Muffin's lead, she would be fine, George said. Freeman looked bored, then irritated. The physicist has an aversion to dogma, and George comes close to being dogmatic in his dietary beliefs. George persisted in the lesson. He seemed insensitive to his father's irritation, or aware of it, maybe, but determined to present his views without compromise. I thought I could feel the thaw reverse, and the ice begin to form again between them.

But generally things went smoothly. Freeman was interested in the Hanson Island people, both as George's friends and for themselves, and he made a study of them. He liked life on the island.

The physicist and I were given simple tasks within our powers. Freeman was made woodcutter, and he chopped away with a precise economy of motion and considerable satisfaction. Healthy, repetitious, outdoors labor is perfect work for a theoretical man. My job was kelpcutter. I worked in the seaweed tangles at high-tide line, cutting cords of kelp and transporting them by wheelbarrow through the forest to the compost pit. The big kelp stalks had a life of their own, like pythons not quite dead, and I often had to stop the wheelbarrow to wrestle them into submission. I got sandy and sweaty and I struggled like Laocoön.

I looked up once to see that Freeman had set down his axe and was watching me, amused. "You look like you're loading intestines," he observed, brilliantly. I could think of no comeback. He suggested that we knock off, as it was almost time for lunch. I set down my wheelbarrow and we went inside.

George sat on the Spongs' floor, repairing a chainsaw, the parts spread around him. Others were gathering for lunch. We watched George work and we talked. Linda Spong and Maureen Berry spoke about canning salmon, about food prices, about the Indians of Alert Bay, the nearest village. Mrs. Spong was almost afraid in Alert Bay nowadays, she said. The Indians were getting militant. George talked about chainsaws, then about epoxy. Emily listened to everything, as was her habit, and she said very little.

Freeman and Dr. Spong talked science. Spong asked about the Institute for Advanced Studies. Was Freeman's work there theoretical? "Yes," said Freeman. "I'm very much a theoretical scientist. As you can see." He nodded toward his son, the practical man, surrounded by chainsaw parts on the floor.

George grinned and agreed: "He's not helping fix this saw."

Spong asked what Freeman's day at the institute was like. The main chore, answered Freeman, was with the select group of invitees that come to Princeton each year. "Mostly I listen to them. I nod my head at opportune moments. Occasionally I tell them when they're off track. And I'm free to do my own stuff."

"What is your stuff?"

"Astrophysics. I'm an astrophysicist. I started as a mathematician."

"What kind of problems in astrophysics?"

"I'm interested right now in galaxies. There's a big problem with how disk-shaped galaxies stay together. They appear to be gravitationally unstable. It's a clean mathematical question—what holds them together?"

"Epoxy," said Emily, so quietly that only I heard.

45

Don't Touch It

It was raining. Emily returned in the downpour from an errand in the Dyson camp. On entering Spong's door she hung up her raincoat.

"Did you look into the tents?" Freeman asked.

"No."

"I suppose they're hopelessly waterlogged by now."

"I doubt it," somebody said, but Freeman was not reassured. After a few minutes of thinking about it, he decided to walk over and check the tents. Emily watched as her father put on his raincoat.

"I think your tent is the kind that leaks if you touch it," she warned. *"So don't touch it."*

46

Clarion Profundus

We sat one night around the Spongs' table sipping anise tea. Some of us sat on chairs made of log rounds, some on a bench worn smooth by many seats of pants. It was an old scene, I thought. The lantern above cast a Stone Age light. In its amber circle was Stewart Marshall, bearded, brown-faced, barefoot. His hands were speckled by his various pigments. He might have been a Cro-Magnon who had spent the day painting bison on cave walls. Beside him was Nina, barefoot too, except for her bangle. There was doe-eyed Muffin, and sane-eyed Linda Spong, and George gazing like a shaman into a fire, and Emily with her lids at half-mast. We were like a tribal group from long ago. From beyond the circle of light came Yashi Spong's regular breathing. He had fallen asleep the instant his father laid him on the bed. A long day, begun early and spent outdoors, was behind us.

In the circle of faces, Freeman's stood out. His was paler than the others, and was something else besides. I fancied that I saw in his features an angularity, an acuity, that resisted the mellowing influence of the light. The lantern could not Stone Age him. If we really were Paleolithic people, I thought, Freeman would be the one who tomorrow invented iron.

Someone started a joint around. Most of the tribe dragged on it, a few just passed it on. The marijuana made one circuit and was in the middle of a second when George, about to pass it beyond his father, held it out to him in afterthought. "You're part of the circle, but I guess . . . ?"

"No thank you," said Freeman.

His tone woke me. There was a hardness to it, as when a pick hits bedrock. I had heard nothing like it since Freeman entered George's country.

The moment extended. I saw, or thought I did, that this was the way it would always be. The Dysons, father and son, had narrowed the gap, but each at this moment had come to a final frontier of his territory, and could go no farther. They would continue to orbit each other at this distance. George had known, surely, that his father would refuse the drug, but he had insisted on completing this normal gesture of his life. At the bedrock ring of his father's reply, he had not flinched. A tension lingered. A second joint began to circulate, but for me the first, proffered and refused, still hung in George's hand, fixed in the amber of the lantern light.

Over the hydrophones came the call of a killer whale. First one note, then a chorus as others in the pod answered. There were more whales than we had heard before. We ran outside onto the point and watched them come. The tall black fins passed between shore and the dark sliver of *Mount Fairweather,* anchored out. The whales came within twenty yards of the rock beneath our feet.

Spong had rigged hydrophone speakers in spruces on the point, and whale sound surrounded us. We heard both the submarine calls and the sound of the blowing. The sensation was peculiar, like having one ear in the water and one out. Spong's equipment was good, the amplification strong, and it was hard to tell which sound was real, which electric.

The blowing was a sympathetic sound. It spoke of lungs and the sweetness of the night air when you finally come up for it. It was like us, human, but on a larger scale. The underwater singing was alien. Human analogies broke down so badly that I couldn't even guess where in its body the whale made the noise. Do they use their blowholes or is it somewhere in their throats? The range of the instrument is extrahuman and it runs off our scale at either end.

I shut my eyes and listened.

There came a bass shuddering, like a castle door, stone and iron, swinging ponderously open. The whale entered the door, climbed to the top of a tower, and opened a higher door. There was a long deep sigh, like a giant—Neptune?—turning over in his sleep, then a sound that scraped the very bottom, dreary as a record played as slow as it will go. The whales shifted effortlessly. They moved through a middle range of Bronx cheers, pig grunts, and fartings, then one whale moved higher still to an anxious, multiple noise like that made by a litter of nursing puppies. Listening, I was almost certain that some of the sounds were experimental. The whales were sending out scribbly signatures to see how they sounded. There was humor in it too, I thought. I listened to several obscene symphonies of the sort a grade-school wit, one hand in his armpit, his elbow pumping, might make in tuning up his instrument. For a moment I thought I had measured the mood of the whales. Then, from the middle of the comedy, out of all the dyspeptic mumblings and coarse imitations, came the trumpet call. It was as pure and beautiful a note as I had ever heard.

I opened my eyes. George was running with Emily down to the Spongs' small kayak. They jumped in and paddled out fast toward the whales. It was a phosphorescent night, and boluses of pale fire swirled back from their double paddles. They left behind twin contrails of light that quickly faded. The whales had moved beyond the buoy, and George and Emily followed, disappearing in the darkness. For a while we heard the double dip of their blades, then that too was gone.

At first George could not find the pod. Then, casting about, he saw two large shapes near the shore to the north. He moved to within forty feet, where he made out a pair of whales resting side by side, so close to the rocks that they could have touched land with their flukes.

George hesitated.

At a moment like this, in George Dyson, hesitation was odd. A goal of the Hanson Island people is to get as near *Orca* as possible, and one of their tenets is that killer whales have no interest in hurting people. But George ventured no nearer. Was it the presence of his sister in the kayak?

"*Orca* teaches you about fear," he would say later, admitting that he had felt that emotion for the first time in his life with whales. *Orca* reminded him that night of fear of the water and its cold, which he had temporarily forgotten.

It was not *Orca* so much that impressed Emily. Yes, the whales were very close, she would say later. Yes, one came up very near the kayak. But what she liked best was the time George anchored. He seized a bulb of kelp, held the kayak against the tide, and scouted for whales. While he looked around, Emily looked down. The tide streamed past, its dark pace illuminated by tracers of phosphorescence. The plankton sparked on like novae, excited at points where the current met the resistance of kelp or the hull. The light faded quickly, turning milky, like the light of nebulae. The plankton mirrored the constellations that were appearing now through holes in the clouds above. As the plankton streamed sternward, it seemed to Emily that she and her brother must still be paddling hard.

The trumpet call unrolled, echoing like an alarum down a corridor, a long stone corridor in a palace made for Titans. There was, I could tell, an enormous beauty in the sound, but I was not quite feeling it. I felt the nameless dissatisfaction I had experienced a year before, paddling past Angoon in the full moon with humpbacks blowing near me. I was just missing something big.

I wondered if Paul Spong felt the same. Perhaps that explained his reticence in talking about killer whales. With whales you came up against a wordlessness. There were no words to describe that singing. I invented some Latin for it, *Clarion Profundus*. But that didn't do the job. It wasn't even grammatical. It wasn't even Latin.

The tendril of sound unraveled over the bottom. It traveled through the night waters and right up my spine. I had heard it on records, and I had heard it several previous nights on Hanson Island, but I was still not prepared for it. It was a communication from an unexpected quarter, and it raised goosebumps. It was a nonterrestrial intelligence, it was probing the void, it passed without discovering us. The other intelligence that Freeman seeks is right here on Earth, I thought, but we have never really connected with it.

The flutes and cries of the Hanson Island people were annoying. I wished they would shut up so we could listen. Paul Spong's piercing *Eeeeyaaah!* did not bother me, nor did Linda Spong's high, sweet, fading *Hellloooo!* Both calls were practiced, both were natural in the conviction that whales were hearing. The tentative little cries of two of the island's women visitors set me on edge. "Hiii," they piped. They were hearing themselves. They were unsure all this wasn't ridiculous, a one-way conversation.

I looked over at Freeman, wondering if he, too, was annoyed.

He stood apart, hands clasped behind him, staring out at Blackney Passage. I saw him glance up at the clearing sky, then down again toward the whales. A moment passed. Eyes seaward, he groped in his pocket. He found his spectacles. He put them on. He gazed up again at the stars.

M-31

It was the first night on Hanson Island that stars had appeared. Our dome of cloud was not perpetual, after all. Through rents in it, the constellations glittered.

Heading homeward to the Dyson camp, Freeman walked deliberately some distance behind Emily, who carried the flashlight. "A meteor!" he said. He walked twenty steps down the beach, then saw another. "That's the third I've seen! It's a shower."

There was no city glow here to dull the stars, and their brightness excited him. He dallied, trying to keep his distance behind Emily and the flashlight. He was looking for M-31, the only galaxy in the Northern Hemisphere, outside our own Milky Way, that is visible to the naked eye. M-31 shows only on a very clear, dark night. Freeman peered hard at the patch of sky in which our neighbor galaxy hurtles toward us.

Emily looked back. She shined her light at Freeman, then up at the stars. Her beam made a nice comment, I thought, graphing the thrust of her father's life. But Freeman was annoyed. He asked her please not to shine it at him. For a while Emily desisted, and then, to be a pest, or just forgetful, she hit him with the beam again.

"Emily! Please don't shine that light at me!"

It was the only time I ever heard him speak sharply to anyone. Emily quit. The beach narrowed, then ended in boulders slippery with rockweed. Freeman had to look to his feet. He had to step carefully on this Earth again. "The time for stargazing is over," he said. He was poking fun at himself, but I heard real resignation there, too.

Rescue

On the morning of their last full day on Hanson Island, Freeman and Emily lingered with George over spruce tea. I sat with them, sipping too. We heard a distant motor, and out in Blackney Passage a small boat came into view. The moment it rounded the point, George straightened. "Those guys have some guts," he said. "Going against the tide in that open boat." He took his binoculars from their leather case and studied the boat. Magnified, the passengers were still just dots at either end. The spray beat up, white and rhythmic and higher than the men, each time the bow socked the waves. The sound of the outboard came fitfully, whining like a far chainsaw bucking a log too big for it. "It's good they have life jackets on," George said. He swung the binoculars slowly, following as the boat approached a place where the tide rip was bad. "They'll never make it through that rip," he predicted, and two seconds later the boat vanished. The chainsaw noise ceased.

Before us was the big, silent, empty arm of the sea. Inanimate, it ripped and ran on its way out.

For an instant we sat still, unable to believe that the thing had followed so closely on George's prophecy. We waited for the wind to bring us the sound of the outboard again. The wind did not. George rose slowly to his feet, keeping his binoculars fixed on the spot where the boat had been. Then he began moving fast. He stuffed the binoculars back in their case, and together he and I vaulted down the shore boulders and ran, slipping and sliding, across the rockweed and wet stones of the beach. A small kayak waited there, and we stumbled with it into the water. We paddled out to the buoy where Paul Spong's rubber Zodiac was moored. I untied the Zodiac's painter while George started up its outboard. The engine started with the second yank—a miracle, for that particular outboard. Once we were past the offshore kelp beds, I went forward, where my weight would help the Zodiac get off and plane. The boat got off, and we skated out into the tide rips.

It was a confused, unpredictable seascape. A patch of water, oily smooth one moment, would begin to rip the next. The surface rolled with waves here, was marbled with upwellings there. One stretch would speed us along, the next would grab us by the collar. "There're eddies all over," George said. We cast about for the missing boat, but saw no sign of it. We saw no sign of the missing men.

"I'll bet they're loggers," George called, above the outboard noise. "When they got into trouble, they speeded up. That's what they teach them—when in doubt, power up."

Several times we thought we saw a man, but on drawing near, the bobbing head proved to be a log or a seabird. Blackney Passage, when seen from shore over cups of spruce tea, does not look like much, but when you are out in it, trying to find somebody there, it becomes a big piece of water indeed. Time was running out. The men had been in the water for twelve minutes now, and survival time this far north is not much longer. I tried to use the knowledge to make my eyes sharper.

At last George spotted the yellow of a life jacket and he turned toward it. As we came up, we saw the boat underwater, turning slowly in the eddy that had caught it. It was upside down, floating two feet under. One man sat forward on the keel, his chest out of the water. The other man, older and bulkier, floated aft, his legs trailing darkly over the white of the submerged hull. Only the head of the aft man was out of water. He seemed at first to be kicking feebly, but on drawing closer we saw that it was just the current moving his legs. He had given himself up to it. He extended his hand to us, in glacial slow-motion. We took him under the arms and hauled him in, horsing his big logger's belly over the side and rolling him to the floor. He lay without moving. His eyes had a dead-fish glaze.

"I thought that was the end," he said. "I'm too old for this." He was about sixty.

The younger man had more strength left and came in easier.

When we had finished attaching a towline to the sunken boat, the older man stirred. He reached up, put his hand on mine, and looked into my eyes. I put my free hand on top of his. His knuckles were cold as ice.

He hoisted himself to an elbow and began a slow-motion search of his pockets for cigarettes. It seemed a crazy thing to want, a cigarette, but then I'm not a smoker. He found a pack of Players and looked to me for help. I unwrapped the foil for him, took out a cigarette, and put it in his mouth. He searched his pockets for his lighter, but the sea had washed it out. His big hand moved up slowly to his mouth and closed on the cigarette. He flipped it overboard. "Don't need it anyway," he said.

He began to think, but not very clearly. He remembered that there had been a gas can in the boat. He asked if we could go back and look for it. We explained that we had been lucky to see the men themselves. We would never find the can. He understood and nodded. He lay back on his elbow, looking out at Blackney Passage. "When I saw these boys coming, I thought the Lord had come," he said, addressing the tide rip, or the far shore, or nothing in particular.

His name was Bill. The younger man was Bernie. They were boom-men from a nearby logging camp. Bill more than anything was glad to be alive. "I don't know about you, Bernie, but I'm saying my prayers tonight." Bernie more than anything was embarrassed by his boatmanship. It was he who had been at the tiller. He kept going over the accident in his mind, trying to unflip the boat there. "Gee, I never expected that boat to flip the way it did. I still can't understand it. We got it turned up once, but then it flipped right back." He asked George what he should have done differently. George answered that he should have cut his speed. Had he simply shut off the engine, he would have been fine. Bernie was surprised. When the rip had roughened, he said, he had throttled up.

Bernie claimed he hadn't been scared. Bill said he had been scared to death.

Bernie was shivering violently. Bill was not shivering at all, and he was proud of that. "Bernie, you're shaking like a leaf. You don't have enough fat on you." The truth was that Bill was just too cold to shake. Later, when the stove on Hanson Island had warmed him to the shivering point, he would shake for an hour, long after Bernie had stopped.

George and I, headed homeward, began grinning. *We had saved two men's lives.* As we neared shore, George snuffed his grin, putting on an impassive, just-another-morning-rescue face. I tried to do the same, with less success.

Freeman hurried down over the rockweed, the first to greet us. He took Bill's hand and helped him from the boat. "I'd be very careful, these rocks are quite slippery," he warned. I wondered how Freeman's odd, prim accent sounded to Bill. Bill was too weary probably to think anything of it. Three times the big boom-man started to fall, but the slender physicist caught and held him up. His arm around Bill's considerable waist, Freeman conveyed him to the Spongs' door.

By the time George finished mooring the Zodiac out and came in, the two loggers were wrapped in blankets and drinking coffee. On entering, George began making sourdough pancakes as if nothing had happened. "I'm impressed by how fast you moved," Freeman told his son. "I was still thinking about what to do, and you were gone."

There was now an embarrassment between Bernie, Bill and me. There had been an intimacy in the rescue. Bill and I had held hands, after all, and had looked into each other's eyes. Now we avoided eyes. We were all uncomfortable, I think, with the idea that there might be some sort of debt. I studied George to see if he shared in this confusion. As far as I could tell he did not.

At that moment, George would tell me later, he was remembering. He was thinking of the dream his father had confided long ago, that nightmare in which the airliner crashes and burns, and Freeman freezes, unable to help rescue the passengers. Freeman had awakened his small son to recount it, hoping that in a similar emergency George would be able to move. That emergency now had come, and George had passed the test. The dream had been George's first memory. It seemed to him that here, in British Columbia, a circle had just been completed, and he was trying to make sense of it all. He was wondering if his father remembered. He decided not to ask.

The closeness of his call had made Bill talky. He was full of gratitude, and it overflowed in words, until finally, with pancakes and coffee inside him, he knew for sure he was going to live, and his sense of gratitude lost some of its sharpness. He was quieter.

"Which one of those boys is your son?" he asked Freeman.

"George. The one who fished you out."

Both George and I had fished Bill out, in fact, but Bill knew which of us Freeman meant.

"That was your best job," Bill said, clapping Freeman on the shoulder.

"Yes," said Freeman. "He seems to have turned out all right."

——— 49 ———
Farewell

The next morning, their last together on Hanson Island, George and Freeman found a place apart and for two hours they talked. George told his father his plan for life. George saw the world as a sick and endangered system, and himself as a sort of leucocyte afloat in it. His purpose would be to clean it up, in part by example. Freeman liked that notion. They spoke of other things. Those two hours of talk, Freeman told me later, were just what they needed.

Then George was loading the boat with the Dyson luggage and taking his father and sister and me to the ferry. It was a pleasant ride. We went around the southern end of Hanson Island, a route we had not traveled before. No one had much to say.

Out in Johnstone Strait a salmon jumped, and Freeman pointed.

"Spring salmon," said George, and with that, only fifteen minutes from the ferry, he seemed to realize how much filling in his father required. He began slowly. It was, he murmured, five years to the day since he first came to this coast. Then his voice rose. In the fifteen minutes left to him, he tried to recapitulate those five years. The stories came fast. He told of the time he worked on a company salmon boat crewed by Indians. The Indians had known nothing about engines, and hadn't wanted to know. They cared even less about the company. They ran all the way from Alaska to Seattle without stopping or changing oil. "It was a death trap," said George. "The fumes! The only place to sleep was around the engine." He told of another boat, on which he worked for a captain who could not read a chart and who drank a fifth of gin a day. "I thought it was a joke at first, about not reading charts, but it was true." Fortunately the engineer could read a chart, and so could George.

George told about another of his captains, a Mormon who had got his captain's papers, and all his previous experience, on Great Salt Lake. In his ignorance of the ocean, the Mormon did everything by the book. The moment the smallest thing went wrong, his nose was stuck in it.

"Did you hear about the barge?" George asked his father. Freeman shook his head. No one had told him of Carol Martin, his horses and cows and his barge trip to Juneau. George hesitated— where to begin that haywire epic? He took a breath and told the story in outline: the lack of radar, winch, and reverse gear; the man overboard; the hay, the horses, the iceberg; the sustained flirtation with disaster. Freeman listened, delighted. George told about the cow going overboard and Carol Martin lassooing it from the deck of the tug, and both Dysons, father and son, simultaneously laughed their silent, shoulder-shaking laugh.

And then we were in Beaver Cove. George was putting us on the ferry. We were all shaking hands and saying good-bye. George was walking up the hill from the ferry slip. I had the feeling, as we watched him go, that the canoebuilder had put something important behind him. He did not look back.

"These past five days have been wonderful," said Freeman on the ferry deck. His voice was pitched above the throb of the engines. His hair blew wildly in the wind. He had not shaved for a week. He was beginning to look pleasantly disreputable. "I must say, I enjoy this outdoor life. I might have been an outdoorsman after all. Of course it's too late for me. But I certainly have enjoyed it."

His stubble, I noticed, had a pattern exactly like that of George's beard—sparse on the sides.

We discussed Paul Spong. Freeman was not sure that Spong's work was science. "It's a religion. It's whale worship. But I suppose it's not so different from what often happens in science. Some astronomers come close to worshiping their telescopes. Telescopes are big, like whales. They're big, precise, wonderful instruments."

His eyes departed, turning inward to follow a thought. Then he came back. "I must say, though, that I'm not very impressed by this business of the *I Ching*. It may be the product of two thousand years of wisdom, but it leaves me very cold." He departed again, wandering off in body this time as well as mind.

Later he found me over a cup of coffee in the ferry cafeteria. "I've learned a lot from this trip," he said. "Not just in getting to know George better. I think in watching George's people I've learned something about what it will take to colonize asteroids."

He gave me a look, and we both laughed.

"I think," he continued, "you would find that the *Mayflower* people were regarded by their contemporaries much as this Hanson Island group is. A bunch of nuts. One or two strong personalities, and the rest sort of vague. One of the things that surprised me is how much these people move about. I hadn't expected that. Will Malloff certainly would be the perfect colonist, as far as technical skills go, but you couldn't expect him to stay in one place. In that sense, with asteroids, you should not look for islands, but for archipelagos. A cluster of places."

Emily arrived and she joined in on the post mortem. She was puzzled by certain of the customs on Hanson Island. "Why would anybody want to make a fast?" she asked, us, wrinkling her nose. "What's the point?"

Freeman explained the point as he understood it: fasting was to free the mind so it could come to grips with more important things than food. Emily did not look impressed. She still smelled good, I noticed. Her nails were clean, her hair neatly brushed, and Freeman and I were shabby beside her. She did not look like a girl who had spent a week in a tent.

I asked if anything about her brother had surprised her. "No," she said. "He's the way I imagined."

I asked the same question of Freeman.

"He's an entirely different person. There's no resemblance. I was struck by how he put Paul Spong's boat in order. And the neatness of his camp. He was so untidy at home."

Freeman smiled oddly and added, "He's certainly a strong personality. He's far more like my father than me. It definitely skipped generations."

Standing at the rail, watching the fiord wall pass, I thought about what Freeman had said. What if the Dyson proclivities skipped generations again? Maybe the starship would be built after all, by someone who grew up in this forest. Maybe the exodus to the stars would begin when the loggers intruded in one of these inlets, causing a grandchild of Freeman Dyson to decide that the time was right to *really* move on. That would surprise the child's father, surely, but fathers have been surprised before.

Envoi

A year later, in July 1976, the big canoe was headed north once more. George was in the stern manhole, steering. My brother John and I were crew. We didn't know how far we were going. Ahead of the dragon prow was the maze of the Inside Passage, and beyond that Yakutat, Prince William Sound, the Alaska Peninsula, the Bering Sea, the Arctic Ocean. Most of that was unknown to us.

The big canoe had been transmogrified. George's conception continued to evolve, and the intervening months had seen big changes. *Mount Fairweather* was now a trimaran. George had added twenty-eight-foot fiberglass outriggers to either side. Outrigger platforms of blond spruce joined each outrigger to the main hull. He had replaced the three wooden masts with a collapsible aluminum A-frame mast, and his three sails with a single large sail of his own design. Having discovered that his Plexiglass bubbles were obstructions to crewmen trying to walk around on deck, he had replaced all but two bubbles with flat, clear Plexiglass hatch-covers, which were strong enough to be stepped on. He had moved the gold coin depicting Saint George and the dragon to the top of the A-frame mast, where on sunny days it glinted. The canoe had lost its Aleut pedigree. It was hopelessly mongrelized. The outriggers and their platforms were Polynesian. The mast and sail were George inventions. The main hull still had classic Aleut lines, but at the bow was one of the remaining Plexiglass bubbles, like the forward turret of a bomber. If the Aleuts had conquered the Russians and everybody after the Russians, if the Aleutian culture had become dominant in the world, if the Aleut Pentagon had gone into building long-range strategic warships, then the warships would have looked something like this.

To our left passed Vancouver Island, to our right the mainland. We were navigating Johnstone Strait, where, four years before,

George had first tested the sails of his three-hole baidarka. A strong southeast wind was blowing now, as it had blown for that earlier test. George was trying out his new sail.

Behind us the strait narrowed with distance and took a turn out of sight. The world seemed to originate at the point of turning. It was a lesson in perspective. The last promontory was the vanishing point, and from out of it the strait's forested walls diverged, growing higher toward us, and the gray following sea ran at us, cresting white, and the clouds blew. The only color left was in the sky, where the setting sun had turned the clouds rosy.

The waves were the heaviest *Mount Fairweather* had encountered. Occasionally she half-buried an outrigger, and now and again the dragon's head at the prow smashed into a wave, sending spray back. There were beads of seawater on the Plexiglass of the forward bubble. Each droplet contained a cold, wide-angle replica of the lesson in perspective behind us. The canoe was traveling so fast that somewhere inside, her aluminum was humming. George thought it was the rudder. He sat like a jockey in the stern manhole, his hands on the steering reins, gazing up at the straining sail, waiting for something to snap.

Nothing did, but George decided finally that he was pushing his luck. He asked me to steer. When I had taken up the reins, he crawled forward, past where I sat in one of the middle holes. He dropped the mainsail and its acreage and raised the twin storm sails and their yardage.

Crawling back in the gathering dusk, he paused on hands and knees beside my hole. He let a big sea chase past us, waiting for a smaller one. I didn't look at him, but I could feel his fear. The fear was a routine part of his day, and it was under control, but I knew it was there. It came off him like his smell of damp wool. The ten-foot crawl back to his manhole was narrow and wet, with nothing to hang on to. If we lurched and he fell in, there was no way to turn back for him. The wind was too strong to paddle against. The water was too cold. The sea was tossing too wildly to find him in.

I remembered a scene from *2001*, a film for which Freeman

Dyson had served as consultant. It was the scene where the doomed astronaut tumbles slowly off into eternal space. The sea around us was nearly as black, now, as that black between the stars. The water was nearly as cold. Lost in the strait, George would have been as absolutely irretrievable. I decided I would just wave good-bye to him. Some kind of salute. Then the sea settled for a moment, and George scuttled back safely to his hole.

The night came on. *Mount Fairweather* did nothing to brighten it. We were an outlaw boat, running without lights, for George had not got around to installing them. We sailed cryptozoically down the middle of the strait.

The clouds thinned and the stars came out, first Venus and then Orion. There had been a light on shore, but now it was gone. I looked back for George. He was still there, sitting in silhouette against the following sea. I could not make out his face. I looked ahead. The Earth had vanished in darkness. The only proof of the planet was the ghostly froth of the near waves. George's dragon prow pranced onward into a sea of stars.